IMAGES
of Rail

BLACK RIVER & WESTERN RAILROAD

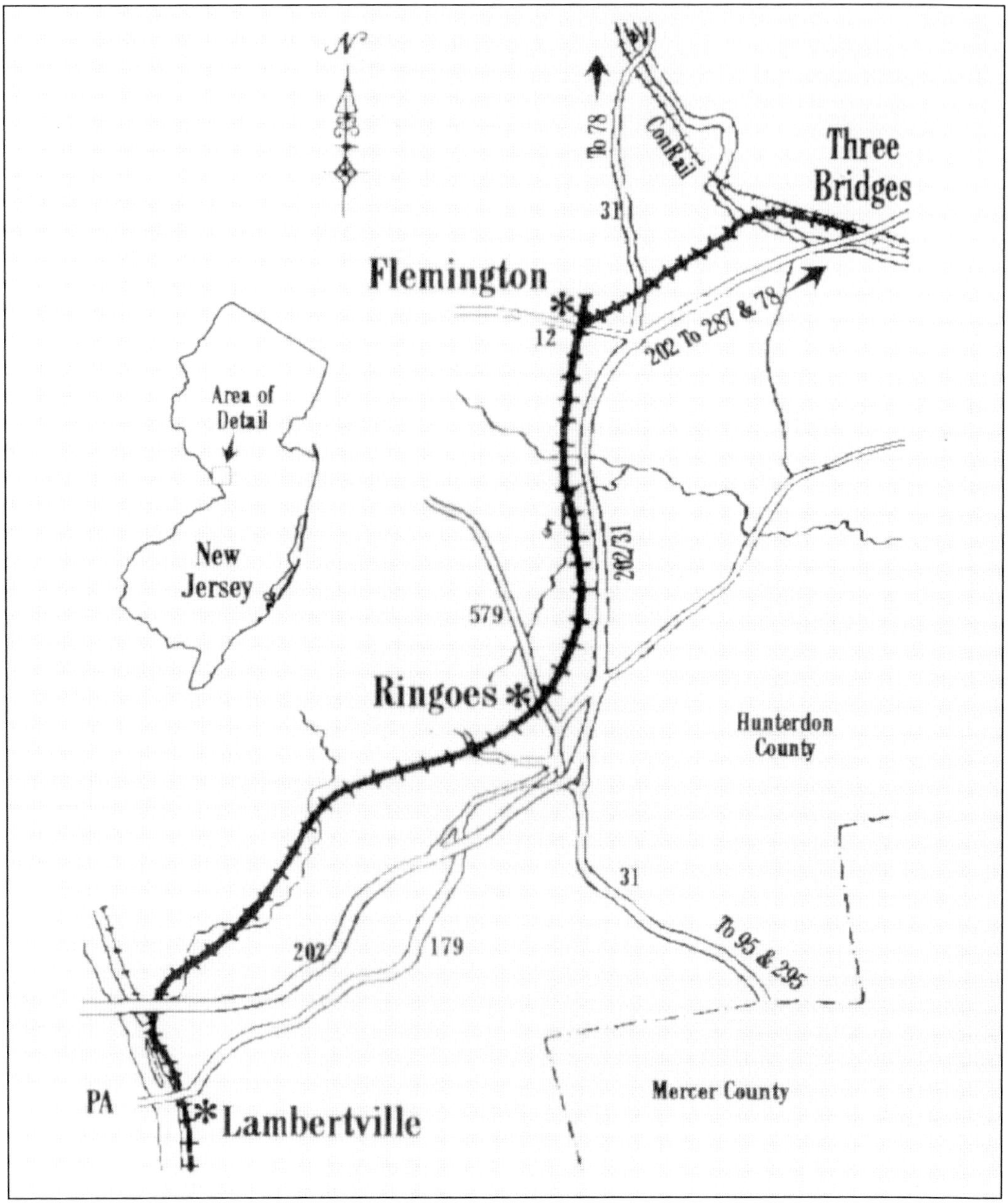

This is the route of the Black River & Western Railroad. (Author's collection.)

On the Cover: Steam engine No. 60 heads south pulling a string of wooden coaches while the engineer watches the train for any problems. (Author's collection.)

IMAGES
of Rail

Black River & Western Railroad

Jerry J. Jagger

ARCADIA
PUBLISHING

ISBN 978-1-4671-2412-6

Published by Arcadia Publishing
Charleston, South Carolina

Printed in the United States of America

Library of Congress Control Number: 2016947829

For all general information, please contact Arcadia Publishing:
Telephone 843-853-2070
Fax 843-853-0044
E-mail sales@arcadiapublishing.com
For customer service and orders:
Toll-Free 1-888-313-2665

Visit us on the Internet at www.arcadiapublishing.com

This book is dedicated to all the volunteers and personnel involved with the Black River & Western Railroad over the past 50 years.

Contents

Acknowledgments

This book would not be possible without the support of many involved in the operation of the Black River & Western Railroad. While it would not be practical to mention everyone involved, there are many who have influenced this project. Borne out of a need to preserve the past history of the railroad, this book is a continuing understanding of the past. Too often, our history is lost when former members pass and their recollections and stories are lost. This journey started with the passing of John Konn, whose railroad stories I will miss. John was a railroad man whose love of steam and railroading in general influenced my decision to collect and catalog as much of the past history as possible.

Many of the early photographs were taken by past volunteers who are deceased and whose photographs are part of the collection of the Black River Railroad Trust. Nelson Tower, past secretary, documented much of the early years of operation on the Flemington branch of the railroad. Lloyd Arkinstall, weekend engineer, photographed much of the Chester operation, and Norman Cole, past vice president and former conductor for the Lehigh Valley Railroad, photographed the early operations at Black River & Western.

I need to acknowledge the help and support of the Whitehead family, the Bishop family, and the Burenga family, along with railroad historian Pete Reimer, John Warrick, Carl Hostler, and James Hager, whose support and encouragement have helped to make this book possible.

Unless otherwise noted, all images are from the author's collection.

INTRODUCTION

William R. Whitehead, the founder and president of the Black River & Western Railroad (BR&W) from 1959 until 1967, wanted to build a tourist railroad to give his children and others the opportunity to see for themselves the old-style iron horse that built America. Using an abandoned railbed that ran behind his property, he made an agreement with the utility company that owned the right-of-way to lease it for $50 a year.

The roadbed that ran that behind the Whitehead property in Oldwick, New Jersey, was part of the old Rockaway Valley Railroad. The Rockaway Valley Railroad was organized in 1888 as a line between Whitehouse and Watnong near Morristown. The railroad operated for only a few short years. Having little or no ballast, it was nicknamed "the Rockabye Baby Railroad" for its roller-coaster grade. The last train that operated on the rail line was in 1913, and there was an unsuccessful attempt to reopen the line in 1914. During World War I, scrap prices rose, and the decision was made to scrap the rail to aid the Allied cause.

The Whiteheads purchased scrap rails from the Ontario & Western Railroad Company, and railroad ties were donated by Creosoting Works of Manville, New Jersey. Some of the original ties, plates, and spikes from the old Rockaway Valley Railroad were used as they began digging up the right-of-way. Other railroads provided spikes, ties, hooks, picks, crowbars, and lanterns to use in their family project. The family spent weekends cutting the overgrown weeds, grading the right-of-way, hauling railroad ties, and putting iron rails in place. By the late summer of 1959, about 600 feet of track had been laid. Wanting something to run on the line, they purchased a small former New York, Ontario, & Western Railway motorized track car. By late 1959, the New Jersey Department of Transportation notified Whitehead that his backyard railroad was in the path of future Highway 78 and would be condemned. When a request to build an overpass over or tunnel under the railbed was refused, the possibility of extending the railroad in the Oldwick area ended.

Also in 1959, William Whitehead's search for a steam engine to operate on a planned tourist railroad in New Jersey saw the purchase of 1906 Alco, 2-6-0 Class 10C Mogul configuration steam engine No. 565 used by the Dansville & Mount Morris Railroad. The steam engine was purchased at a cost of $2,500, terms were arranged, and the deal was sealed with a handshake. Needing a place to store the newly purchased steam engine, Whitehead leased 200 feet of track on the Chester Hill Branch of the Central Railroad of New Jersey. The branch line was built in 1876 to serve the iron mines in that area, extending five miles from Long Valley to Chester and seeing rail traffic dwindling early on when the iron mines ceased operations.

Once the engine arrived in 1960, William Whitehead and Lloyd Arkinstall, a former fireman on the New York & Long Branch Railroad, started a fire in the engine and waited for the steam to come up. Over the next several hours, the engine was run back and forth over the short stretch of leased track. William Whitehead is quoted as saying, "There was no generator so there was no headlight. I stood out there with a red lamp so Lloyd would know when he was coming to the end of the track. We operated up and down that length of track—I guess it was well after twelve o'clock at night."

In late 1960, steam engine No. 565 made an actual "unauthorized run" down the line between Chester and Long Valley. After they cleaned, painted, and oiled the engine, she was fired up and the volunteers climbed aboard riding wherever there was room, such as the locomotive's pilot and tender. The run was made to much fanfare, and photographs were taken. Once some of the photographs were printed in the newspaper, the Interstate Commerce Commission immediately shut down further operations of the engine until it was properly inspected, since the idea of a 1906, uninspected 200-psi steam boiler with people hanging all over it created quite a stir. Arrangements were made for the inspection, and the front of the boiler was opened. It was determined that extensive and costly repairs would have been required to bring the steam engine back into service.

Wooden passenger cars began to arrive at the railroad in 1960–1961. All the cars were wooden tongue and groove and were painted green with yellow trim and black roofs. "Black River & Western" in yellow lettering ran along top of each side of the cars.

On January 17, 1961, the Black River & Western filed for a certificate of incorporation with Sheldon Fruchtman of Union, William Whitehead of Oldwick, and Mildred Portuguese of Newark signing the papers. The railroad would be named Black River & Western, with the name coming from the Black River, which the railroad crossed just west of Chester. The "Western" was added because it sounded like an old-time railroad. The railroad was incorporated "to establish and conduct a general amusement enterprise and to furnish amusement to the public."

The project was short-lived since both the Chester and Long Valley Planning Boards rejected the proposal for a short amusement ride. It was believed that the steam railroad trips would bring noisy tourists, and that the noisy, smoky steam engines would scare the cows.

In July 1961, the Black River &Western moved some of the equipment to Gladstone, New Jersey, for use in filming *The Miracle Worker,* a movie about Helen Keller starring Anne Bancroft and Patty Duke. While the producers wanted to use steam engine No. 565 in the movie, the Central Railroad of New Jersey (CNJ) would neither transport nor allow the operation of the locomotive out of Chester. Only some of the Black River & Western coaches appears in the movie.

But troubles would persist as the Central Railroad of New Jersey planned to abandon the Chester Hill Branch right-of-way. With the threat of being landlocked, the Black River & Western Railroad tried to negotiate a price to purchase the rail line from Chester to German Valley, now called Long Valley. By March 1962, abandonment of the property was approved and Black River & Western scrambled to offer the Central Railroad of New Jersey $32,000 for the right-of-way and tracks in Chester, expecting favorable terms. The Central Railroad of New Jersey rejected the offer and September 9, 1962, was the last day the railroad would be on the track in Chester. With the lease terminated, the equipment would be moved to temporary storage at Taylor Iron in High Bridge. Searches for alternate sites found the railroad looking at a location in Canaan, Connecticut, and locations in Sussex County, New Jersey. By 1963, circumstances would again see the equipment moved, this time to Flemington, where it would be stored on sidings of the Central Railroad's South Branch line, most notably the siding next to Flemington Glass.

The incorporation of the railroad allowed funds to be raised for the purchase of another steam engine. Carl Conover, who had been hired as the railroads master mechanic in Chester was given the task of locating another steam engine and, in 1963, found an engine that was for sale on the Great Western Railway. The Great Western had a 1937 Alco consolidation type 2-8-0 steam locomotive No. 60, offered at a sale price of $9,000. Having been overhauled in 1958, the engine was stored in A-1 condition, and arrangements were made to purchase and ship the engine by rail from Colorado to New Jersey with Conover on board the entire route. In 1964, it would arrive and be stored on the Flemington Cut Glass siding along with the other equipment belonging to the railroad.

In 1964, William R. Whitehead, Samuel Freeman, and Albert E. Blomquist (chairman of the Hunterdon County Planning Board) and County Freeholders Linton Alles, William Amerman, and Ralph Muller, along with George C. Vaughan, New York regional manager of the Pennsylvania Railroad, arranged for a leasing arrangement with the Pennsylvania Railroad that allowed a tourist train to operate from Flemington to Lambertville on the Pennsylvania Railroad's Flemington Branch. The Flemington Branch was built in 1854 by the Flemington Railroad and Transportation Company as an agricultural line. Freight was the main business of the rail line, and in the 1920s, the line had become the second-largest milk shipping line on the Pennsylvania Railroad, where 6,000 gallons of milk per day were shipped from local farms to the markets in Philadelphia. By 1964, thirty-five years had passed since passenger service was discontinued on the Flemington Branch for lack of revenue. Freight traffic had dwindled to just three trains per week. Black River & Western agreed to pay $5,000 a year and rehabilitate the railroad line for passenger service while the Pennsylvania Railroad would continue to operate freight service over the line during that period.

On March 27, 1965, the Jersey Central Railroad delivered the Black River & Western equipment to the recently leased rail line in Flemington. The equipment would be ferried to the home base of Ringoes by the little Mack engine that the railroad had obtained in November 1963. By April 1965, the railroad was ready to be shown off, and a trip for the stockholders was planned. Unfortunately, the steam engine had not yet passed all its inspections, and the little Mack engine was put into service for the event. Pulling two passenger coaches, the little engine made runs over the line on April 3 and 4, with the first trip reserved for the stockholders and their families, who were treated to tours of the equipment and a box lunch; later trips were run for prospective investors. The engine found the train a little more than it could handle, since the top speed for the trip was around five miles per hour, and the engine had to make periodic stops to let the engine cool down.

On May 16, 1965, then New Jersey governor Richard J. Hughes christened the start of passenger service by giving a short speech and cracking a champagne bottle over steam engine No. 60's rear drive wheel. It was estimated that 400 paying passengers, along with the governor and his entourage, rode the first trip. During the first year of operation, an estimated 20,000 passengers were handled by the railroad.

Throughout the 1960s, passenger excursion service flourished. Five trips between Flemington and Ringoes were run on weekends and holidays, and a sixth trip was added as needed. Special school trips were offered on Mondays and Fridays, and steam engine No. 60 and the wooden coaches would be used for various media commercials and film shorts. Additional equipment was sought after and added to the railroad's inventory. By the end of 1969, while tourist passenger service continued, the railroad would enter another phase of its operation, which was expansion into freight service and becoming a common carrier short-line railroad.

On March 16, 1970, the Black River & Western Railroad took over the ownership and operations of the entire Flemington-Lambertville line by purchasing it from the Penn-Central Railroad. The Federal Railroad Administration had also embargoed the South Branch line of the Central Railroad of New Jersey between Somerville and the Tenneco plant in Flemington due to poor track conditions and the derailment of tank cars. The FRA further implemented an emergency service order that directed Flemington-bound Central Railroad of New Jersey traffic to be rerouted from Trenton to Lambertville and handled by the Black River & Western to Flemington. CNJ crews then operated over the South Branch line from Flemington to the two remaining customers, returning the outbound cars to the interchange at Turntable Junction in Flemington.

On April 1, 1976, Conrail took over the Penn-Central Railroad, and everything changed. Service south of Lambertville to Trenton was stopped since it was not included in the final system plan and was not needed. In 1976, the primary interchange between the Black River & Western and Conrail was changed to Three Bridges, but no decision to close Lambertville interchange had yet been made. Conrail freight trains ran along the Delaware River until November 12, 1978, when the line from Milford to Trenton was abandoned. Freight for the Flemington line was then delivered at the interchange in Three Bridges.

Passenger excursions continued throughout the 1970s, 1980s, and 1990s. Two steam train operations between Flemington and Ringoes began in 1972 using steam engines No. 60 and No. 148. Passenger train service to Lambertville was established in 1973.

In 1985, Black River & Western was handling 1,500 freight cars per year, serving nearly a dozen customers along the rail line. Much of the freight was chemicals and plastics such as polyethylene pellets. Black River had served the Tenneco plant with 500 to 600 cars each year until it closed in 1985.

In 1995, the Belvidere & Delaware River Railway was formed when the Conrail Delaware Secondary line was purchased by the Black River Railroad System to serve customers in the Phillipsburg area of northwestern New Jersey. Freight along the line included wood pulp, pulp board, petroleum, wax, and lumber for companies in Carpentersville and Riegelsville.

By December 1997, a lack of freight traffic and a bleak outlook for the local tourist industry led the Black River & Western to place the line between Ringoes and Lambertville out of service. The last passenger train to Lambertville was in 1998, and the last train into Lambertville to remove equipment was in the year 2000.

The last season that steam engine No. 60 ran prior to its major overhaul was in 2001. Taken out of service, the engine went through over 10 years of work by volunteers until returning to service. During the overhaul period of the steam engine, all weekend passenger excursions were pulled by one of the railroad's diesel engines.

A separate nonprofit entity known as the Black River Railroad Historic Trust was formed in 2001. As a not-for-profit 501(c)(3) organization, the Black River Railroad Historical Trust operates the public passenger trains and events on the railroad. Working closely with the railroad, the trust's mission is to preserve railroad history and educate the public about railroading. The volunteers have been successful in restoring a former baggage car as a small museum at the Ringoes rail yard, along with ongoing acquisitions, restoration, and preservation of historic railroad equipment. A second baggage car was renovated and turned into a workshop. Successful seasonal events are held each year and include Easter Bunny trains and North Pole Express trains.

An agreement was made in 2014 between the Black River Railroad Historical Trust and the Black River & Western Railroad to lease the rail line from Ringoes to Lambertville. By late year, work began to clear the line of brush and to start installing new ties. The process of clearing and restoring the line to service is ongoing, with the intention of restoring service to Lambertville.

On Saturday, May 16, 2015, the 50th anniversary rededication of the Black River & Western Railroad dedication in 1965 was held. With invited guests, many of the original participants in the 1965 ceremony were on hand, including members of the Whitehead and Bishop families. The ceremony included a rededication by cracking a bottle of champagne over the rear driver of steam engine No. 60. Guests were invited for a train ride to Ringoes and a picnic afterwards.

Fifty years of continuous passenger excursions is a feat that few tourist railroads can claim. The railroad started as a steam excursion attraction and grew into a common carrier of freight. The Black River & Western continues its operations with a bright outlook. New planned events, upgrades, and expansions are expected.

One

The Early Years

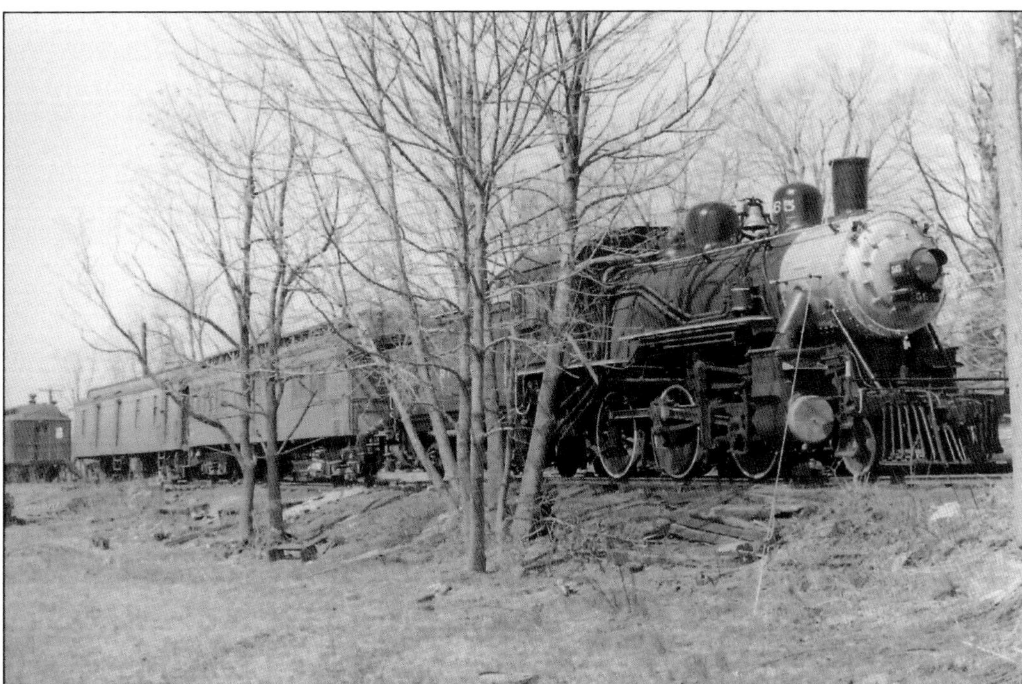

Black River & Western's first steam engine ex–Delaware, Lackawanna & Western (DL&W) No. 565 sits quietly on a siding at Chester, New Jersey, in 1960. The two wooden passenger cars behind the tender are one of the center combine cars and the Railway Post Office car No. 100. (Lloyd Arkinstall.)

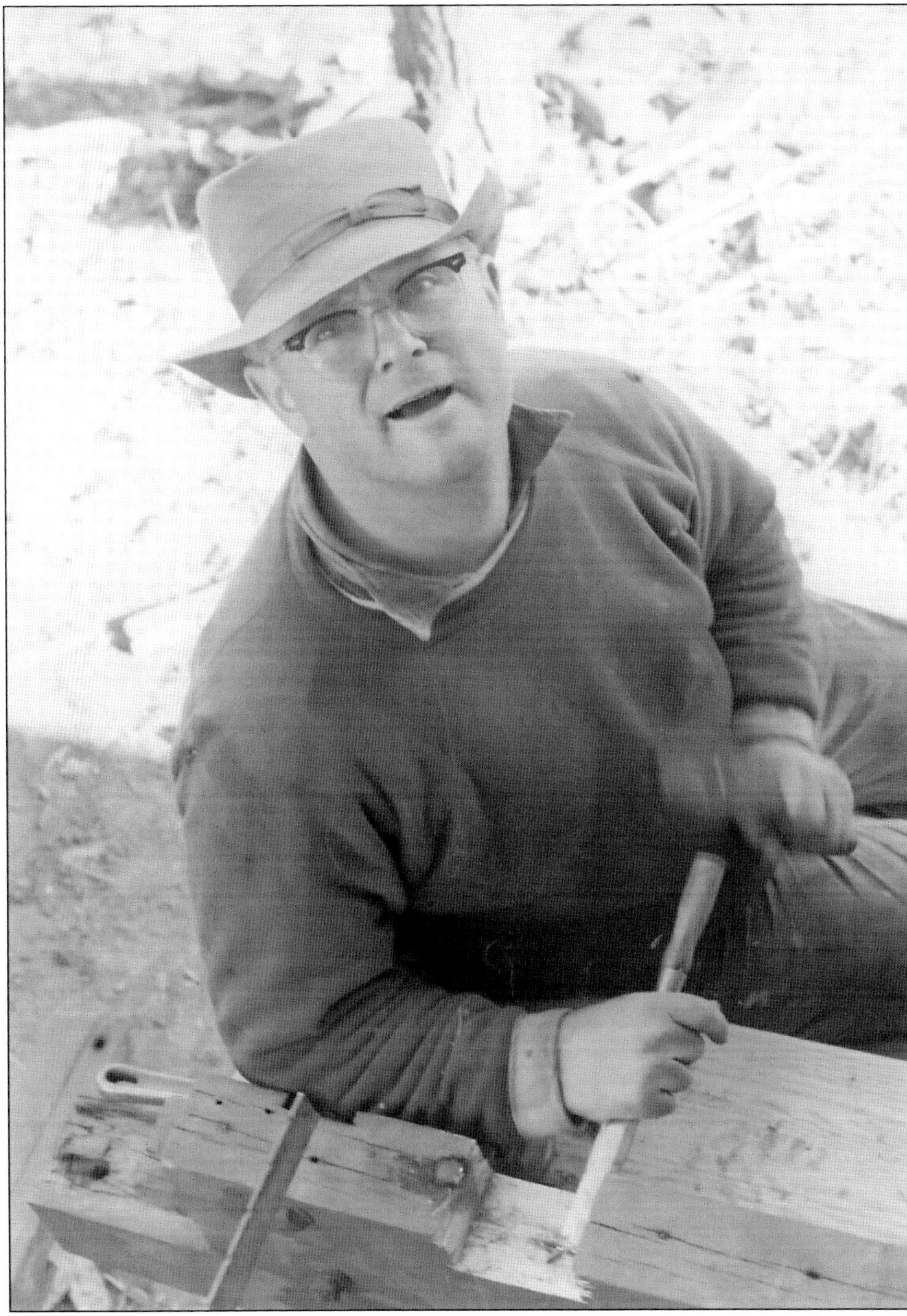

William R. Whitehead dreamed of the day that a steam tourist excursion line would exist in New Jersey. As the first president of the Black River & Western Railroad, he saw that dream become a reality. Ever the salesman, he inspired the volunteers and, through hard work and desire, formed the core of the railroad that would bring steam railroading to New Jersey for all to enjoy. He is shown working on a wooden passenger coach in Chester. Bill Whitehead would spend the next several years working in all aspects of the railroad before leaving in the late 1960s. (Lloyd Arkinstall.)

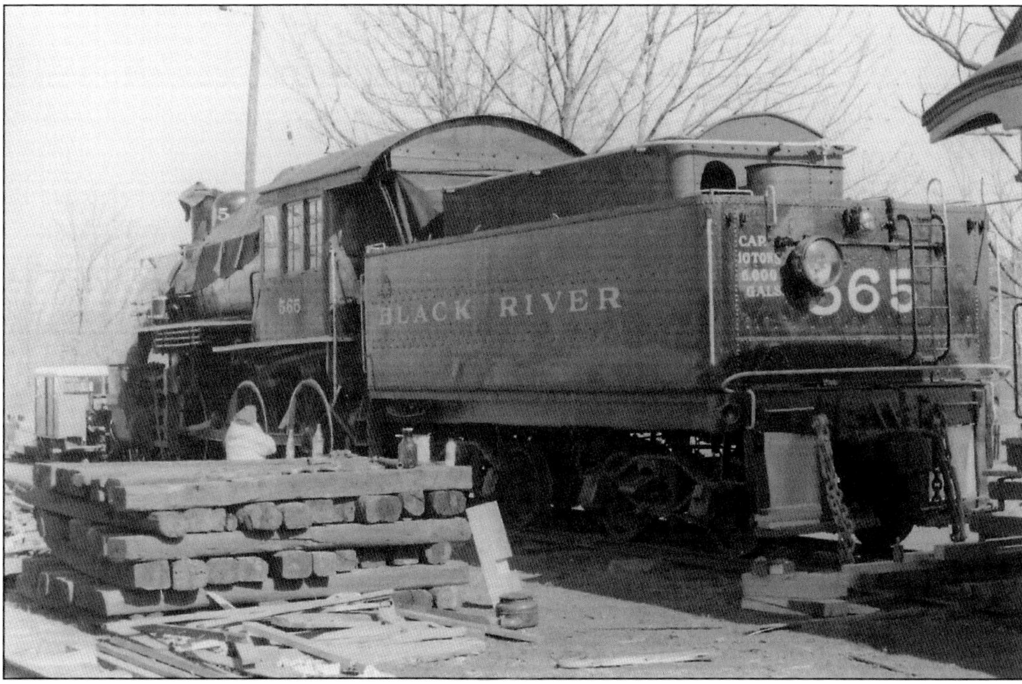

Steam locomotive No. 565 is pictured at Chester in 1961. Note the tower light that has been installed on the tender to act as a backup light for the locomotive. In front of the steam engine is the ex–New York, Ontario & Western Railway speeder, the first piece of equipment owned by railroad. (Lloyd Arkinstall.)

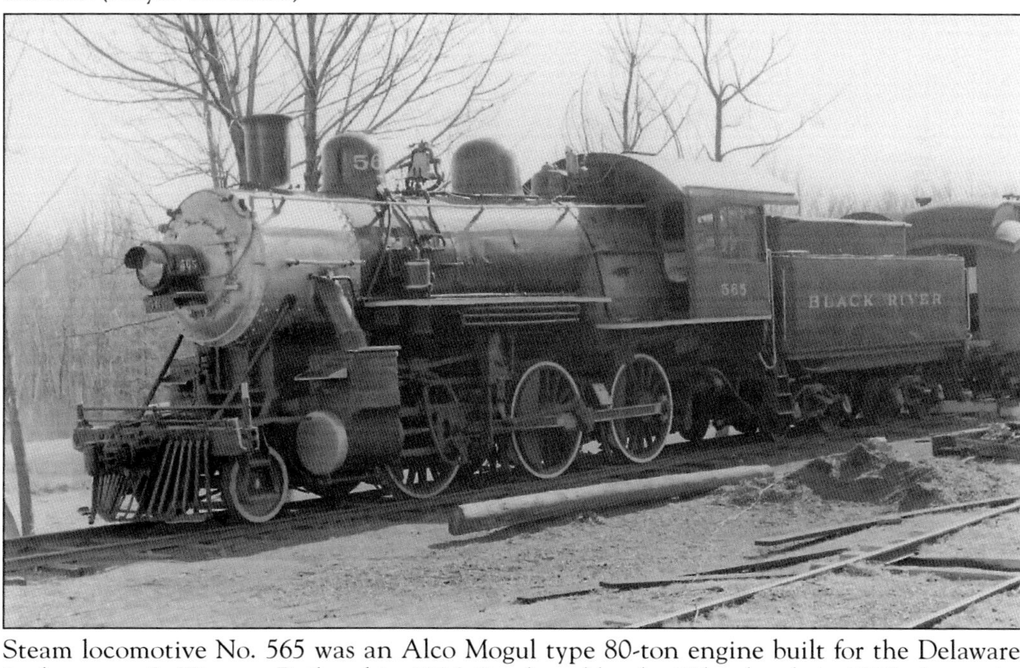

Steam locomotive No. 565 was an Alco Mogul type 80-ton engine built for the Delaware, Lackawanna & Western Railroad in 1906. Purchased by the Whiteheads in 1960, the engine would, unfortunately, not run in passenger operation since it failed the required boiler inspection, resulting in extensive and costly repairs. (Lloyd Arkinstall.)

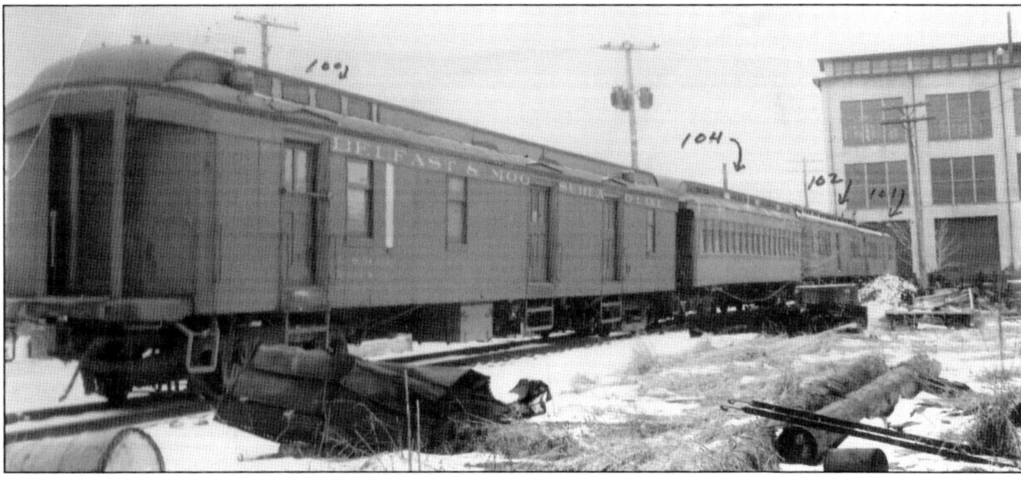

Wooden passenger cars were purchased from the Belfast & Moosehead Lake and Bangor and Aroostock Railroads. Car No. 100 was a former Railway Post Office car built in 1906 that was last used in US mail service in 1959. Car No. 104 was an open platform coach built in 1904 and used as a first-class coach. Cars No. 102 and 101 were center combine cars. (John Bishop collection.)

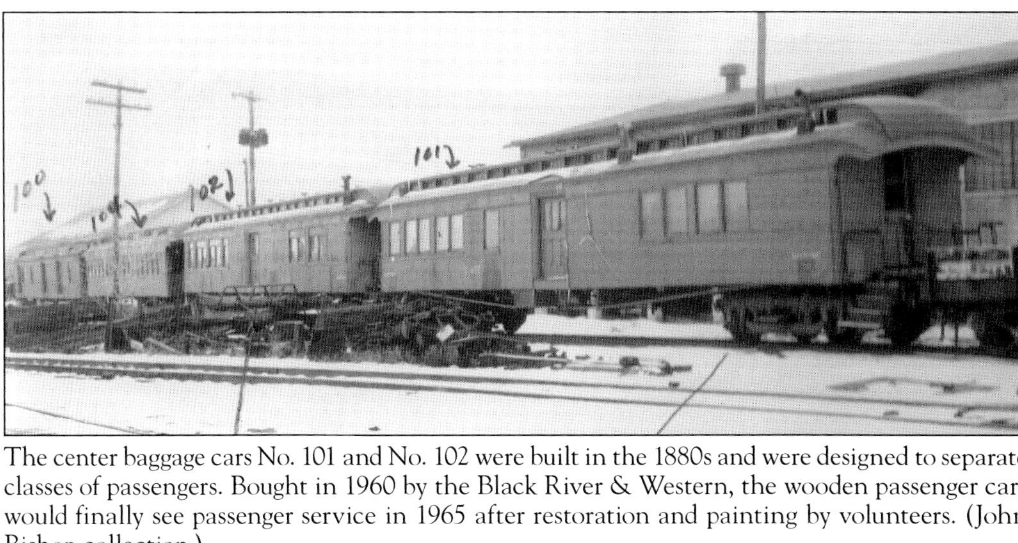

The center baggage cars No. 101 and No. 102 were built in the 1880s and were designed to separate classes of passengers. Bought in 1960 by the Black River & Western, the wooden passenger cars would finally see passenger service in 1965 after restoration and painting by volunteers. (John Bishop collection.)

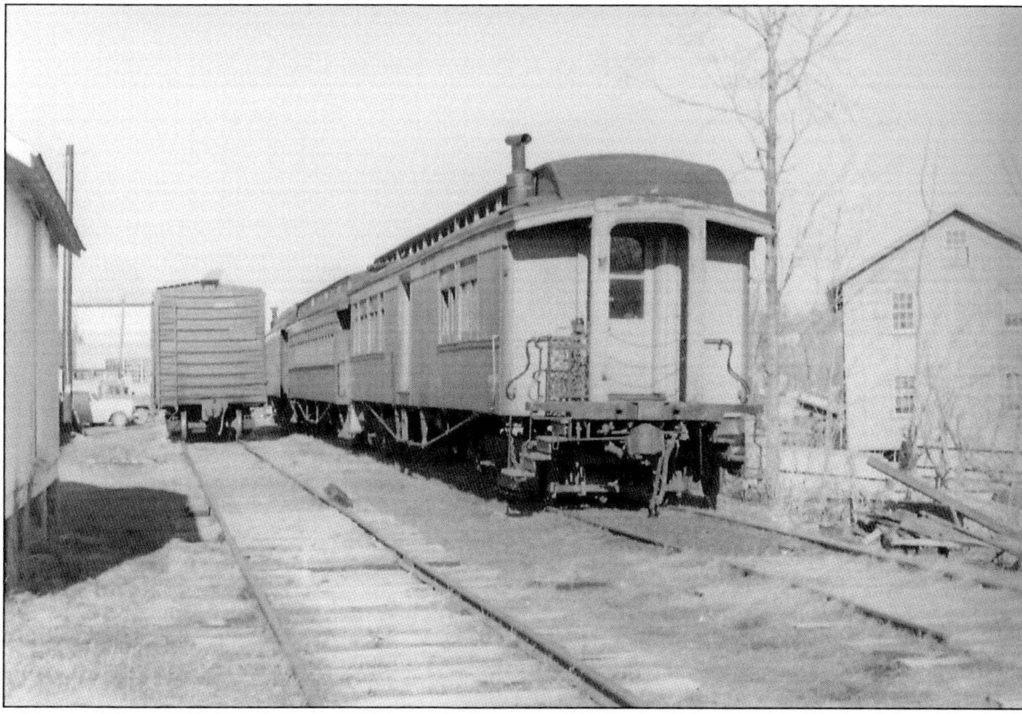

Three of the wooden passenger cars—No. 102, No. 104, and No. 101—purchased by the Black River & Western (BR&W) are shown on a siding at Chester, New Jersey. The Central Railroad of New Jersey still provided limited freight service to Chester during this time, as seen by the boxcar in the photograph. (Lloyd Arkinstall.)

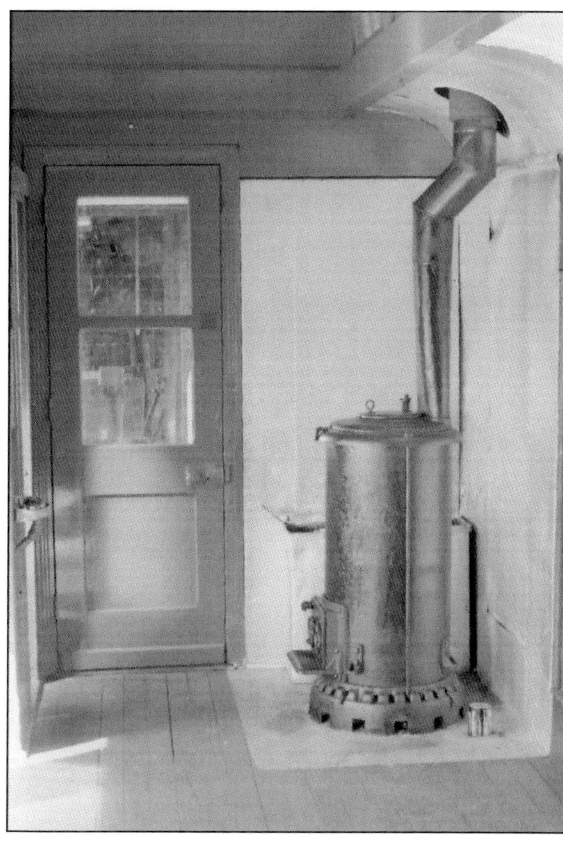

The coal stove inside one of the coaches was used to heat the car. Coal stoves were the main source of heat for the wooden coaches and would continue to be used until their replacement by the steel coaches used today, which are heated by steam. (Lloyd Arkinstall.)

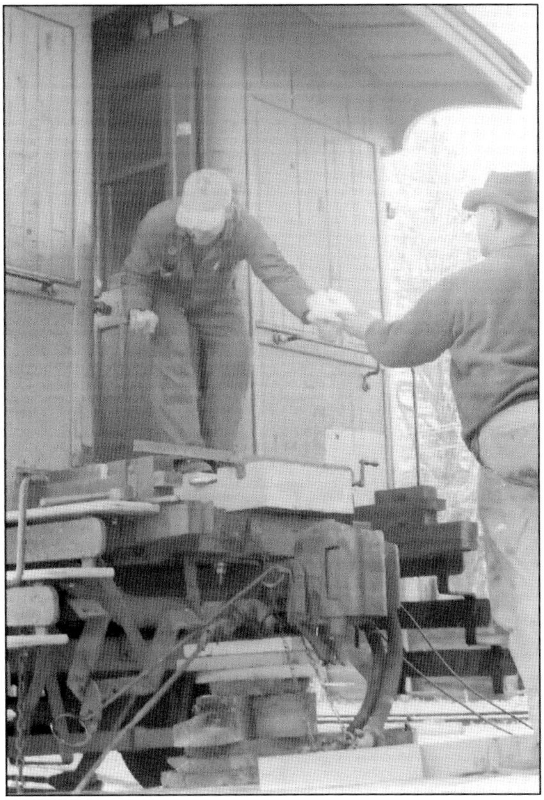

Lloyd Arkinstall and William Whitehead work on the end of one of the wooden coaches. Work on the cars would continue in Chester, where new wooden steps were fabricated and installed along with other necessary repairs to get the cars in shape for passenger service. (Lloyd Arkinstall.)

Combine car No. 102 was a former Bangor and Aroostook Railroad wooden combine built in 1884. One of two owned by the railroad, this type car was designed to separate first-class passengers from second-class passengers by the addition of a baggage compartment in the middle. The car would be painted the signature Black River green with yellow trim and lettering and a black roof. (Lloyd Arkinstall.)

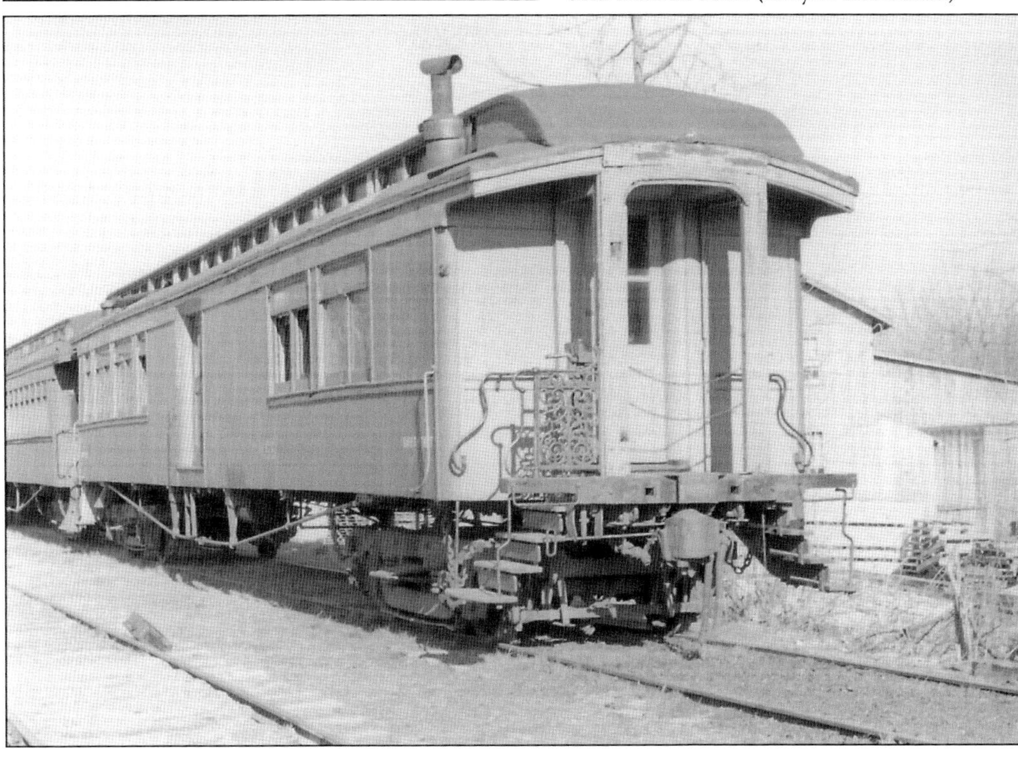

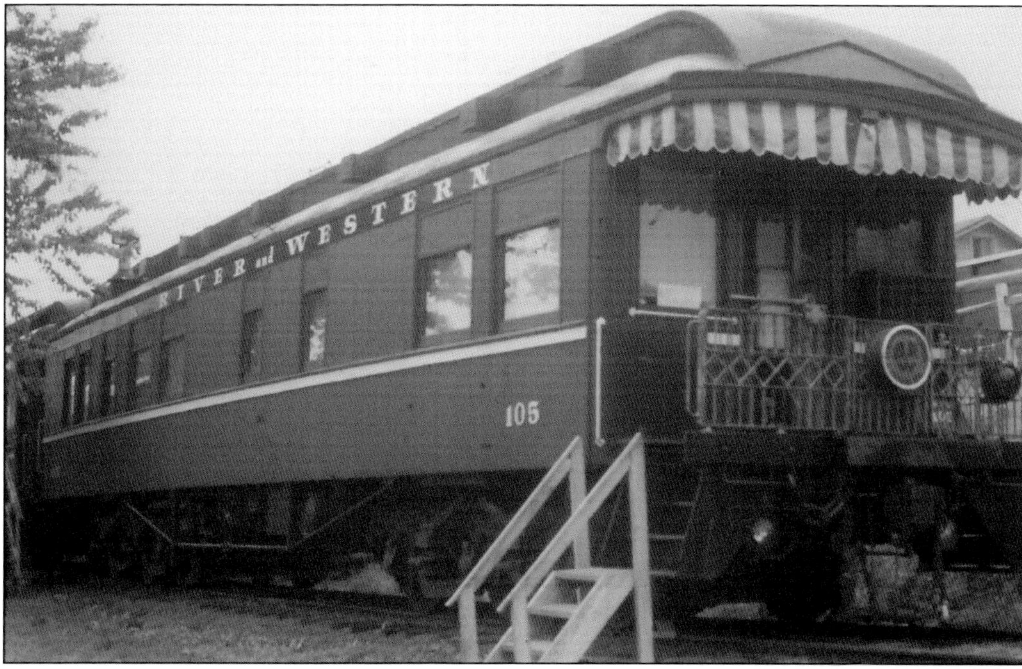

Business car No. 105 is shown on a siding in Ringoes. The former Canadian Northern Railway car was built in 1895 and utilized by the president of that railway for his personal use. The luxury of the car featured living and dining areas, a kitchen, and servant and master bedrooms.

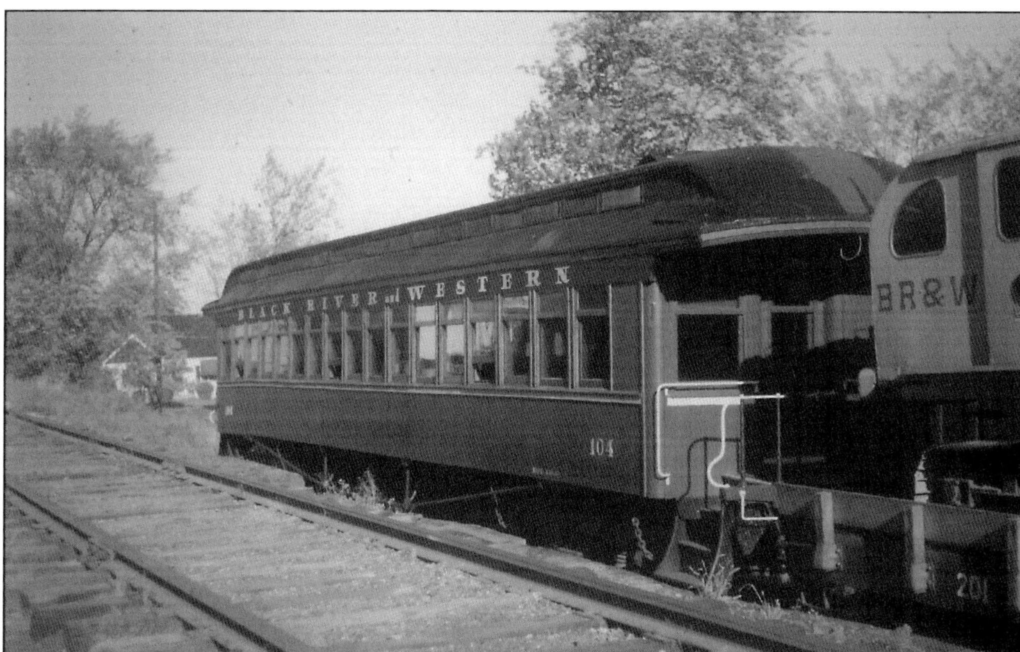

Wooden passenger car No. 104 sits on the siding in Ringoes along with flatcar No. 201. The railroad's crane is shown on the flatcar. The coaches compartment had blue plush seats that had come from one of the Jersey Central's famous Blue Comet train cars.

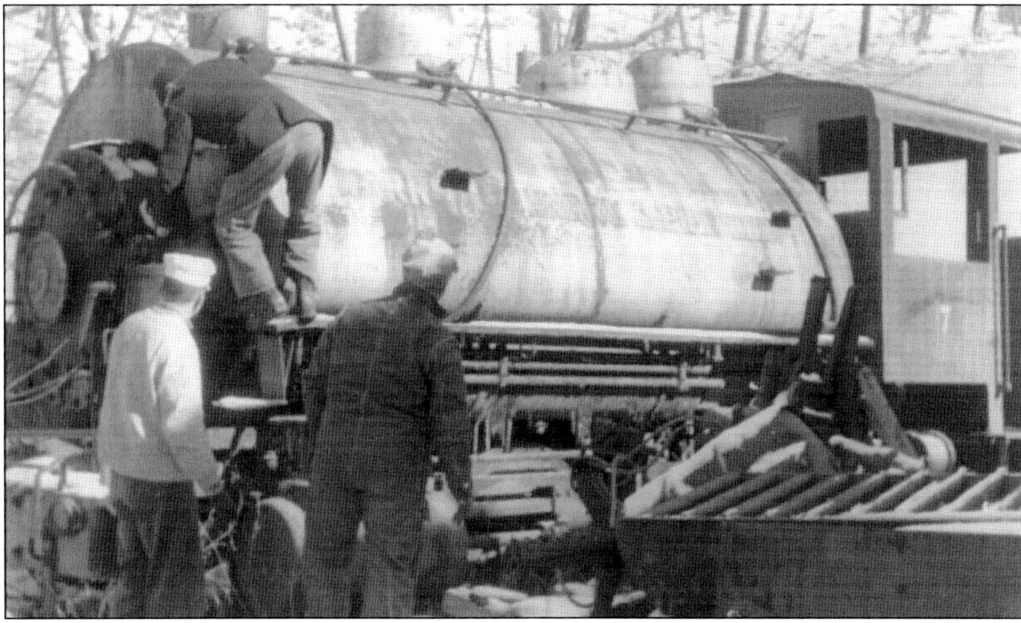

During 1962–1963, volunteers searched for additional equipment to add to the newly formed railroad. With the need for another steam engine as a replacement for steam engine No. 565, Saddle Tank Engine No. 7, located at Warren Foundry in Phillipsburg, was considered and rejected. (John Bishop collection.)

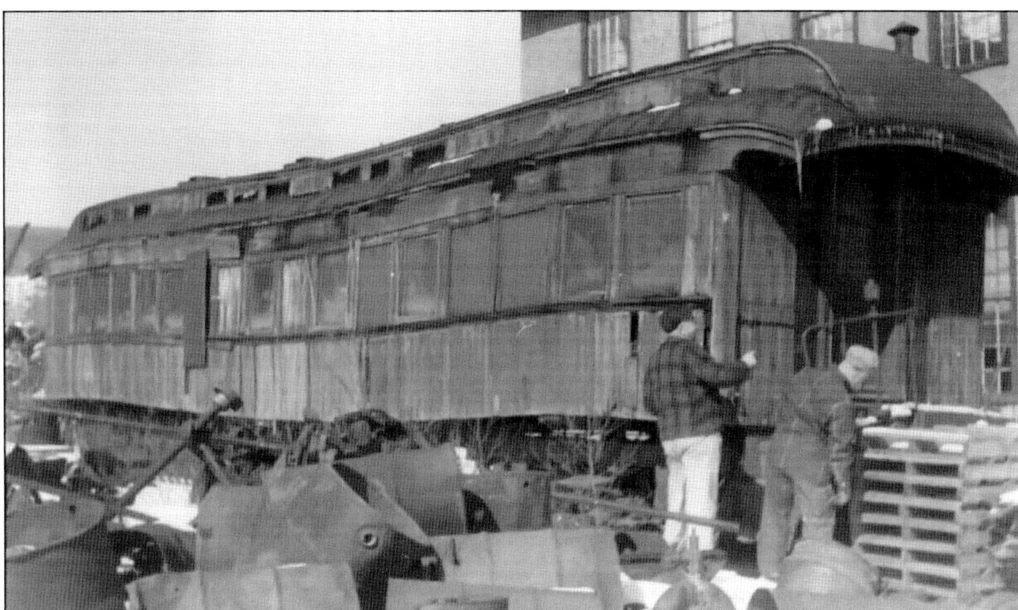

Volunteers look over an old New York & Ontario wooden coach in Carbondale, Pennsylvania, and later rejected the car due to its condition. Similar equipment would be inspected and rejected before the railroad started to obtain steel-sided cars starting in 1965. (John Bishop collection.)

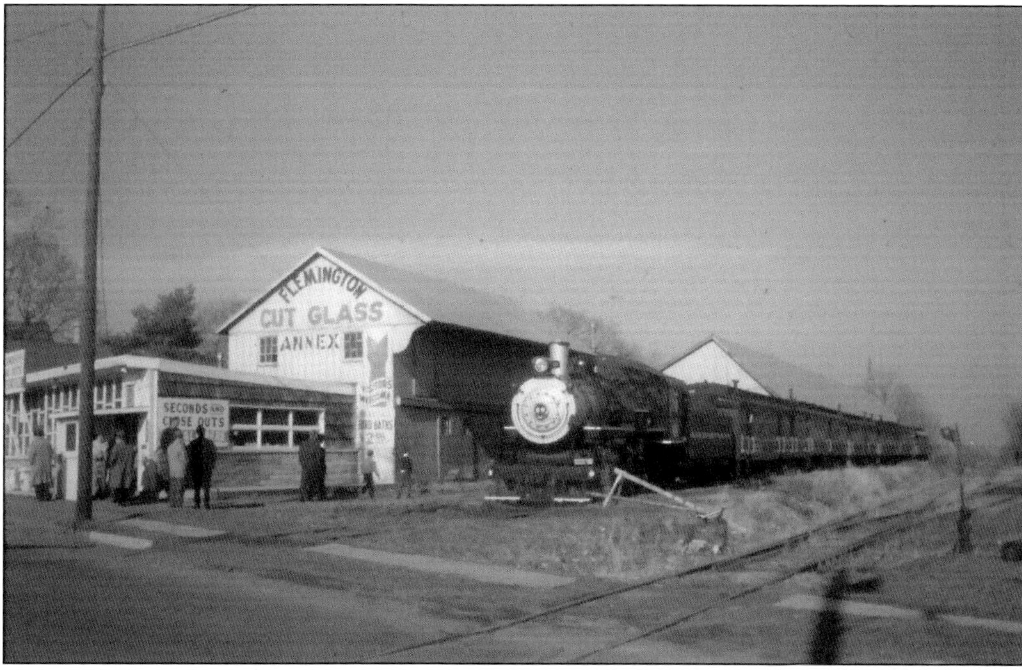

By late 1963, the train set, along with a newly acquired steam engine No. 60, had been moved to Flemington and stored on a siding near Flemington Cut Glass. The volunteers would open the passenger cars to interested members of the public for viewing while continuing to work on the equipment.

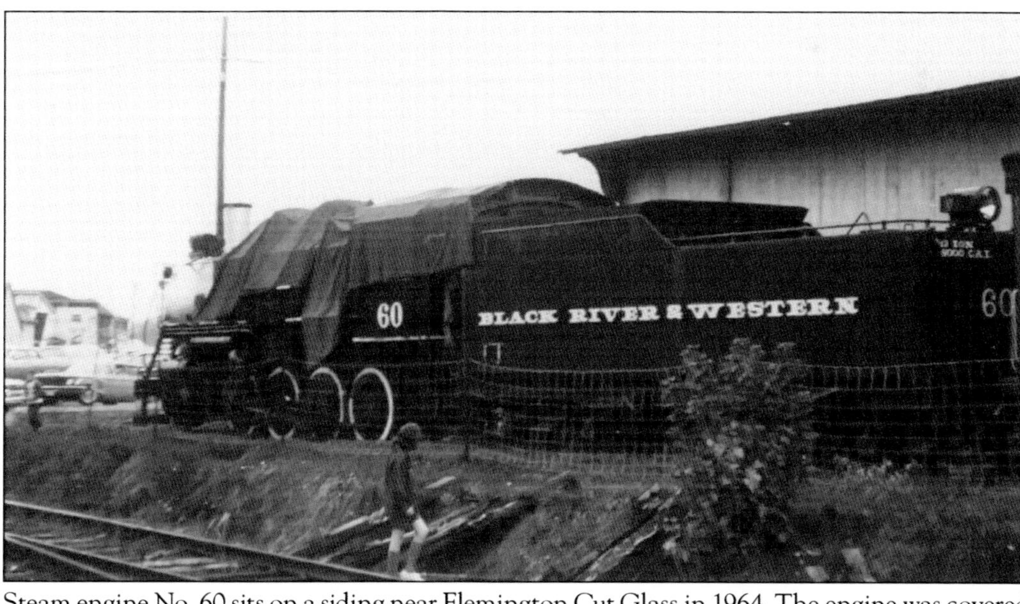

Steam engine No. 60 sits on a siding near Flemington Cut Glass in 1964. The engine was covered with a tarp for protection while volunteers continued to prepare her for service on the expected tourist line. Temporary fencing was used to discourage damage to the equipment.

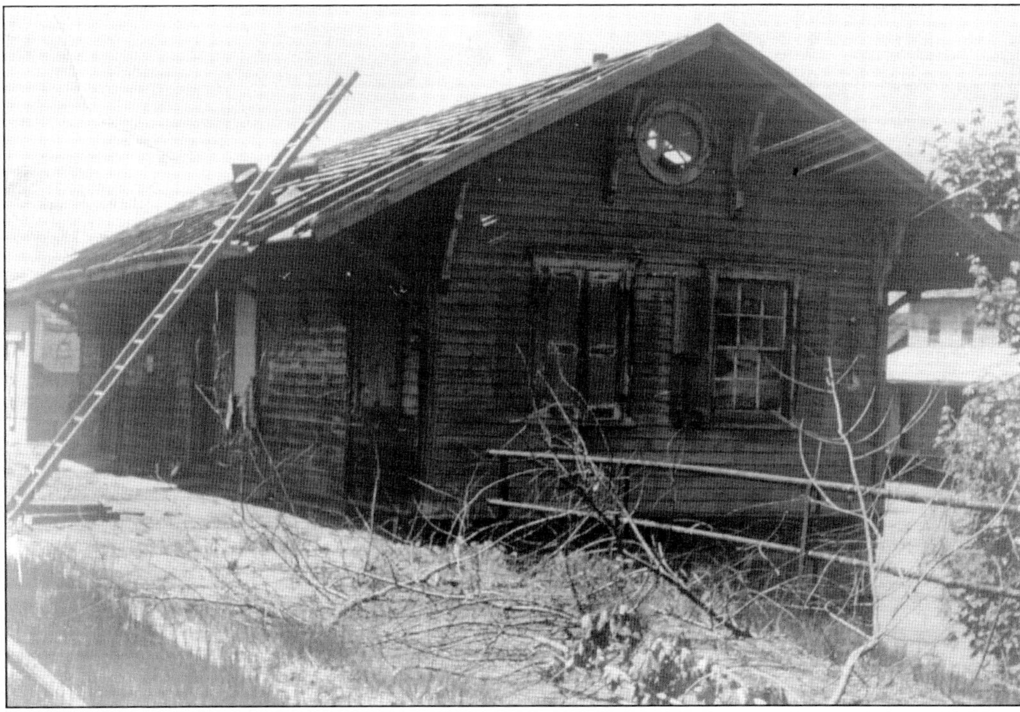

With a lease agreement in hand, volunteers began working on the former Pennsylvania Railroad Ringoes station in March 1964. The station had been neglected for a number of years by the Pennsylvania Railroad, and a complete renovation of the interior, exterior, plumbing, and roof had to be undertaken.

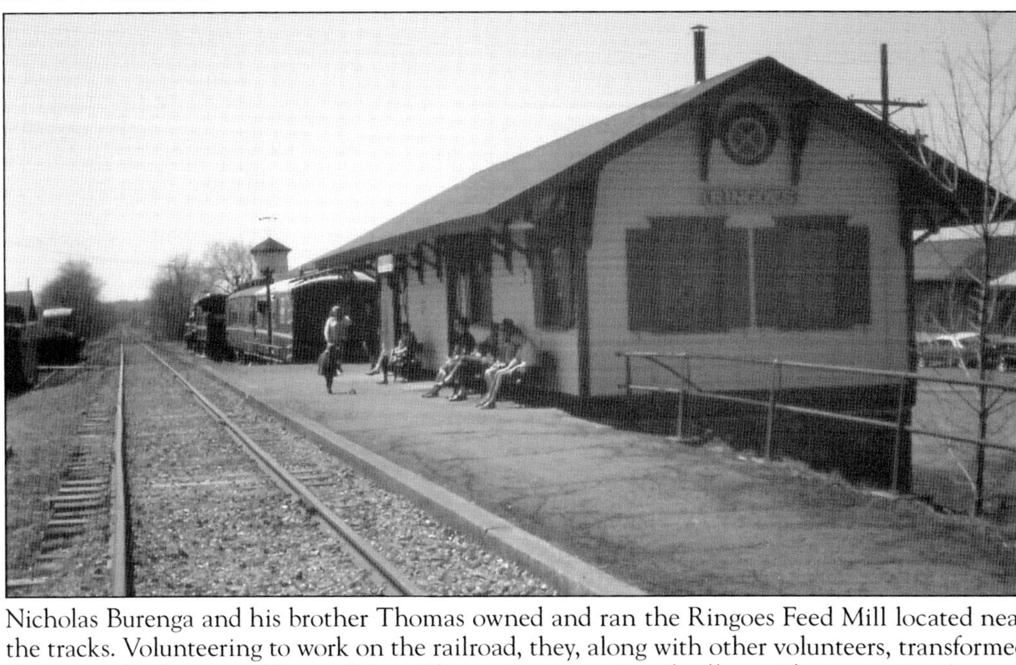

Nicholas Burenga and his brother Thomas owned and ran the Ringoes Feed Mill located near the tracks. Volunteering to work on the railroad, they, along with other volunteers, transformed the station back to a usable condition. The station was painted yellow with green trim. A snack bar was also set up in the station to sell refreshments.

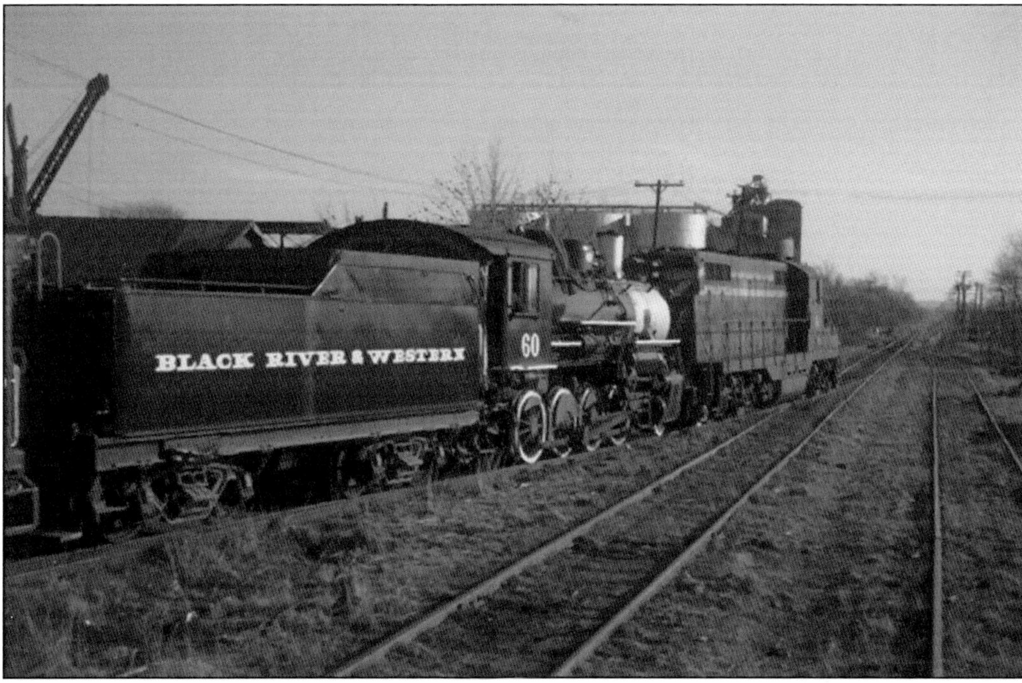

On March 27, 1965, the equipment of the Black River & Western was moved from its storage siding on the South Branch line of the Central Railroad of New Jersey to the Flemington Branch of the Pennsylvania Railroad. Here, steam engine No. 60 is being moved by one of the CNJ's diesel locomotives. (Nelson Tower.)

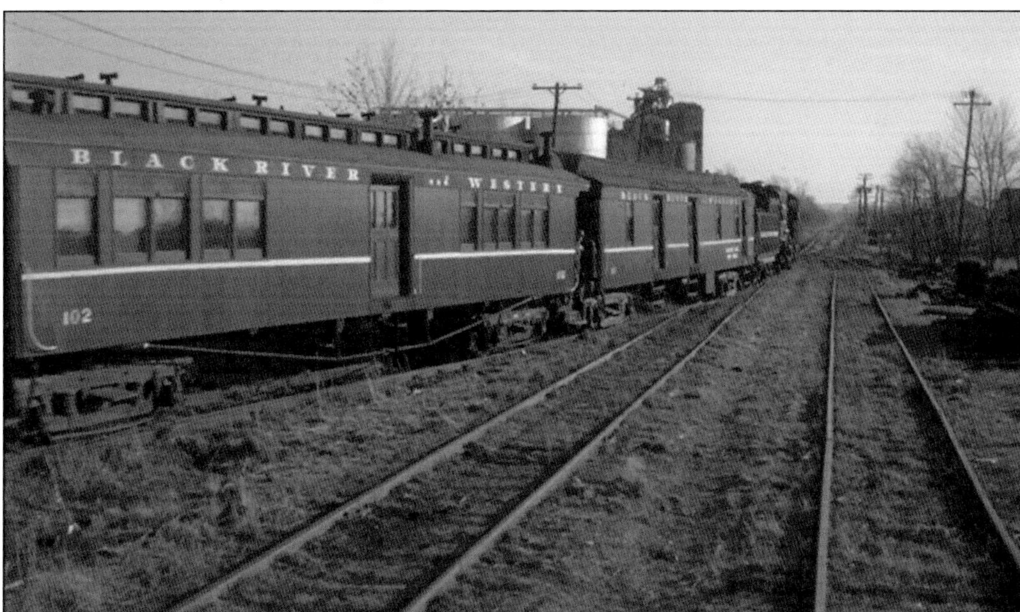

Passenger cars No. 102 and No. 100 trail behind steam engine No. 60 as they are being delivered to the Black River & Western Railroad by the Central Railroad of New Jersey. The consist would be shoved into the Flemington station end of the Pennsylvania Railroad's Flemington Branch. (Nelson Tower.)

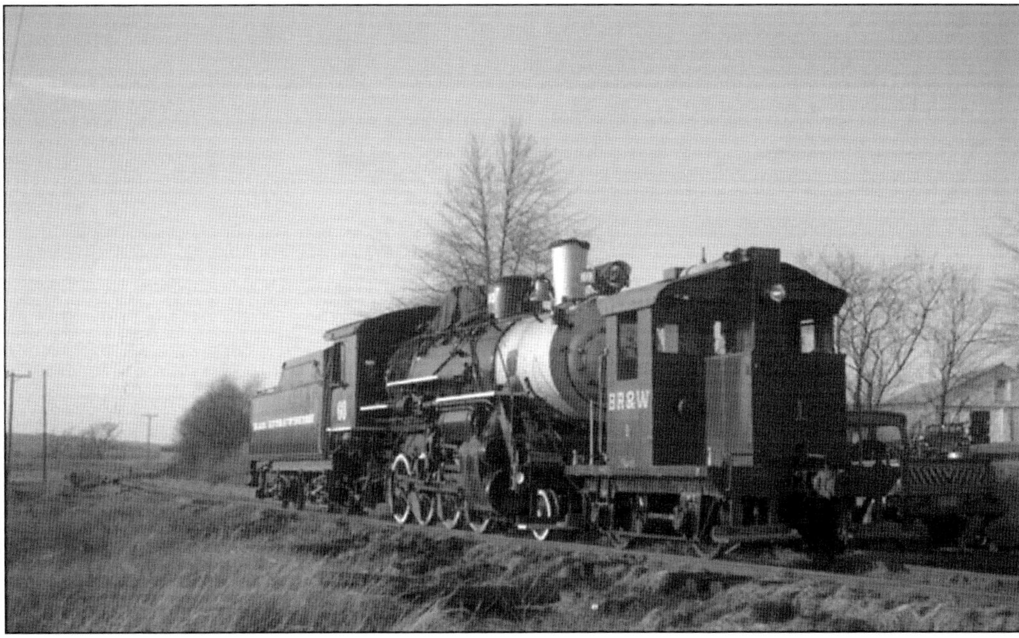

Black River & Western's little Mack engine No. 1 made numerous trips back and forth between Flemington and Ringoes. She is shown here posed at Copper Hill before heading south to Ringoes with steam engine No. 60. Capable of pulling 300 tons at a top speed of 12 miles per hour, the little engine was put to work in a myriad of services. (Nelson Tower.)

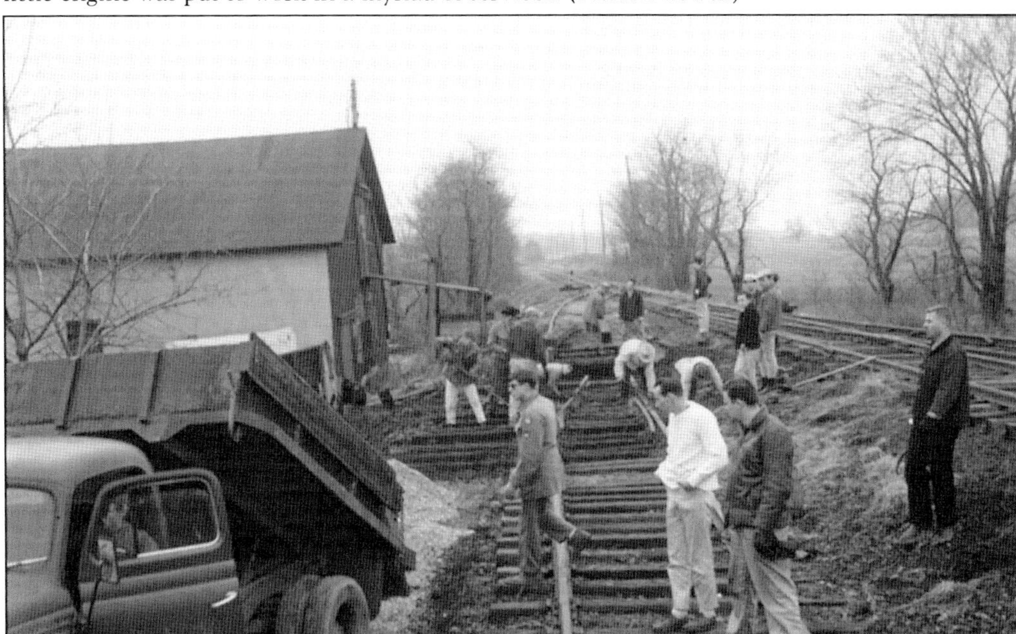

With additional equipment expected to arrive soon, the need for another siding for storage in Ringoes became apparent. Work on a new siding began in March 1965, and the second siding was added to the east side of the main track. This allowed for three storage tracks in Ringoes in 1965. (Nelson Tower.)

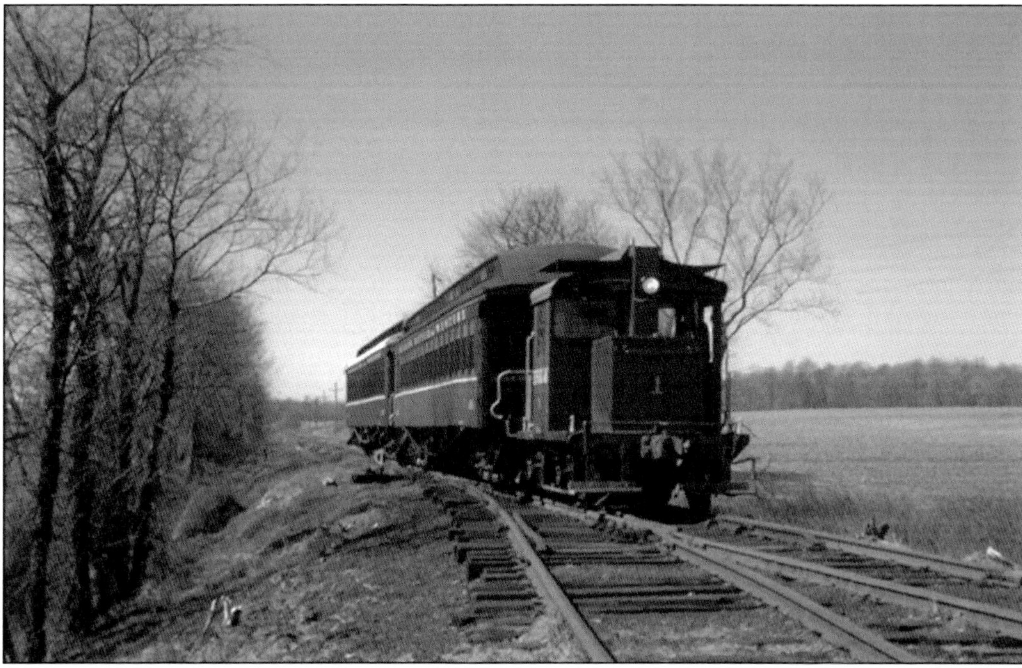

Since the steam engine was not yet ready for service, the little Mack engine No. 1 was called on to pull the first official stockholder trips over the line on April 3 and 4 in 1965. The train was prepared in Ringoes for the event using coaches No. 104 and No. 103. (Nelson Tower.)

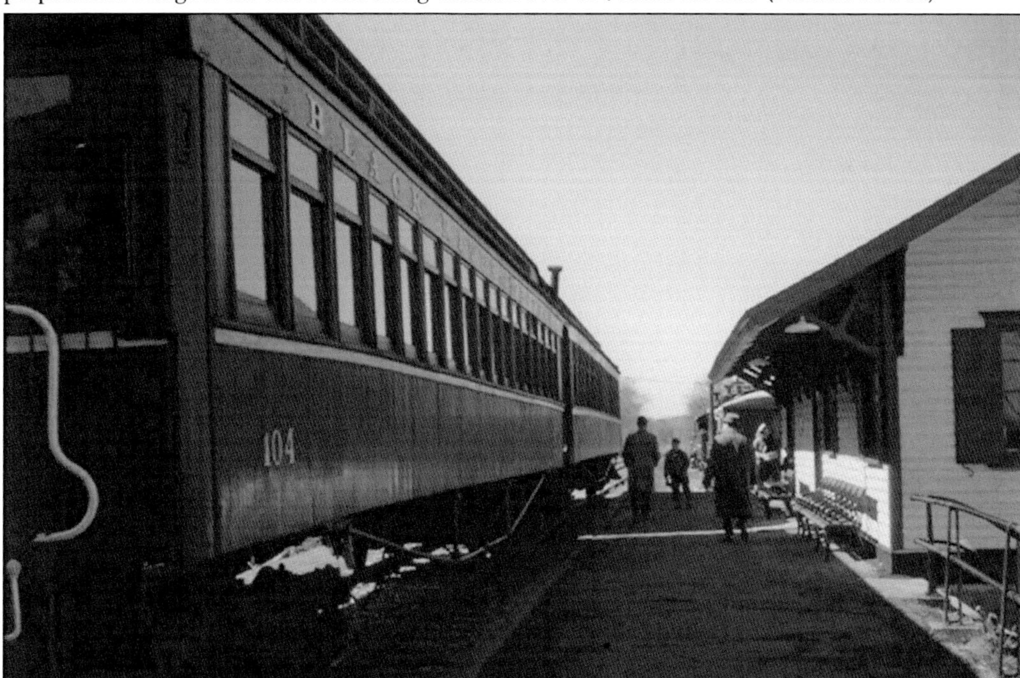

Passenger coaches No. 104 and No. 103 are ready to proceed from Ringoes north to Flemington, pulled by the little Mack locomotive No. 1. They will be greeted in Flemington by an enthusiastic crowd waiting for the first official stockholder trip over the new rail line. (Nelson Tower.)

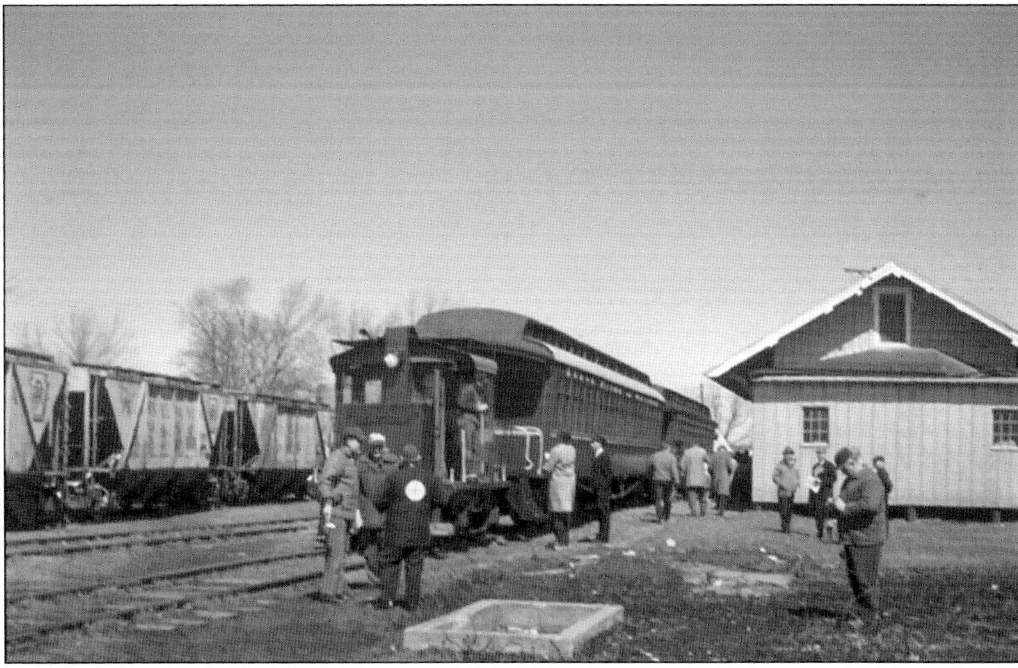

The first train stockholder's train waits at the Flemington station before departing for Ringoes. Stockholders and their families were invited for the first official trip over the new rail line. Later trips were for invited guests and prospective investors. The small ticket office had not yet been placed in Flemington for passenger excursions. (Nelson Tower.)

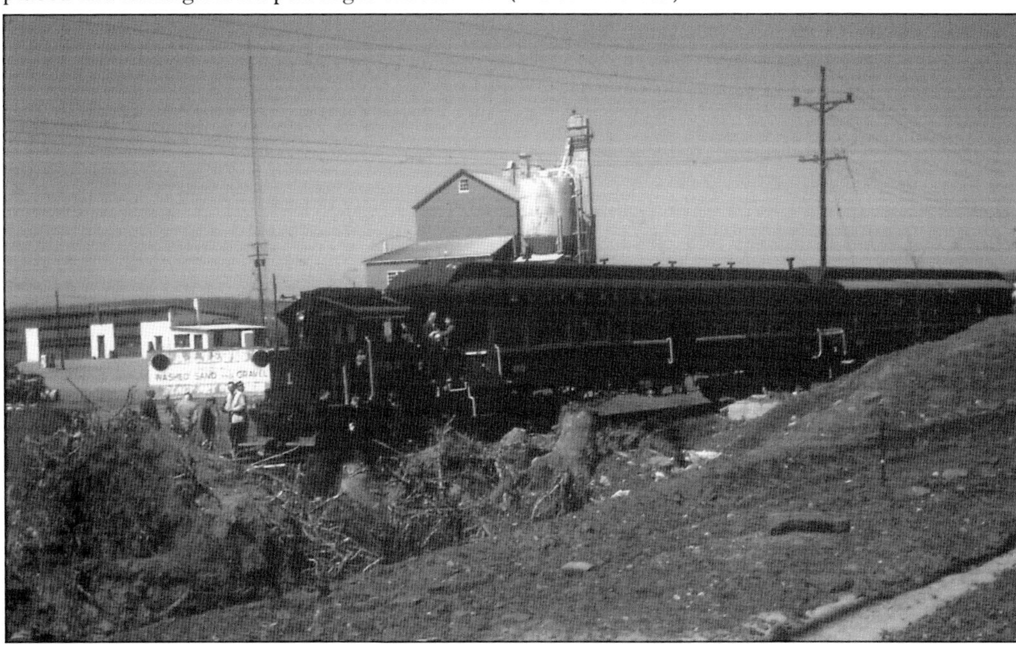

During its trip south towards Ringoes, the stockholders' trip train stops near what today is known as Hogtown to allow the engine to cool down and the passengers to have a chance to stretch their legs. The trip averaged five miles per hour with stops to cool down the locomotive. (Norman Cole.)

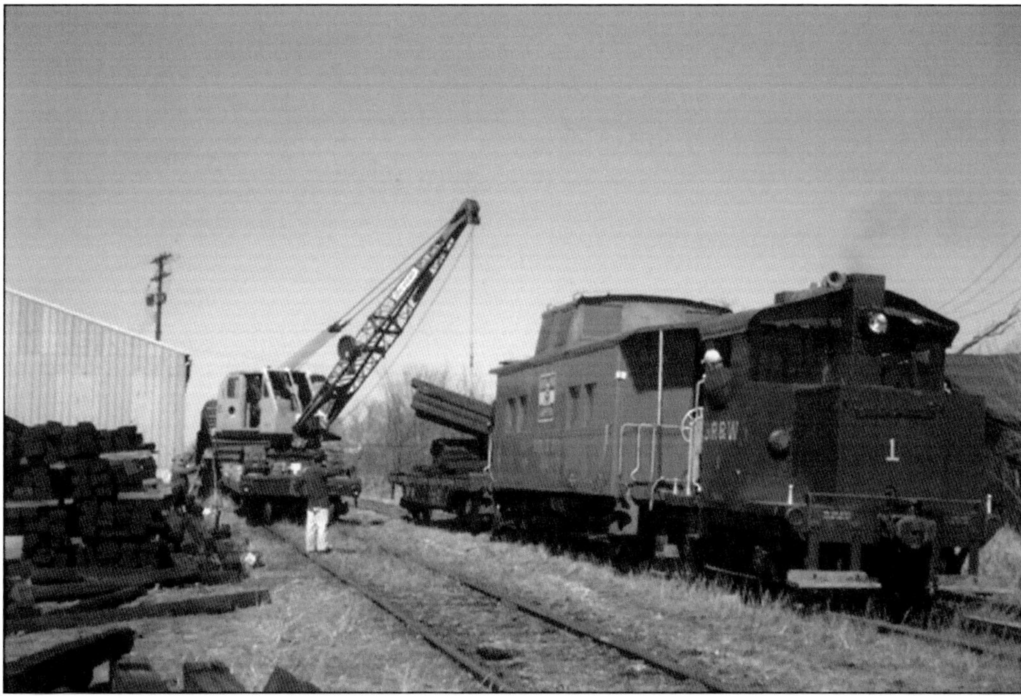

The little Mack locomotive was called on in the latter part of 1964 and the early part of 1965 to move flatcars loaded with railroad ties and rail that would be used in the renovation of the rail line between Flemington and Ringoes. (Nelson Tower.)

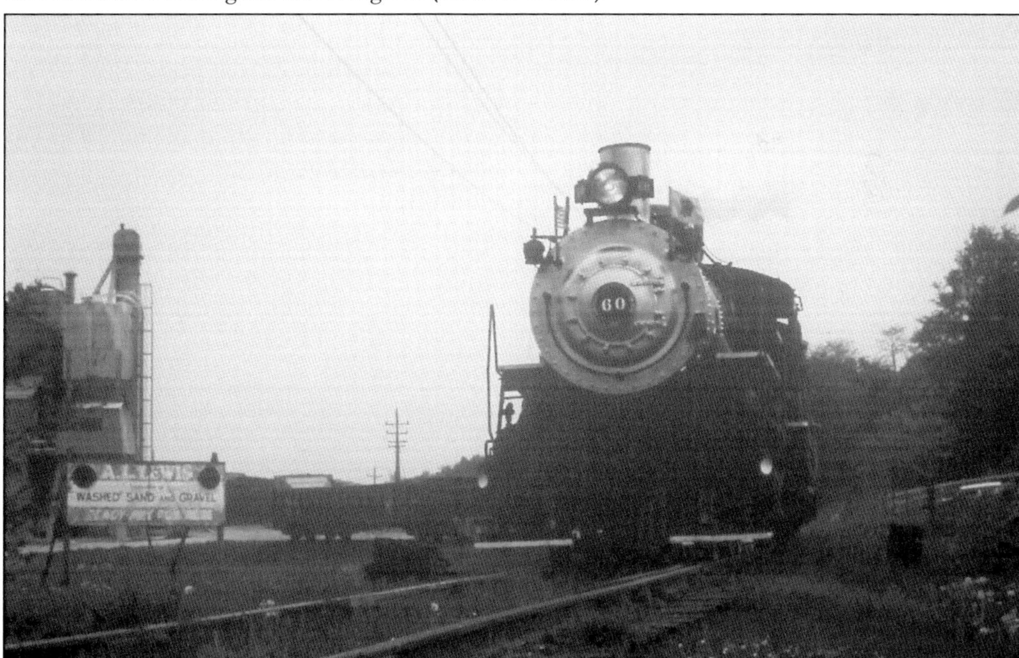

Steam engine No. 60 hauls ballast that had been loaded into a gondola from a local sand and gravel facility in 1965. The ballast would be transferred along the line to other equipment for distribution over the tracks.

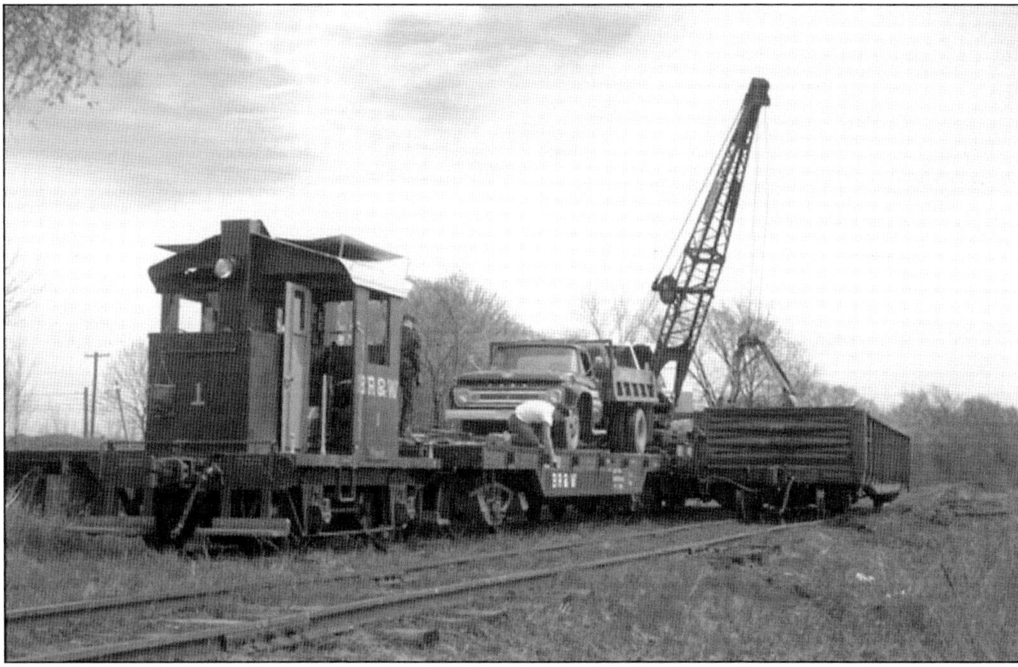

Ballast was loaded into the railroad's dump truck from a gondola car using the railroad's clamshell crane. It was spread by dumping it in spots along the rail line that needed additional ballast, which was a quick and easy way for the volunteers to accomplish the task. (Nelson Tower.)

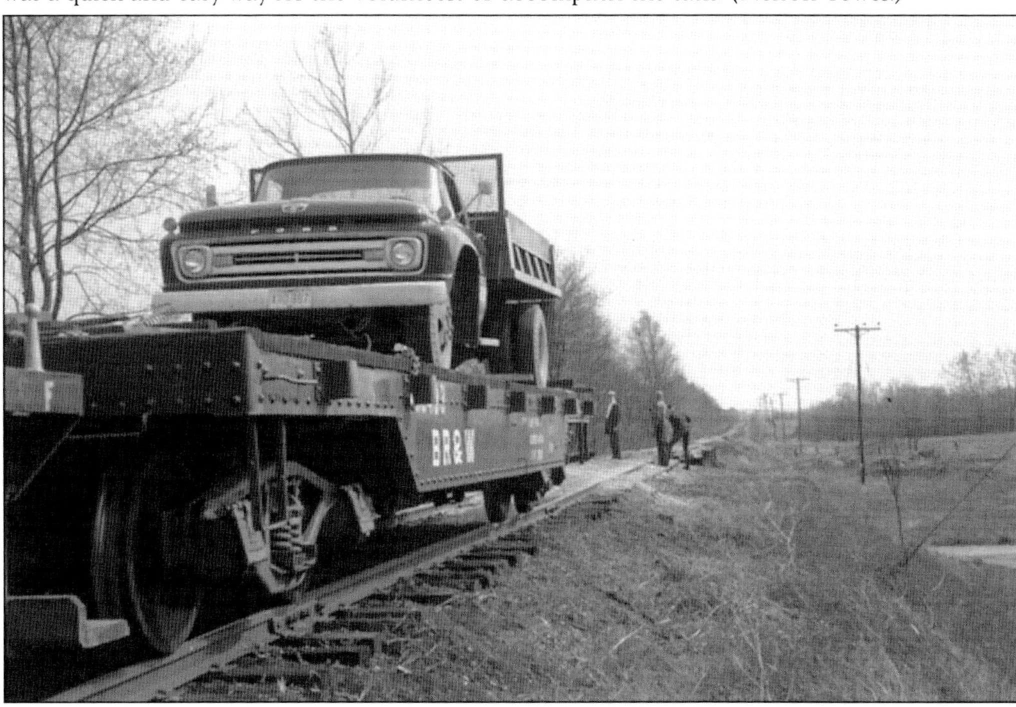

Part of the leasing agreement with the Pennsylvania Railroad was the upgrading of the existing railbed. Black River used the equipment it had, such as this flatcar loaded with a dump truck, to help spread needed ballast along the right-of-way in April 1965. (Nelson Tower.)

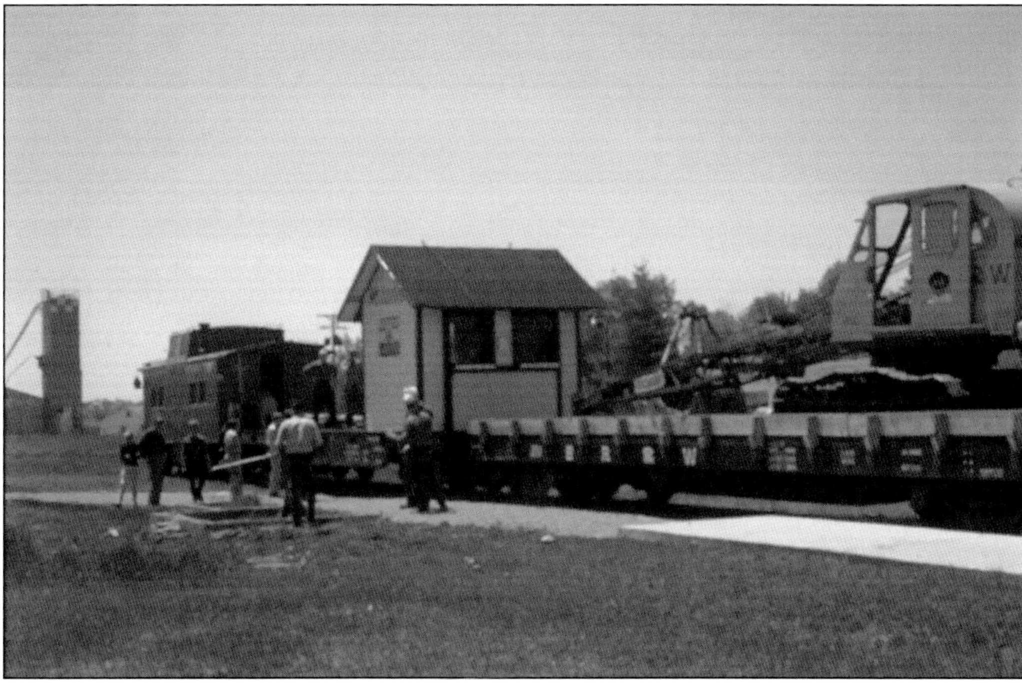

The new ticket office for the Black River & Western Railroad would be delivered on a flatcar and set into place by Black River's crane. The ticket office was built in Ringoes by John Bishop with the assistance of students from Hunterdon High School. (Nelson Tower.)

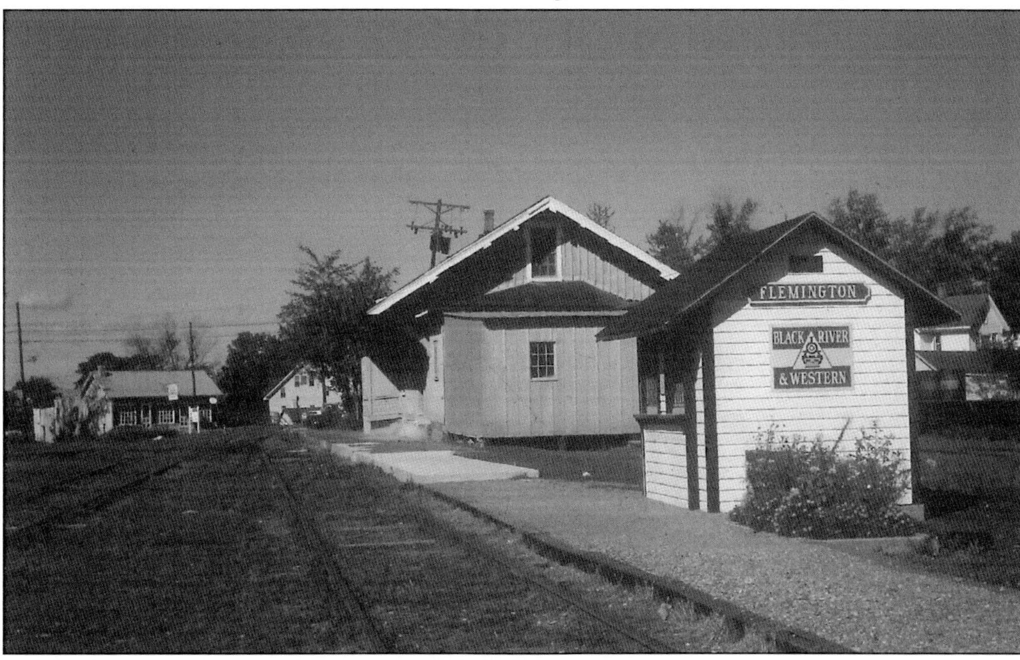

The new ticket office in Flemington is dwarfed by the original Pennsylvania Railroad station in the background. The little office served the railroad for several years, since the railway did not own the original station. The little shack was eventually replaced by one of the wooden coaches as a ticket office.

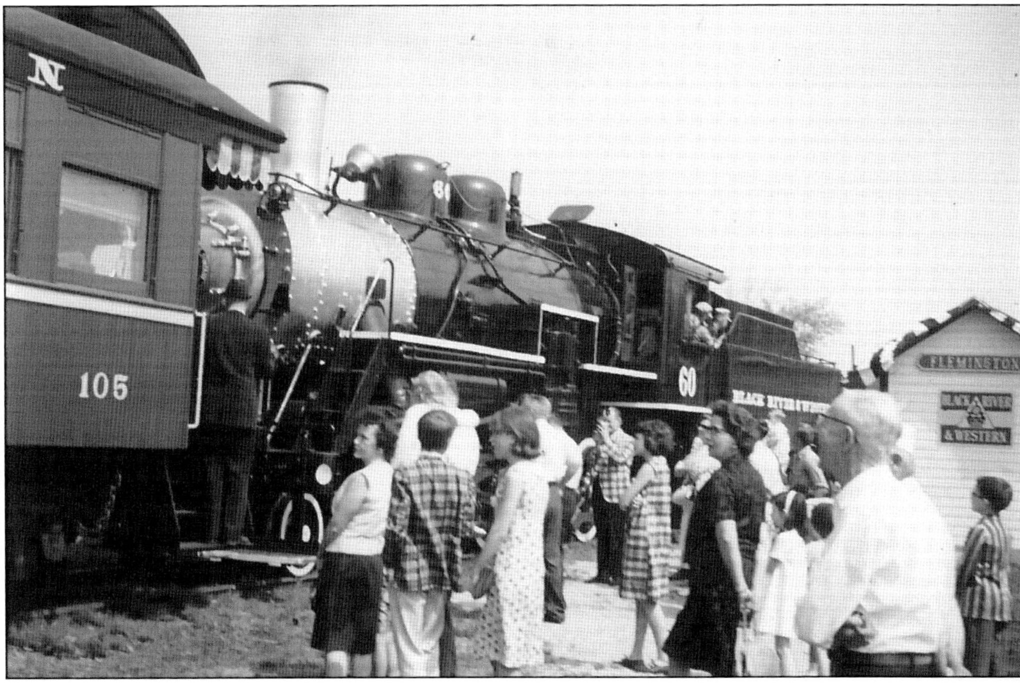

Steam engine No. 60 and the wooden passenger cars arrive in Flemington for the dedication ceremonies that officially began steam excursion service on May 16, 1965. Gov. Richard J. Hughes gave a short speech and then broke a bottle of champagne over the steam engines drive wheel to officially open the rail line. Over 200 people rode the train during the dedication trip. (Dick Hague collection.)

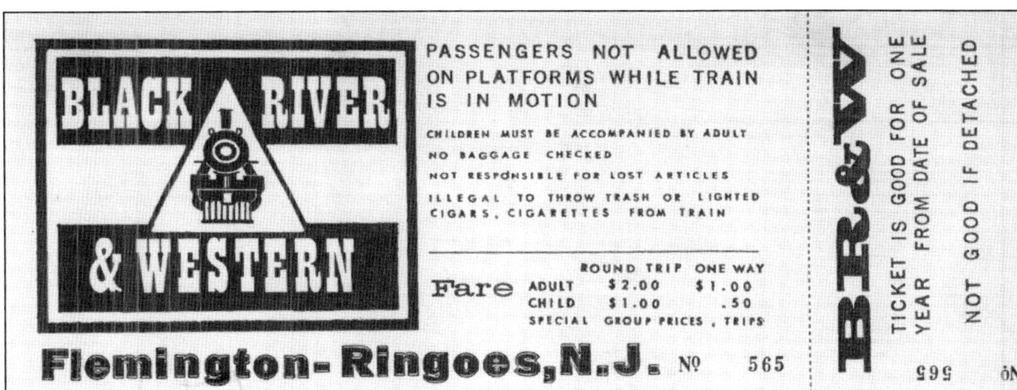

This ticket from 1965 shows the original fares of the Black River & Western Railroad approved by the Public Utilities Commission. The railroad's schedule provided for round-trip excursions between Flemington and Ringoes on Saturdays, Sundays, and holidays.

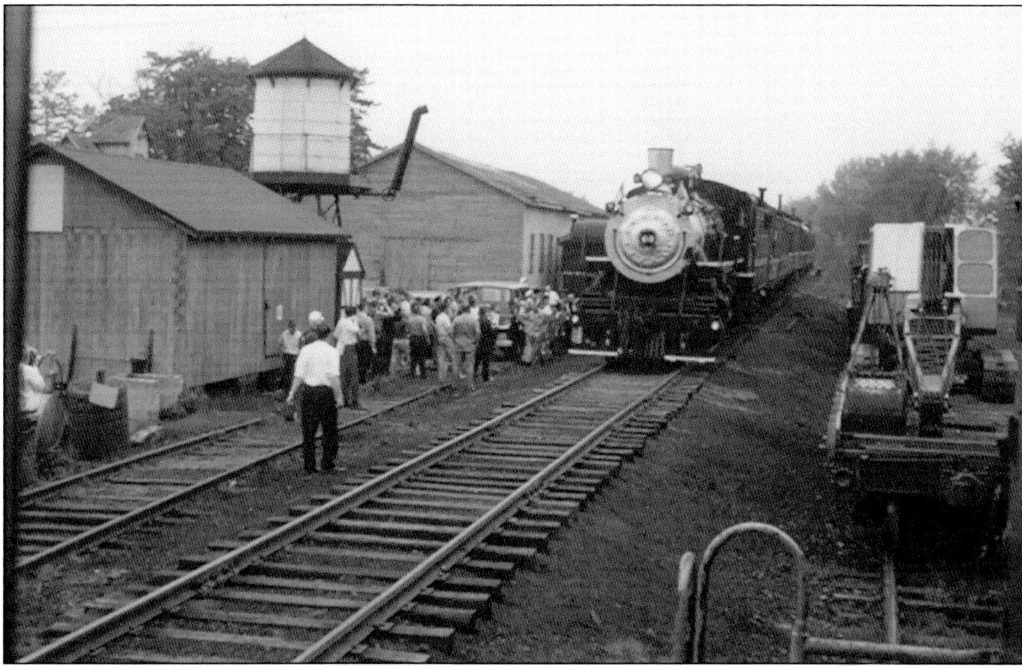

The first official trip of the steam engine was made on May 16, 1965, with then governor Richard J. Hughes and other officials aboard. Steam engine No. 60 and the wooden coaches arrive in Ringoes to an enthusiastic crowd waiting to greet the governor. (Nelson Tower.)

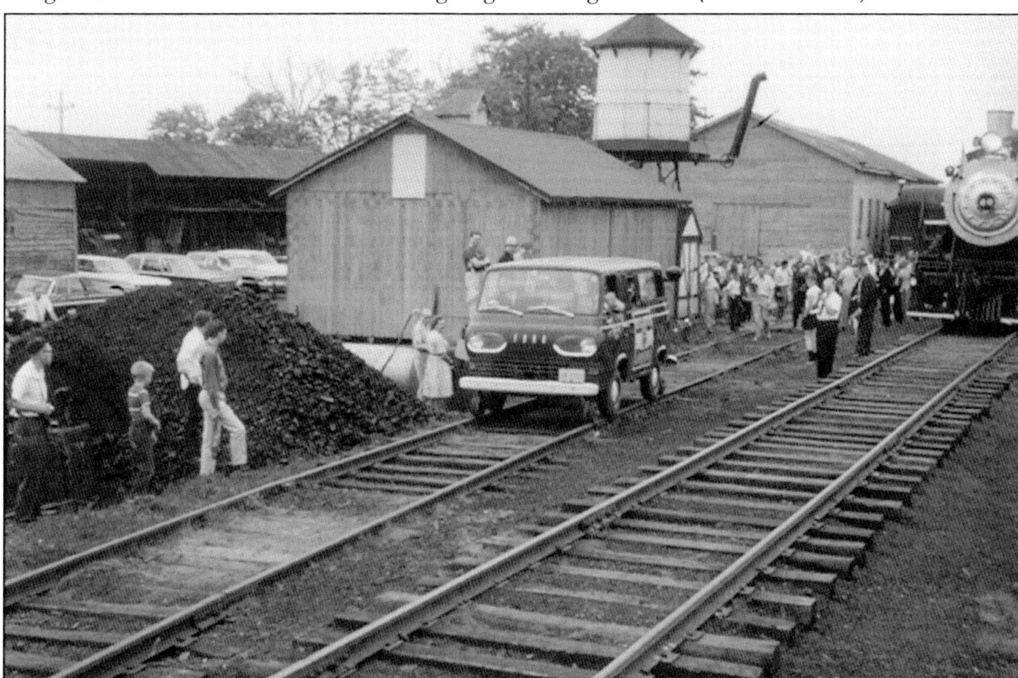

Governor Hughes was treated to a special tour of the remainder of the rail line to Lambertville in the railroad's track van, as service between Ringoes and Lambertville had not yet been upgraded for passenger excursions. (Nelson Tower.)

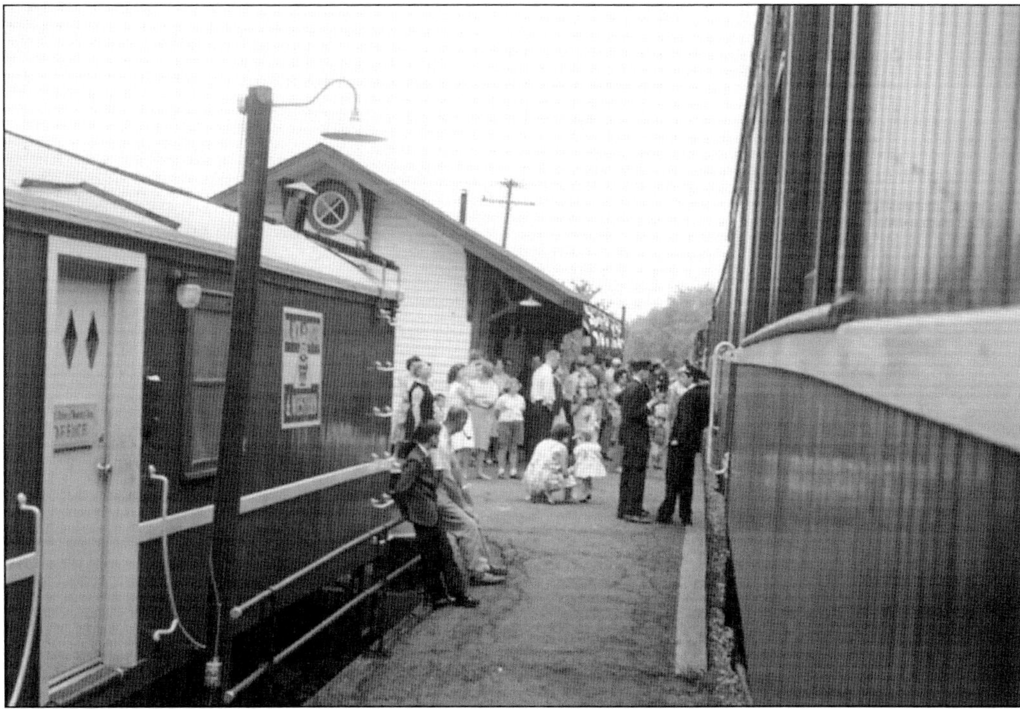

Passengers wait to board the train in Ringoes on May 16, 1965. The station is decorated with pleated banners for opening weekend. The railcar on the left is the railroad's business office car No. 106, an old converted Delaware, Lackawanna & Western Railroad Company (DL&W) wooden milk car. (Nelson Tower.)

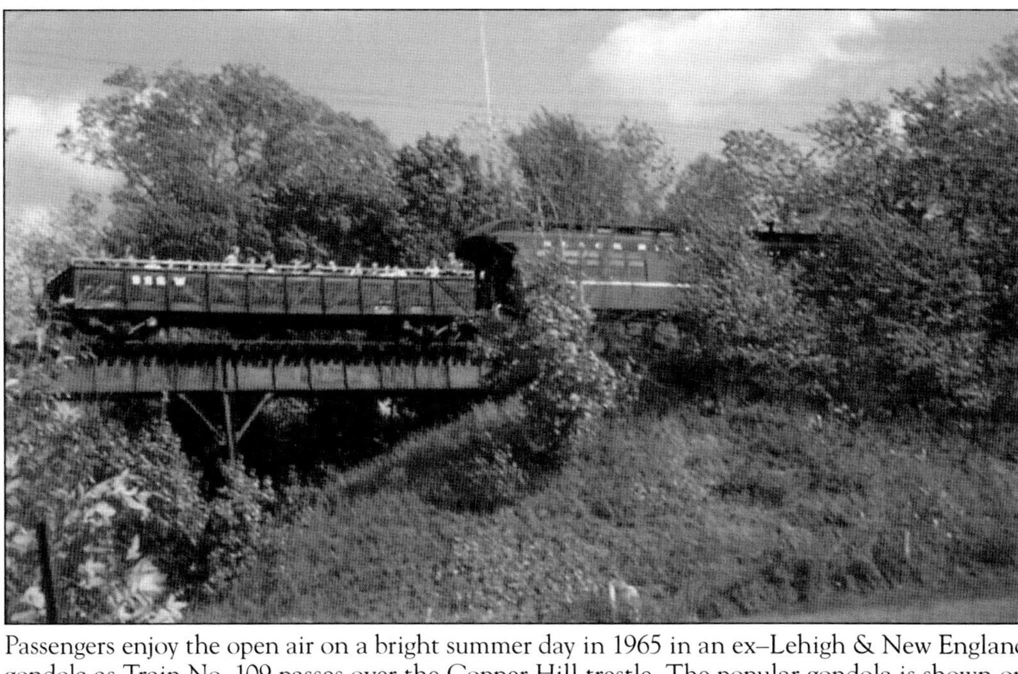

Passengers enjoy the open air on a bright summer day in 1965 in an ex–Lehigh & New England gondola as Train No. 109 passes over the Copper Hill trestle. The popular gondola is shown on the end of the train behind wooden center baggage car No. 102. (Nelson Tower.)

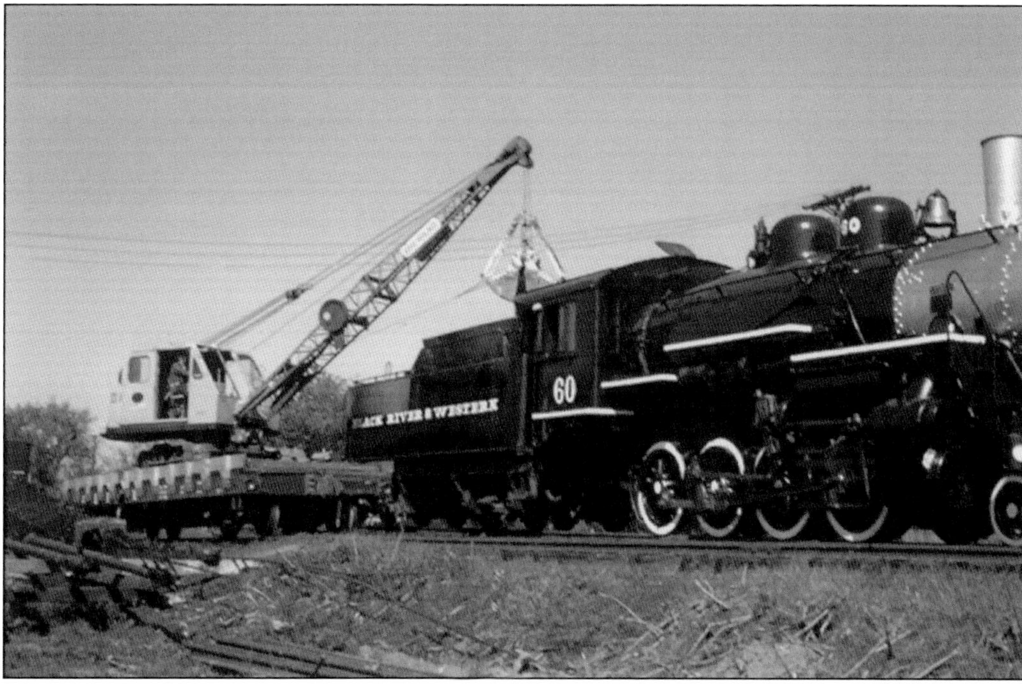

Part of getting steam engine No. 60 ready for service in the morning was to use the railroad's clamshell crane to load coal into the tender. The steam engine's tender was able to carry 12 tons of coal. (Nelson Tower.)

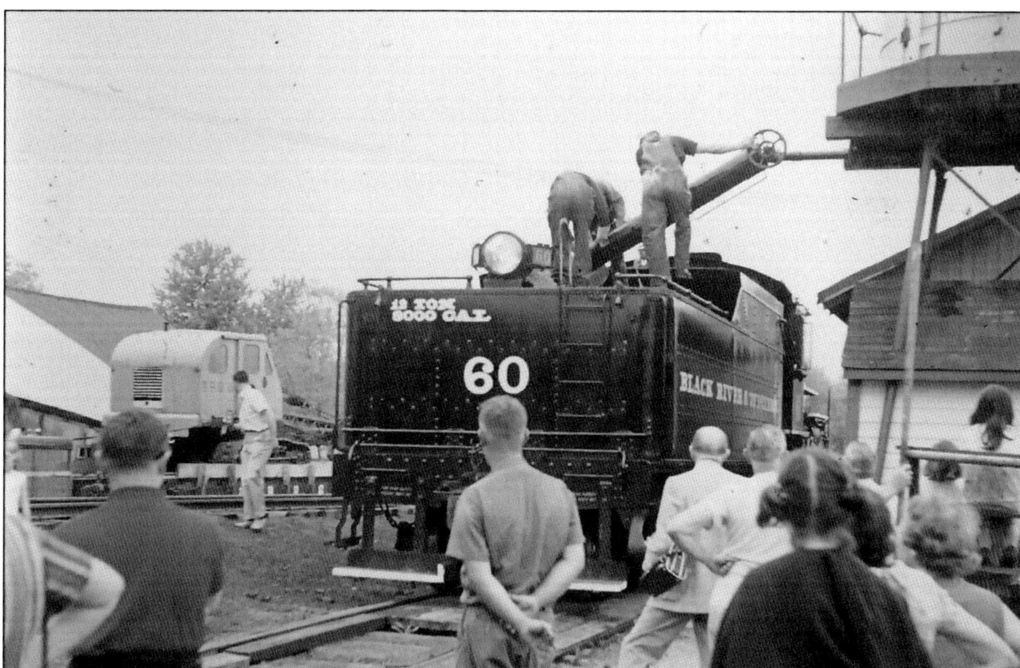

During their stop in Ringoes, interested passengers are treated to the sight of steam engine No. 60 taking on water in its tender from the railroad's water tower. The steam engine's tender was able to hold 8,000 gallons of water. (Nelson Tower.)

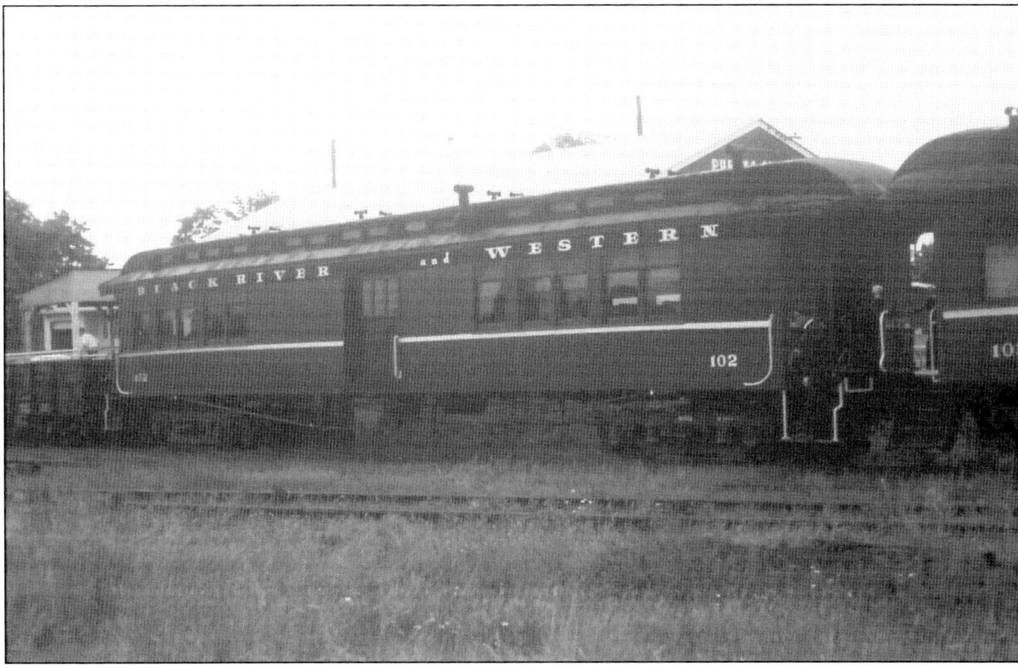

Passenger combine car No. 102 is seen in service in Flemington in June 1965. Conductor John Bishop often referred to this car as "potatoes in the middle, people on the ends." The car was painted green with yellow trim and lettering along with a black roof.

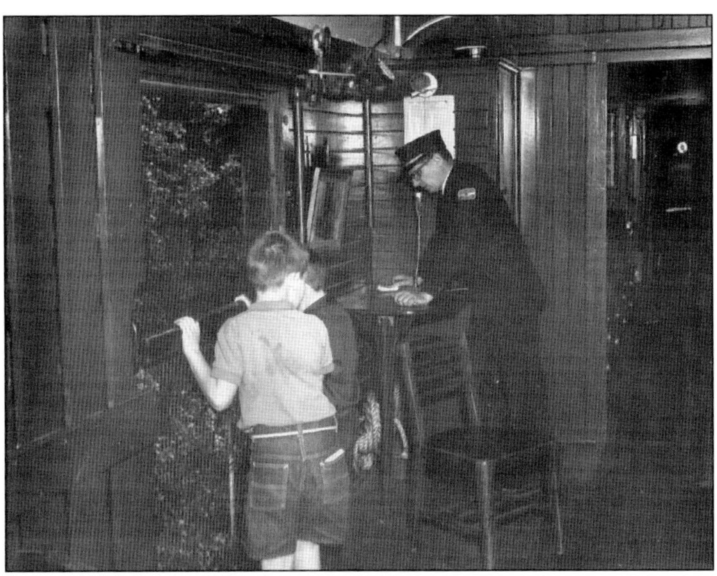

Conductor John Bishop makes announcements over the PA system in combine car No. 102 while two young riders are nearby. Bishop would greet the passengers with an announcement: "Good afternoon, ladies and gentleman, welcome aboard the Black River & Western Railroad." (Photograph by James Thorn, John Bishop collection.)

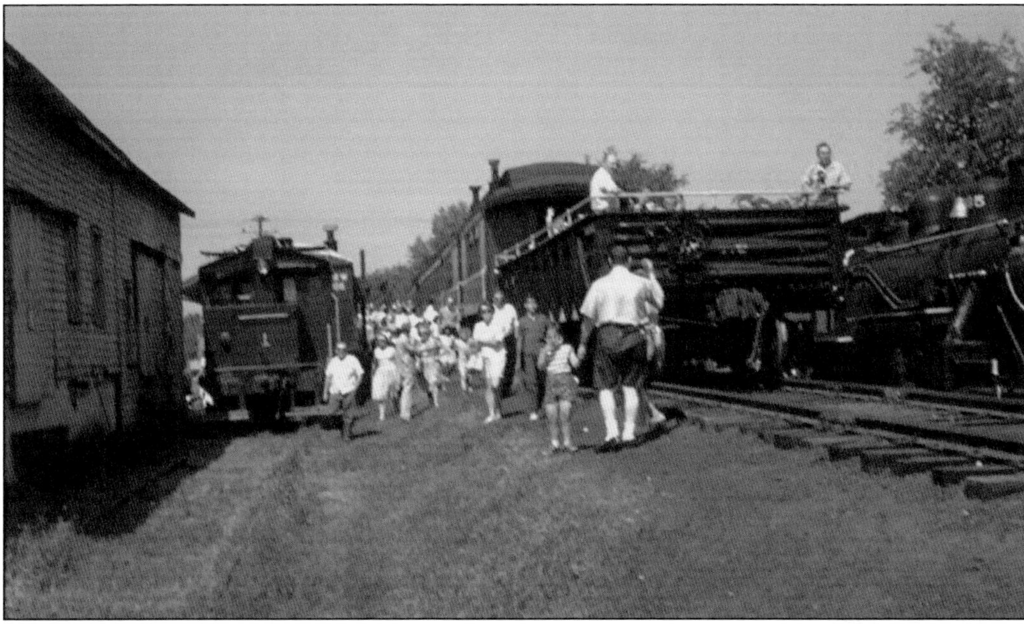

June 1965 saw lots of activity in Ringoes. The little Mack engine No. 1 sits idle on the siding in front of the home office railcar No. 106, a converted wooden milk car. The wooden coaches are starting to be filled with passengers as some ride in the ex–Lehigh & New England gondola that was converted to an open car. (Nelson Tower.)

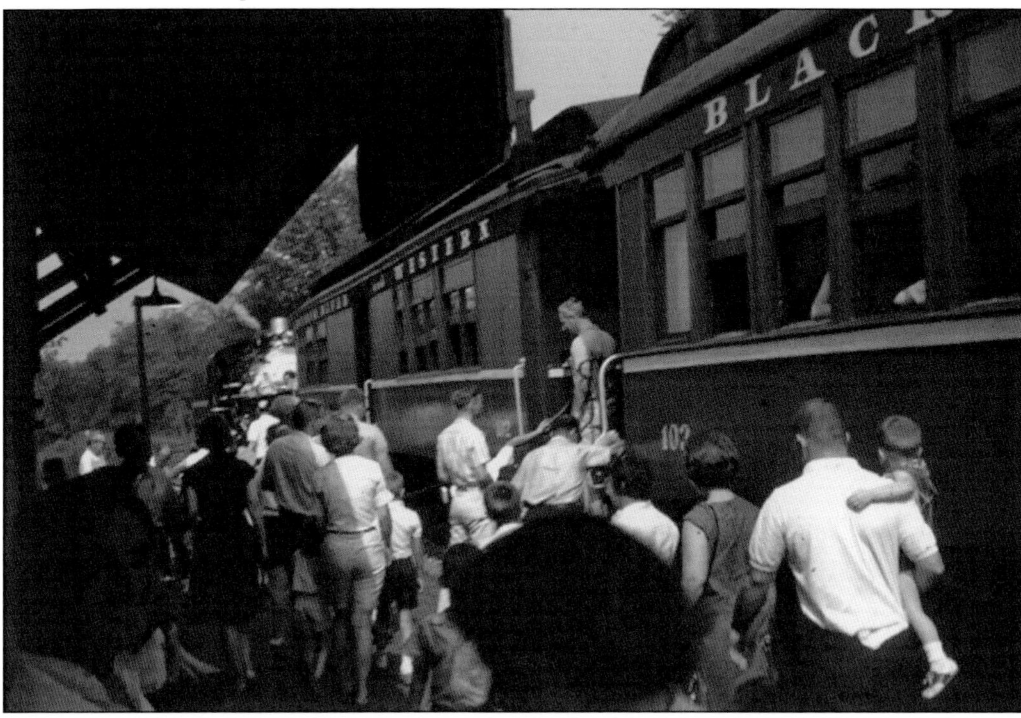

Passengers at the Ringoes station board wooden coaches No. 102 and No. 103 for the return trip to Flemington while steam engine No. 60 waits for signals. During 1965, there was much interest in the steam railroad, as cars were filled with passengers. (Nelson Tower.)

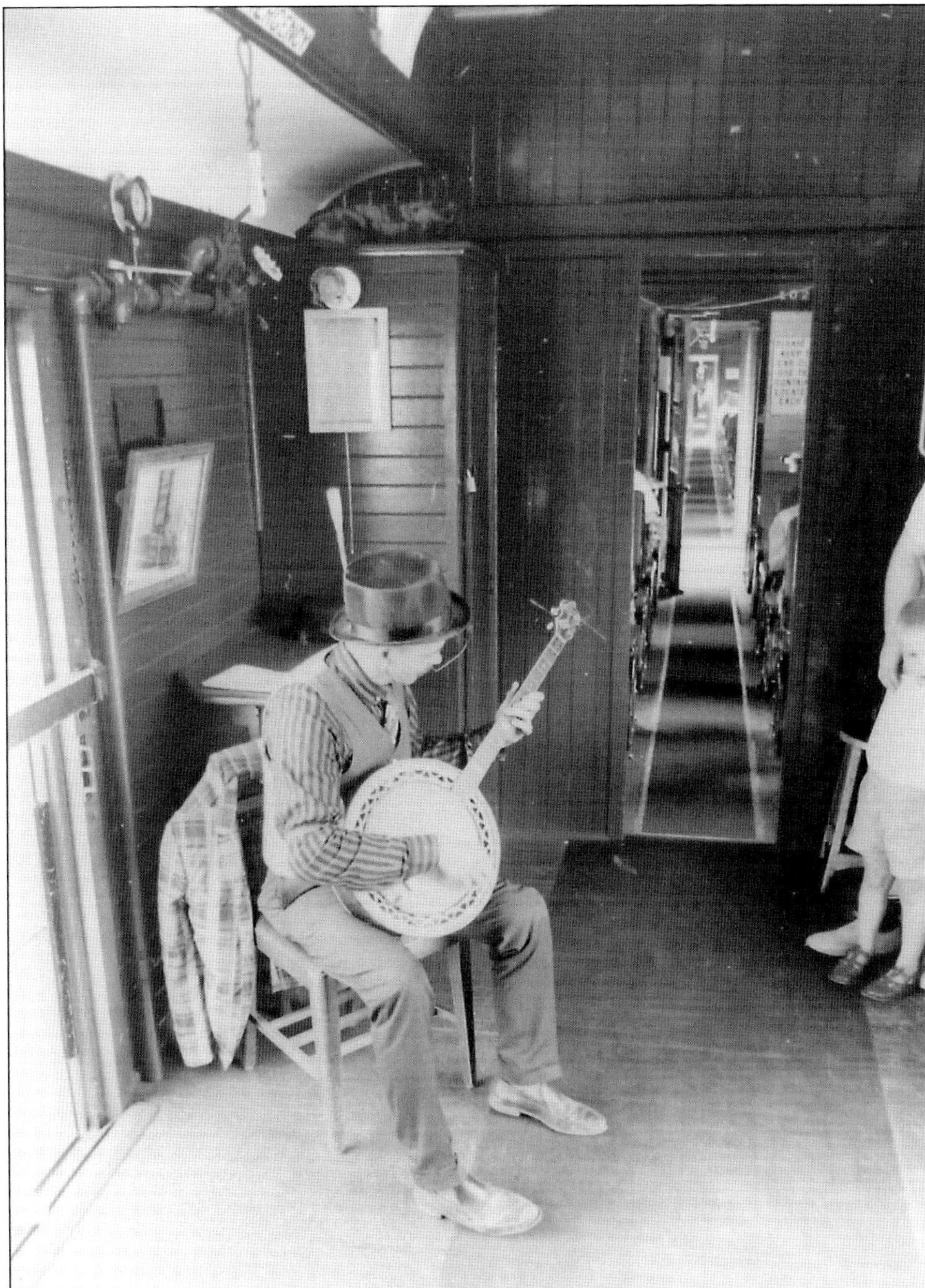

During the 1965–1966 season, an entertainer and railfan named Diamond Paul Jones proposed an idea to sing on the train. On weekend excursions, he would play his classic banjo for the enjoyment of the passengers on the train. Sporting a thick waxed mustache, fancy vest, and hat, Jones established himself in the baggage car No. 102 and play over the PA system. He had a rare talent for music, was a master of the banjo, and had a repertoire of over 2,200 songs memorized. (Jim Thorn.)

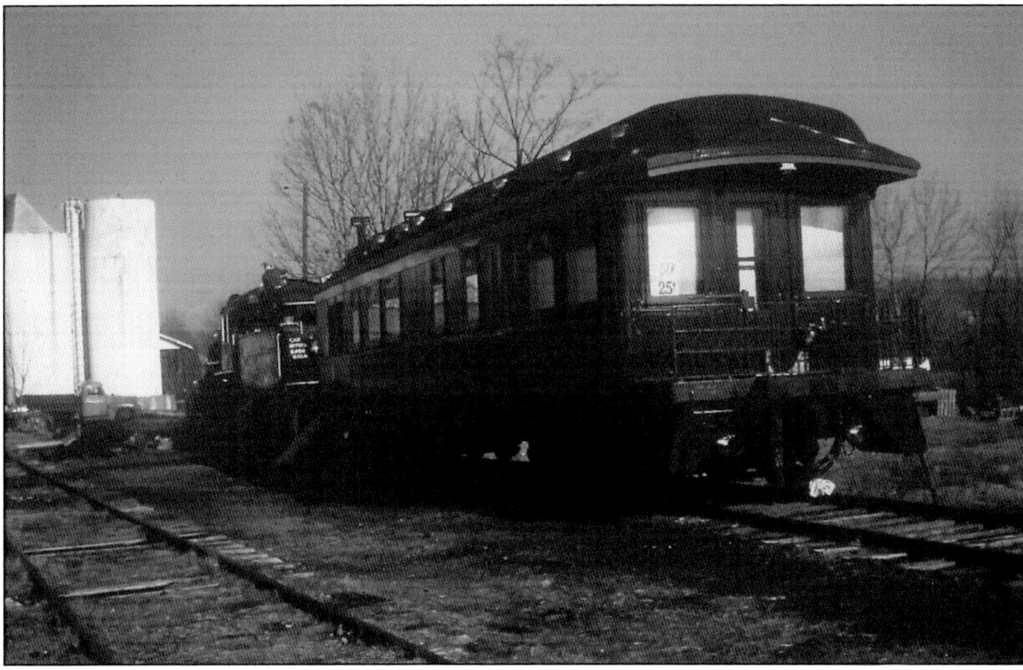

Passenger coach No. 105 and steam locomotive No. 565 sit in temporary storage in Flemington. Business car No. 105 shows the sign for tour prices of the car as 50¢ for adults and 25¢ for children. (Norman Cole.)

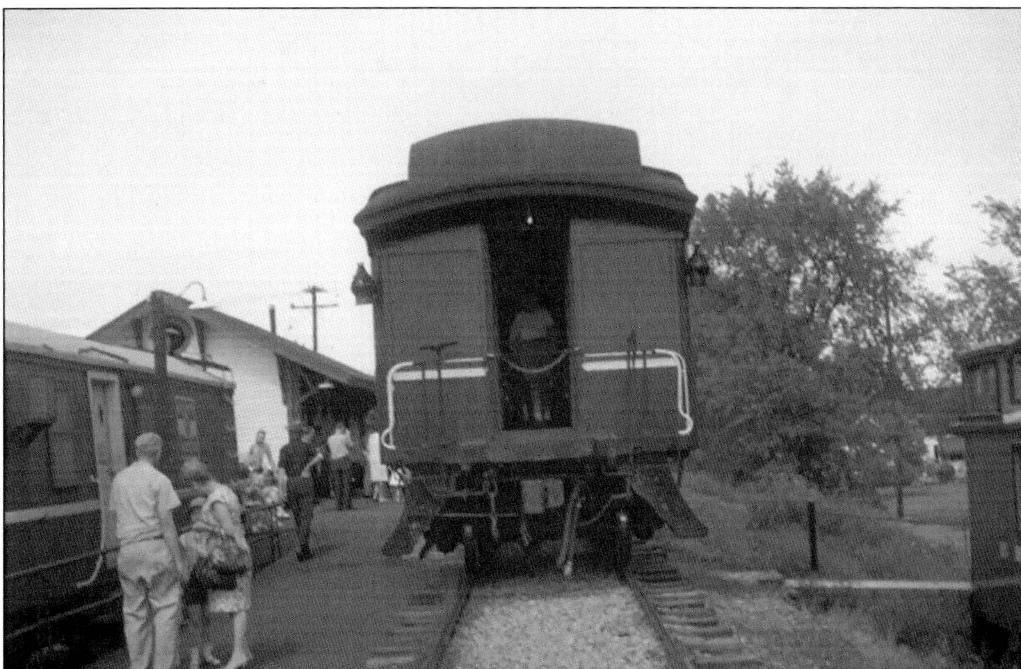

Passenger car No. 101 waits at the Ringoes station while passengers board. To the left is the business office car No. 106, and on the right is the four-wheel caboose No. 1. Note the plank used as a walkway to access the caboose. (Nelson Tower.)

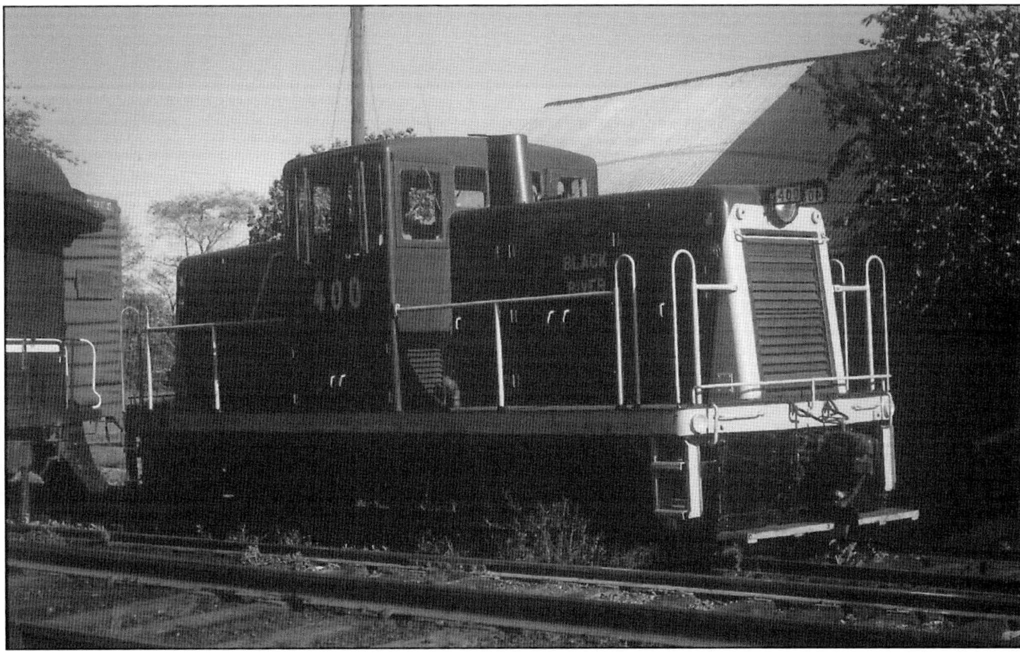

Black River acquired a 1950 ex–Long Island Rail Road 44-ton General Electric center cab locomotive. It was repainted, numbered 400, and used in a variety of duties. Owned by the railroad's treasurer, Samuel Freeman, the locomotive was leased to the Black River & Western Railroad.

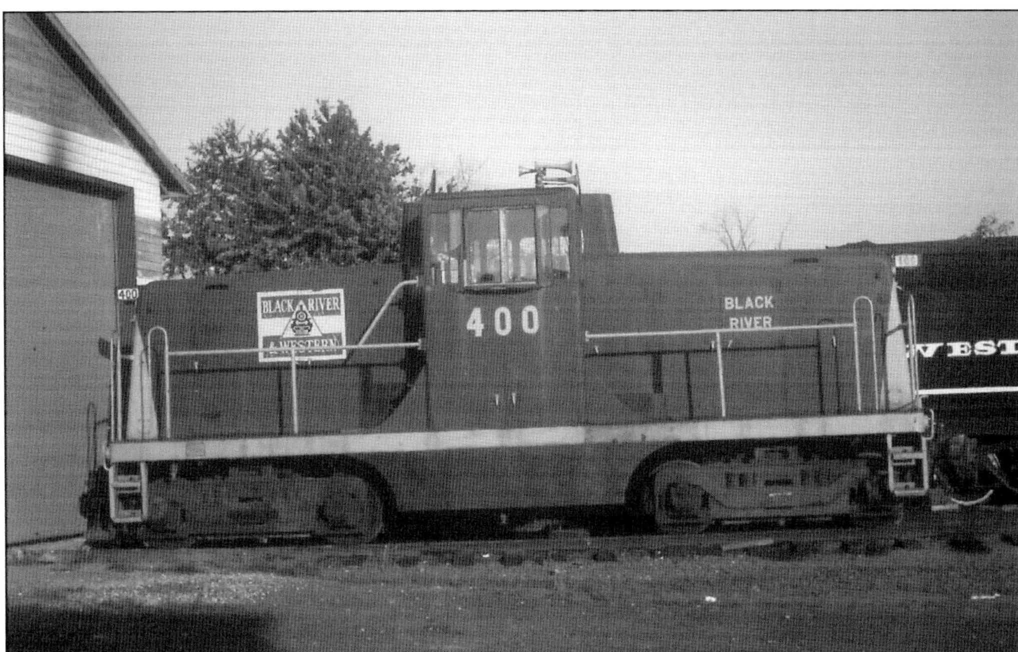

Locomotive No 400 sits on the engine house track with the tender of steam engine No. 60 behind. Locomotive No. 400 would come to be called "Little 400" or "First 400" when another diesel locomotive also numbered 400 was later brought to the railroad.

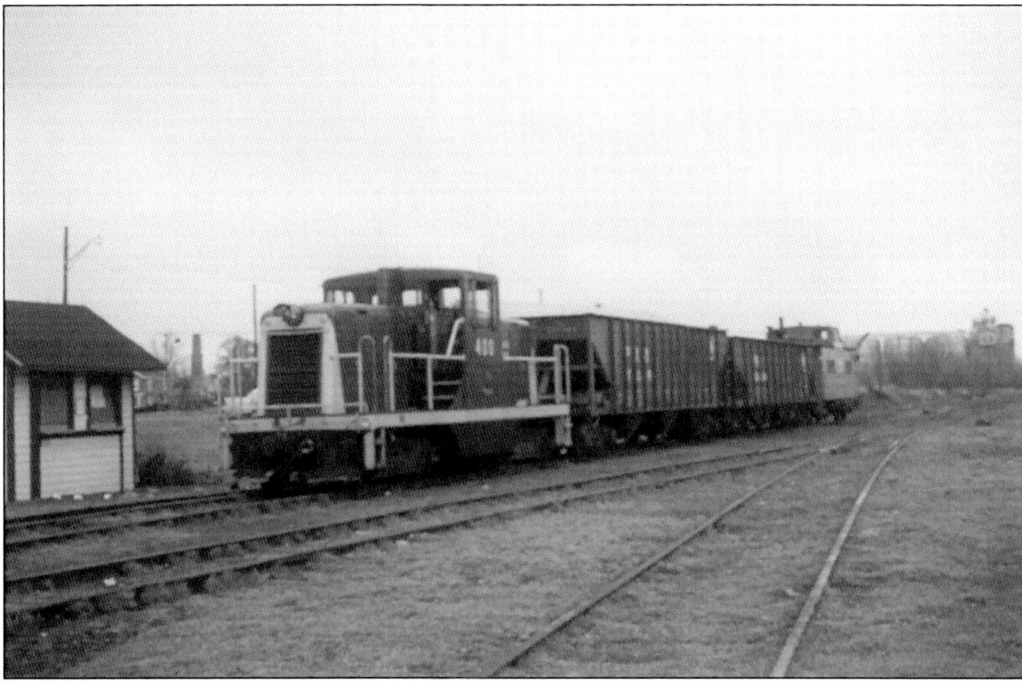

Locomotive No. 400 was called on to move two hopper cars of ballast in November 1965. The locomotive is shown here in Flemington along with the caboose No. 200. The small ticket office in Flemington is on the left. (Nelson Tower.)

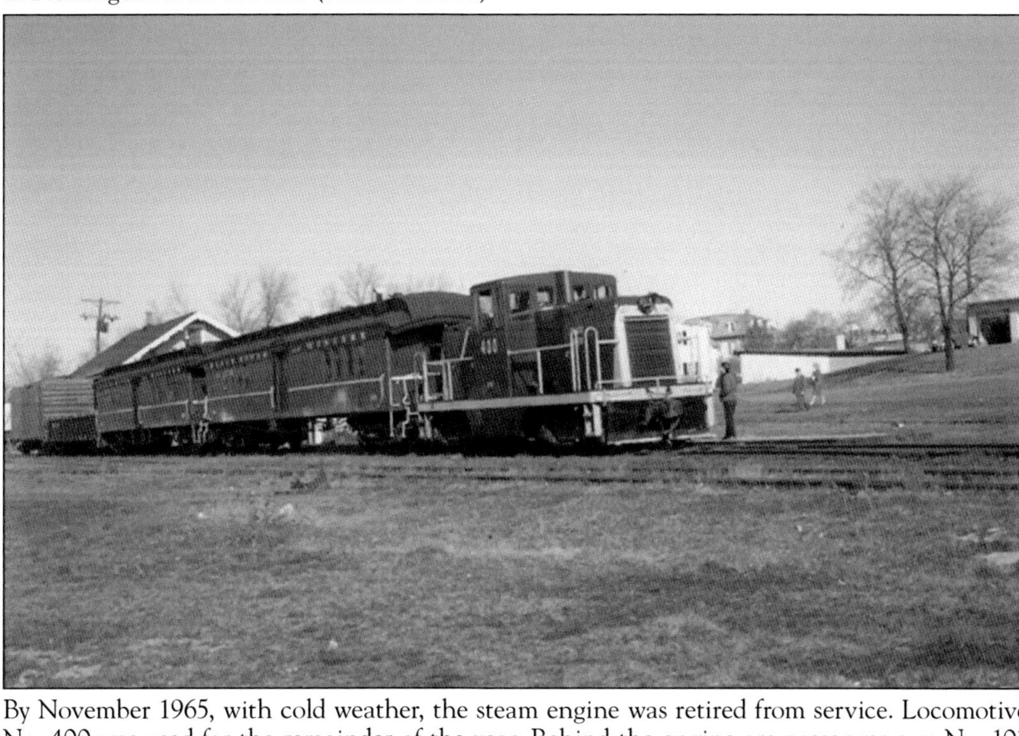

By November 1965, with cold weather, the steam engine was retired from service. Locomotive No. 400 was used for the remainder of the year. Behind the engine are passenger cars No. 101 and 102, along with the open gondola and a boxcar. (Nelson Tower.)

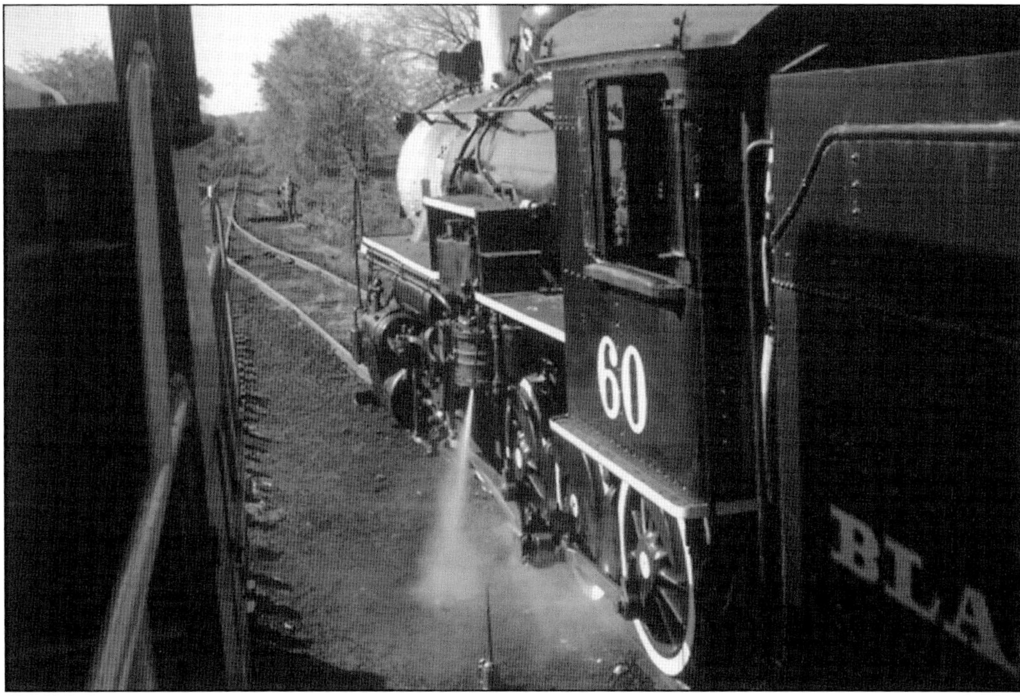

Steam engine No. 60 enters a siding in Ringoes to allow locomotive No. 400 to pull the passenger cars past. Once No. 400 pulled the passengers cars farther down the main track, the steam engine could then be placed on the other end for the trains for the return trip to Flemington. (Nelson Tower.)

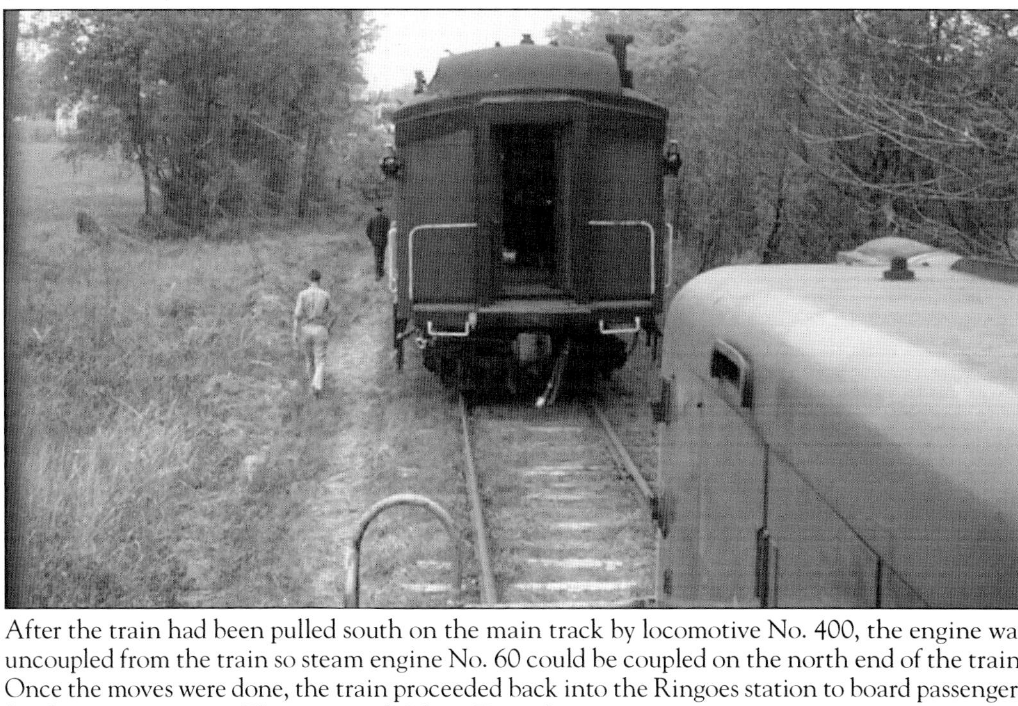

After the train had been pulled south on the main track by locomotive No. 400, the engine was uncoupled from the train so steam engine No. 60 could be coupled on the north end of the train. Once the moves were done, the train proceeded back into the Ringoes station to board passengers for their return trip to Flemington. (Nelson Tower.)

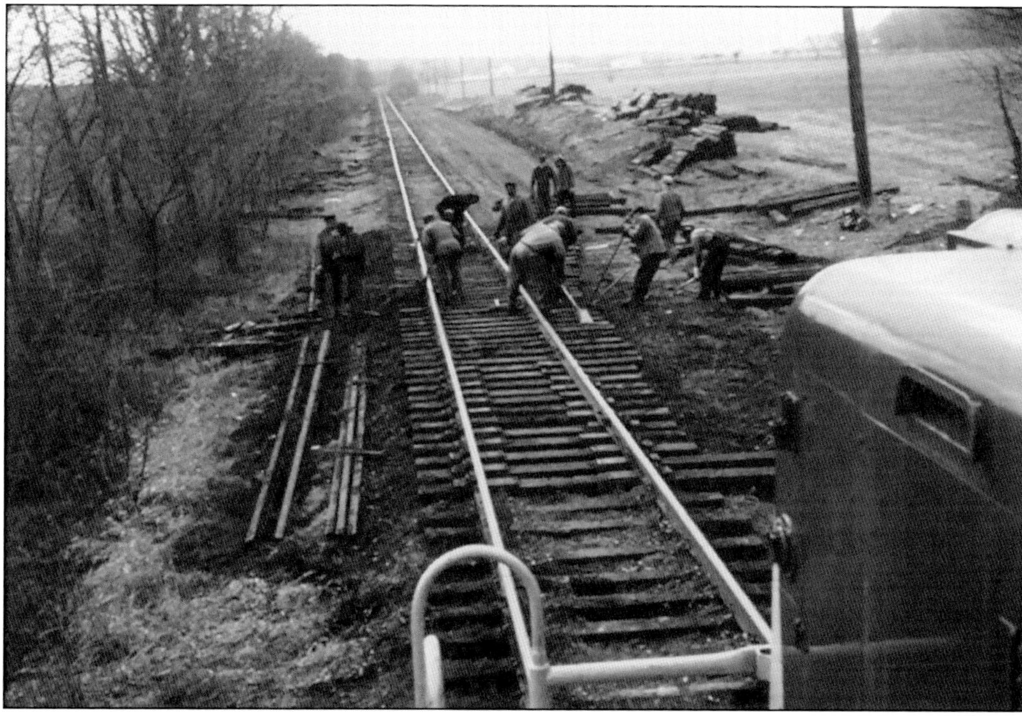

By the fall of 1965, the track gang began work on a new passing siding in south Ringoes. This would allow for the steam engine to run around the passenger cars for its return trip north and eliminate the need to use a second locomotive. (Nelson Tower.)

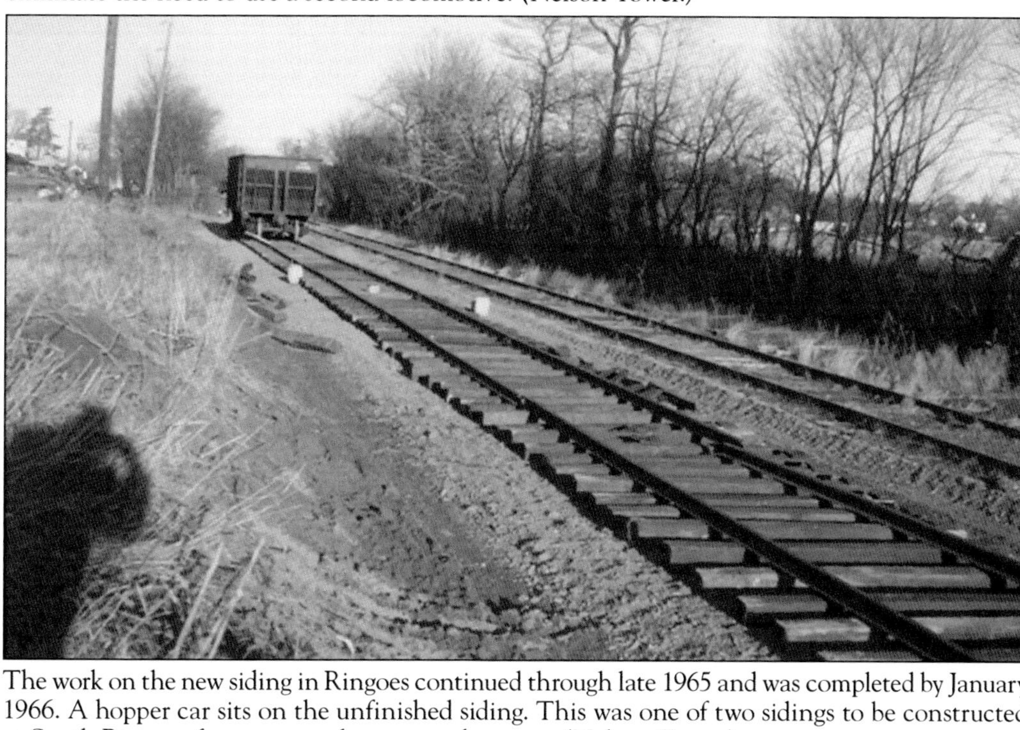

The work on the new siding in Ringoes continued through late 1965 and was completed by January 1966. A hopper car sits on the unfinished siding. This was one of two sidings to be constructed at South Ringoes for runaround moves and storage. (Nelson Tower.)

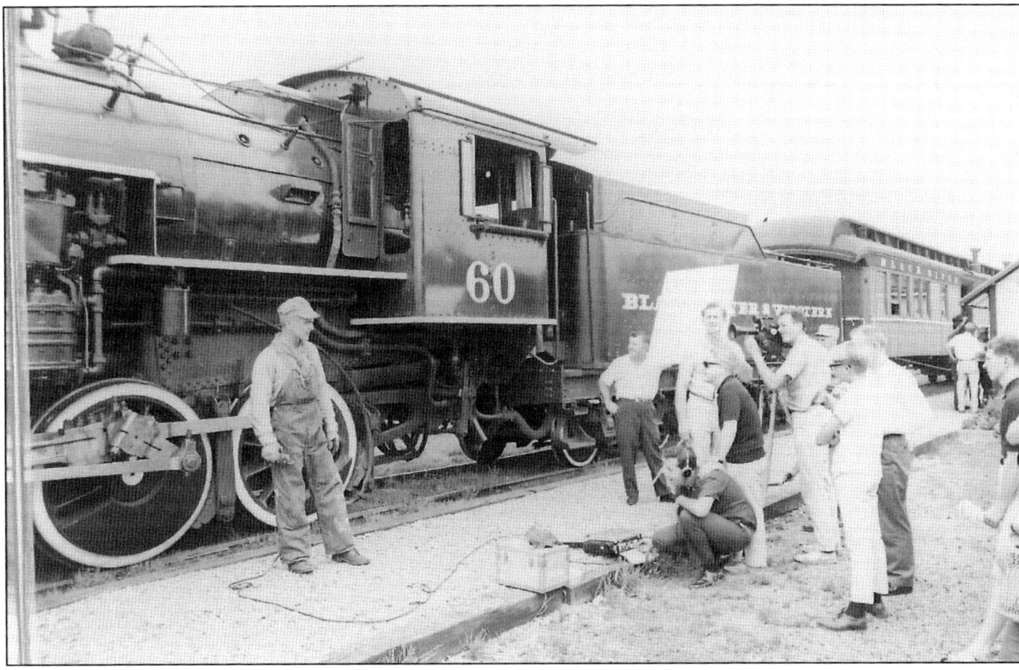

Engineer Lloyd Arkinstall poses for the camera in front of steam engine No. 60 in Flemington during the production of a 15-minute CBS News segment, "Boys will be Boys," filmed on the railroad in 1965. (Jim Thorn.)

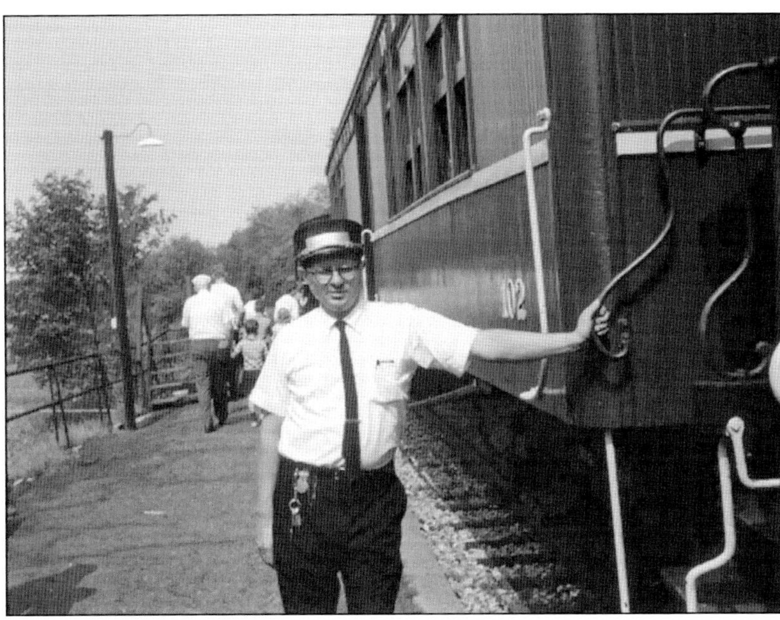

Conductor John Bishop waits to board passengers on coach No. 102 in Ringoes. Bishop served as conductor every Saturday or Sunday and would play a recorded historical lecture about the rail line over the PA system every trip from Flemington.

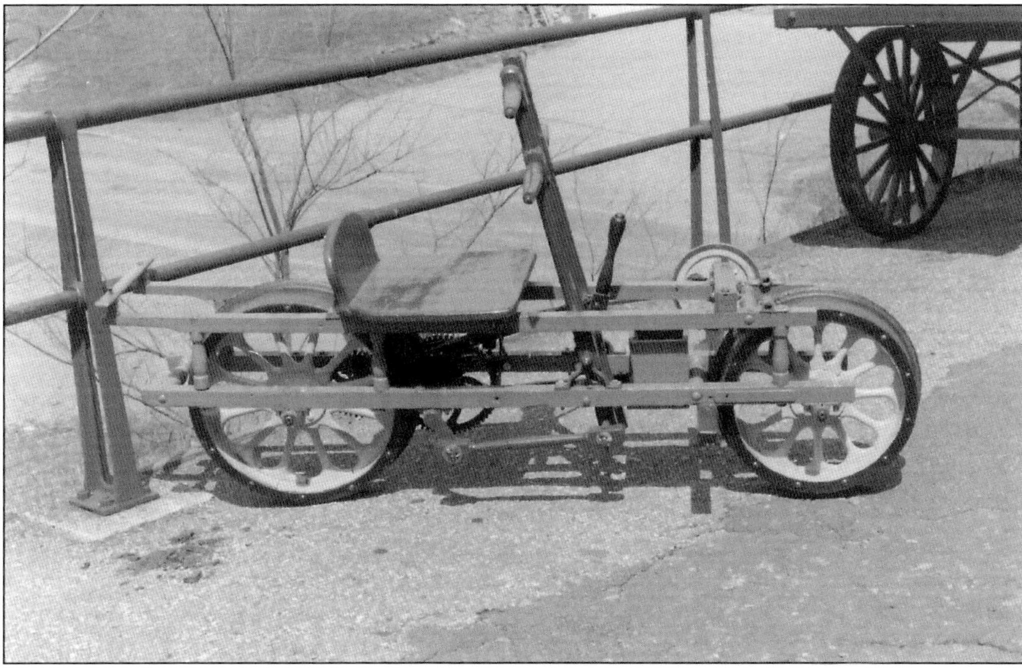

The hand-pump velocipede was restored in 1965 by John Bishop as a school project from only the gears and wheels on hand. The velocipede sat at the Ringoes station platform as a display for many years. The wheel of a baggage cart, seen in the background, was also on display on the Ringoes platform for a number of years.

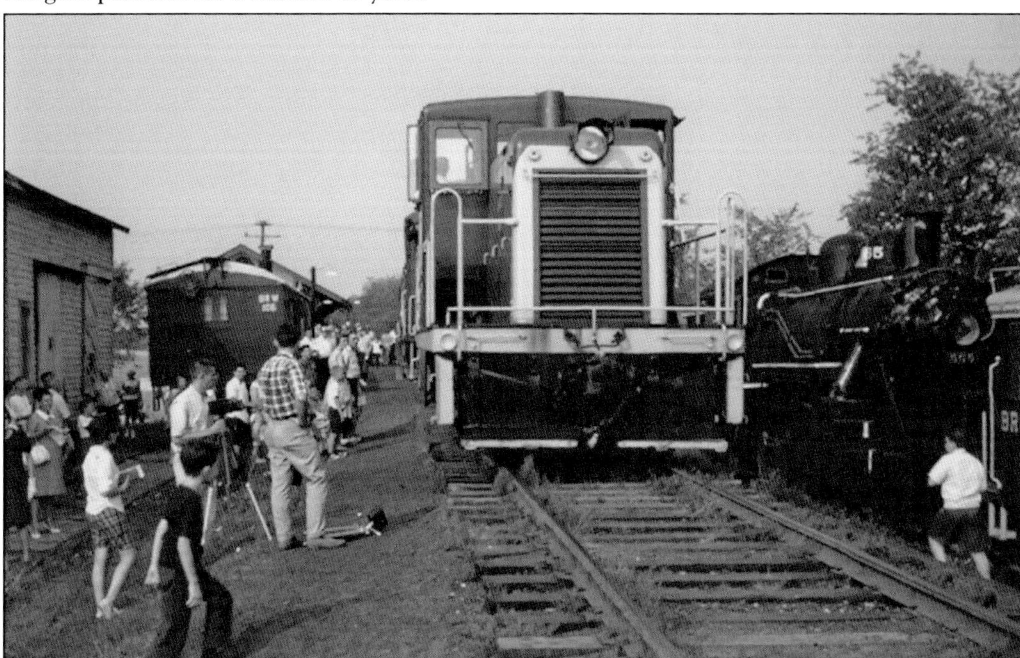

A busy day in August 1965 shows the No. 400 engine with the wooden coaches on the main track. On the left is the business office No. 106, and on the right is steam engine No. 565. The little Mack engine is on the extreme right of the photograph. (Nelson Tower.)

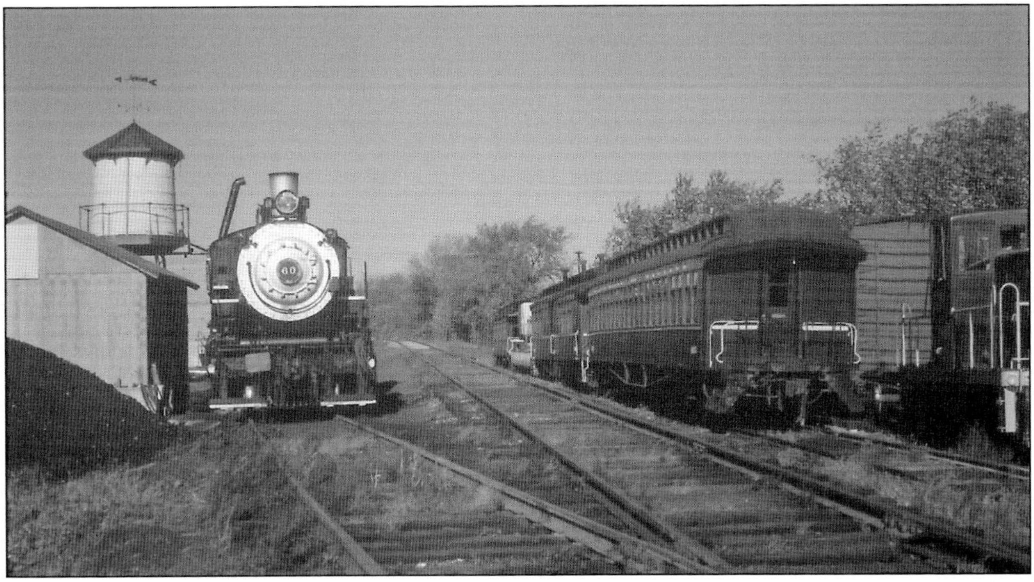

This peaceful October view of Ringoes in 1965 shows an idle steam engine, No. 60. Stored on the siding are passenger cars No. 103 and No. 102, flatcar No. 201 with a crane, and passenger car No. 104. Locomotive No. 400 is on the far right in front of a boxcar.

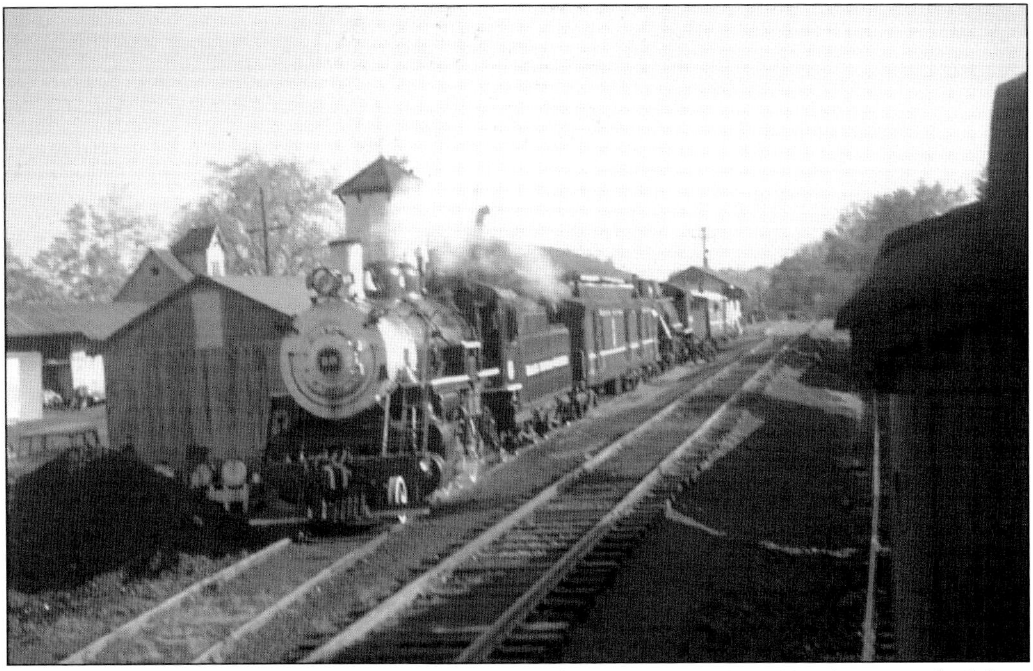

On an early September morning in Ringoes in 1965, steam engine No. 60 is being readied for a day of steam excursion runs. Behind engine No. 60 are car No. 100, the No. 565 steam engine, and the No. 106 business office. The remainder of the train set is stored on the tracks on the left. (Nelson Tower.)

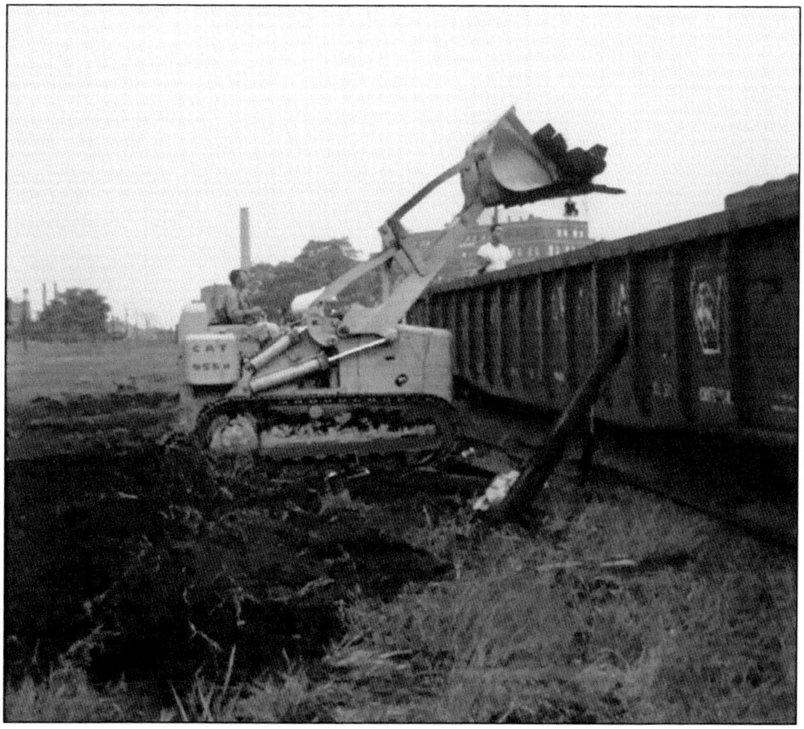

Railroad ties were salvaged from the Pennsylvania Railroad yard at Cass Street in Trenton to be used as replacement ties. Volunteers would load them into a gondola for transport to Ringoes, where they would be sorted for use along the railroad. (Nelson Tower.)

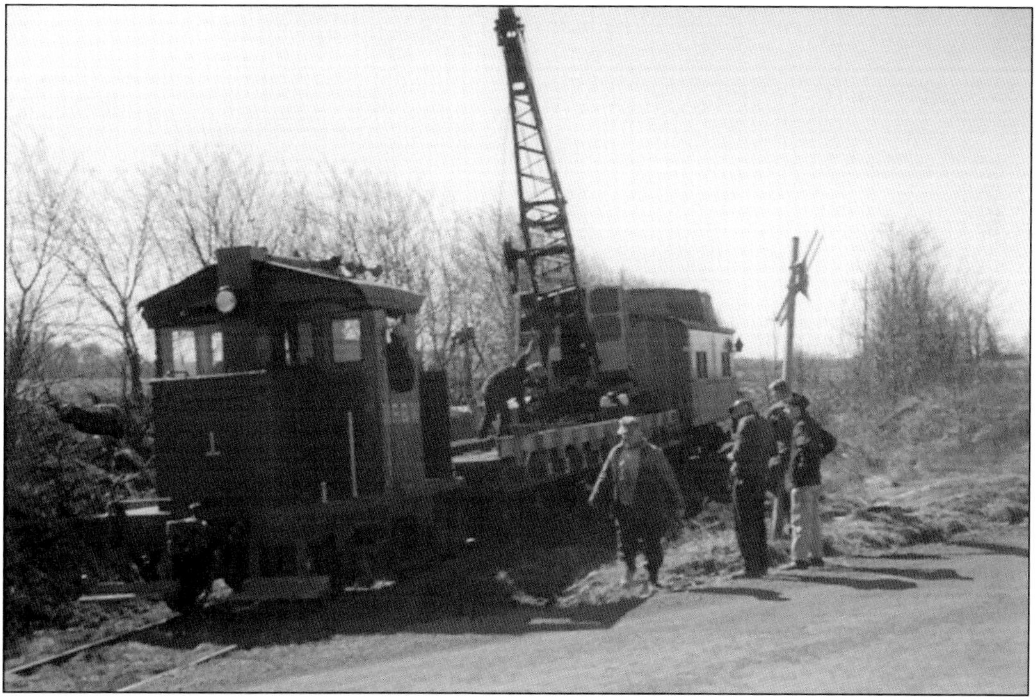

In 1965, the crew sets out rails and ties to be used along the right-of-way near Toad Lane. The little Mack engine would be pressed into service all during 1965. The railroads crane can be seen on the flatcar, along with caboose No. 200 in tow. (Nelson Tower.)

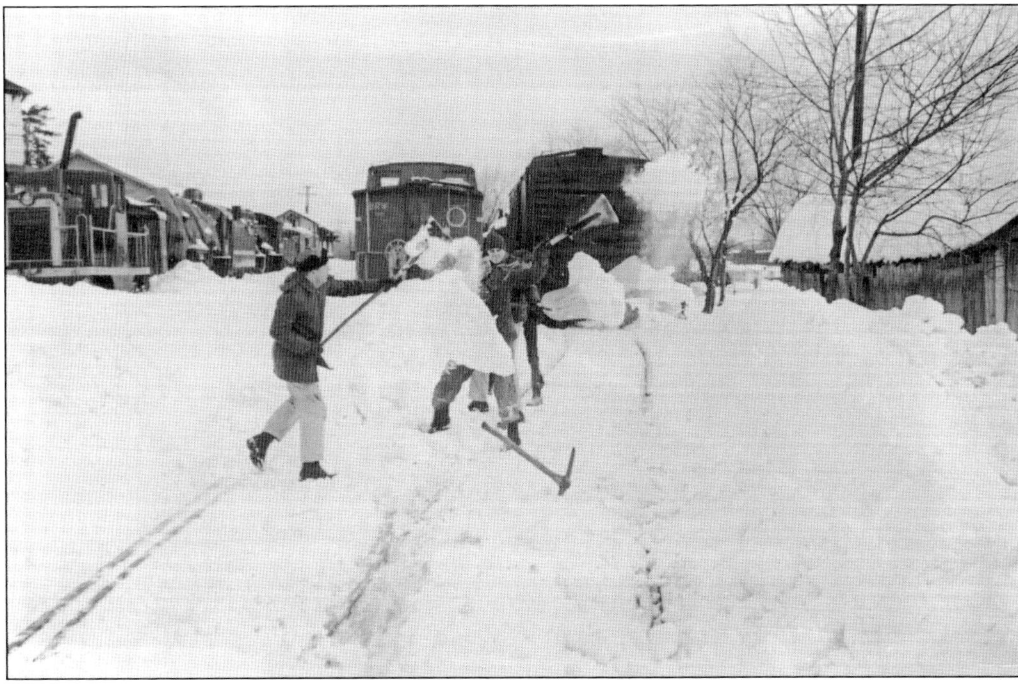

Volunteers dig out the tracks on the siding in Ringoes after the blizzard of January 1967, which did not stop operations on the railroad. On the left are engines No. 400, No. 60, and No. 565. Behind the volunteers is caboose No. 200. (John Bishop Collection.)

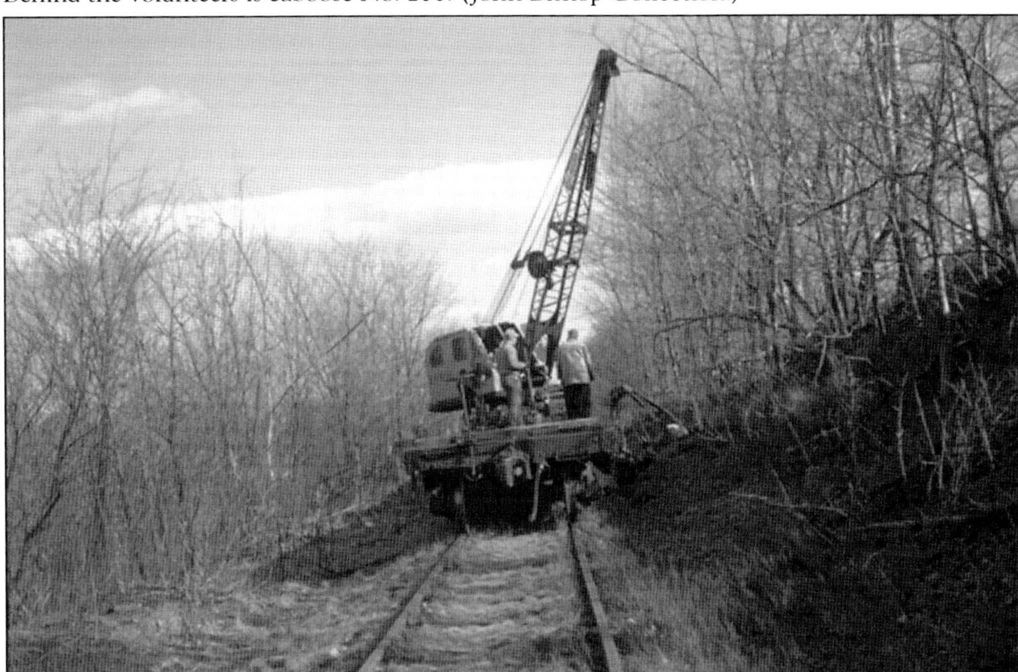

Over the winter, work trains still ran along the line toward Lambertville. The railroads clamshell crane was used to clear parts of the right-of-way. The crane transported on the flatcar was used in a variety of tasks for the railroad. (Nelson Tower.)

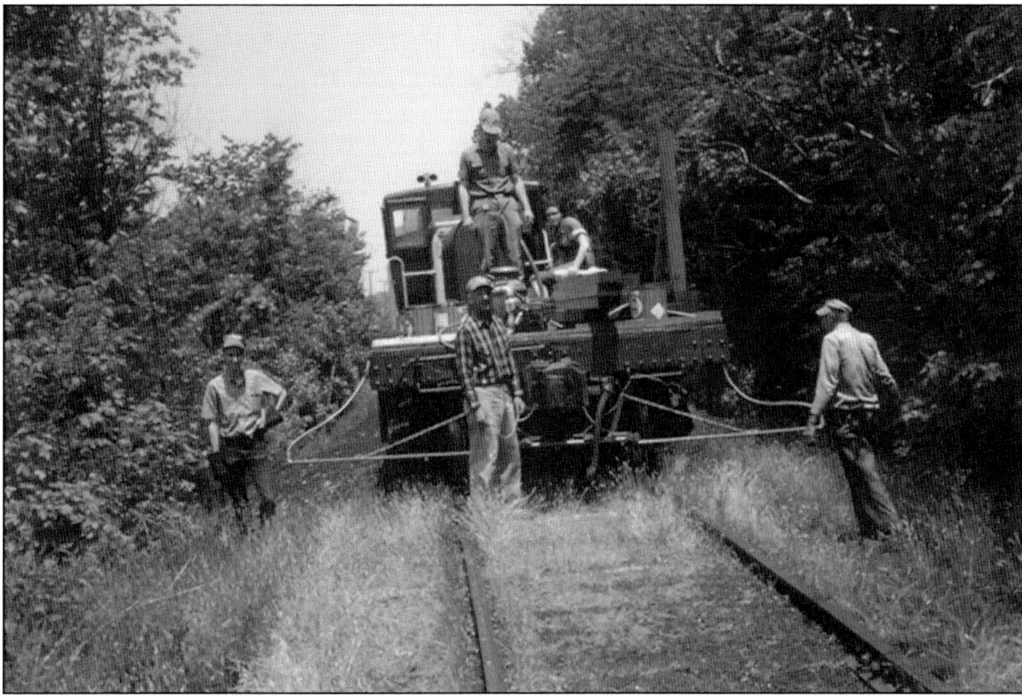

One of the railroads flatcars is outfitted with spraying equipment as the work crew stands ready to spray weeds on the right-of-way in June 1965. BR&W locomotive 400 would be used to push the flatcar along. (Nelson Tower.)

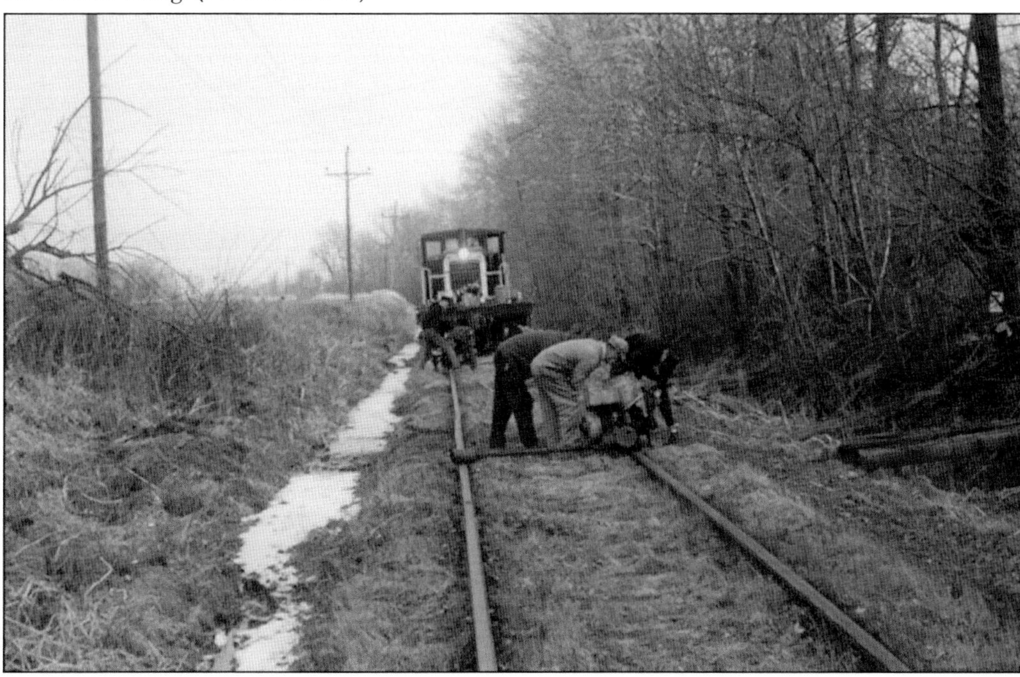

Railroad volunteers work to tighten rail joints along the right-of-way in January 1966. Locomotive No. 400 and a flatcar are used to transport the equipment needed for the workmen to complete the job. (Nelson Tower.)

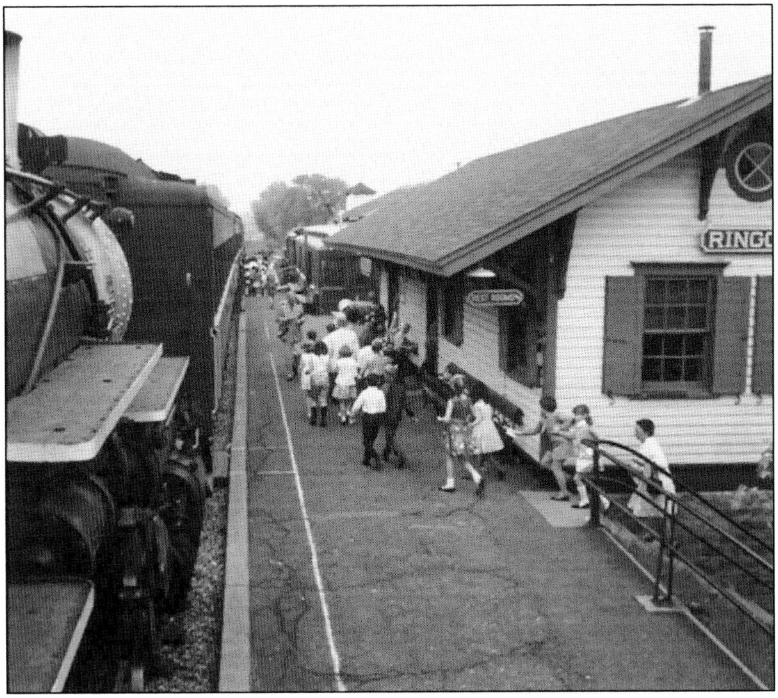

Starting in 1966, school trips were being offered on special trains that ran on Mondays and Fridays. The first two schools to sign up for the trips were the Grant School of Trenton and the Hopewell Township Elementary School. (Nelson Tower.)

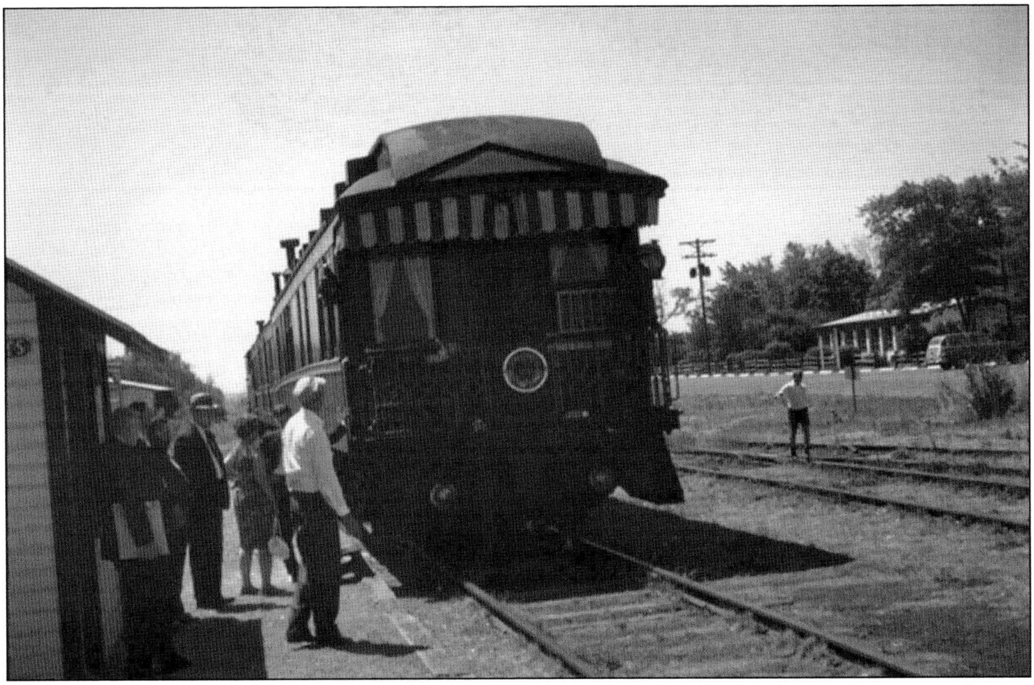

A special trip to honor George Vaughan, eastern region general manager of the Pennsylvania Railroad, who had helped with the leasing agreement of the line, occurred in August 1966 using executive car No. 105 *Seafalls*. Departing from Flemington, the trip included a tour of the line, and dinner was served aboard the train for the guests. (Nelson Tower.)

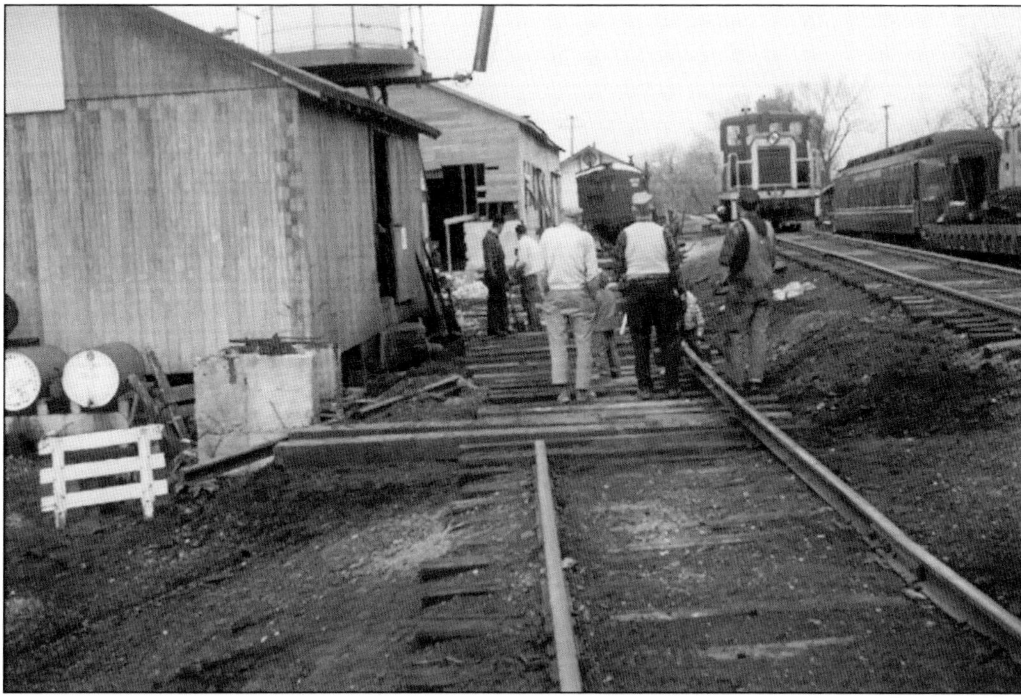

By November 1966, the need for an engine house was met when Nick and Tom Burenga donated a trackside building for the railroad to use. The renovation was done by volunteers Nelson Tower, Samuel Freeman, Nick and Tom Burenga, Harry Reifsnyder, and Ken and Jim Burenga. A new switch was installed to enter the building. (Nelson Tower.)

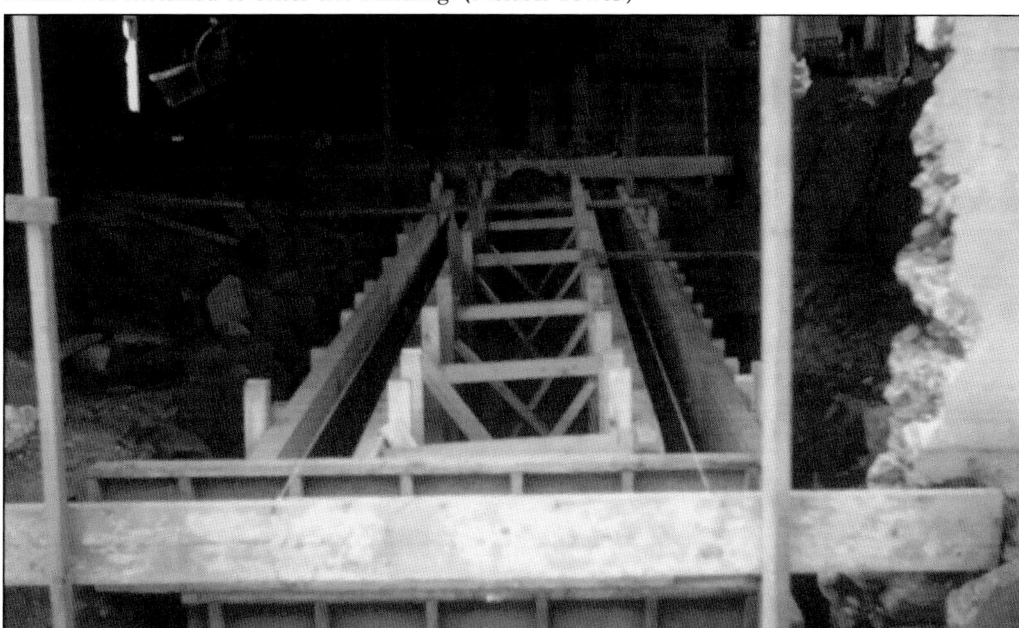

A new servicing pit was installed in the engine house for inspections and work on the railroad equipment. It was 40 feet long and built of concrete by volunteers using jackhammers, crowbars, and sledgehammers. (Nelson Tower.)

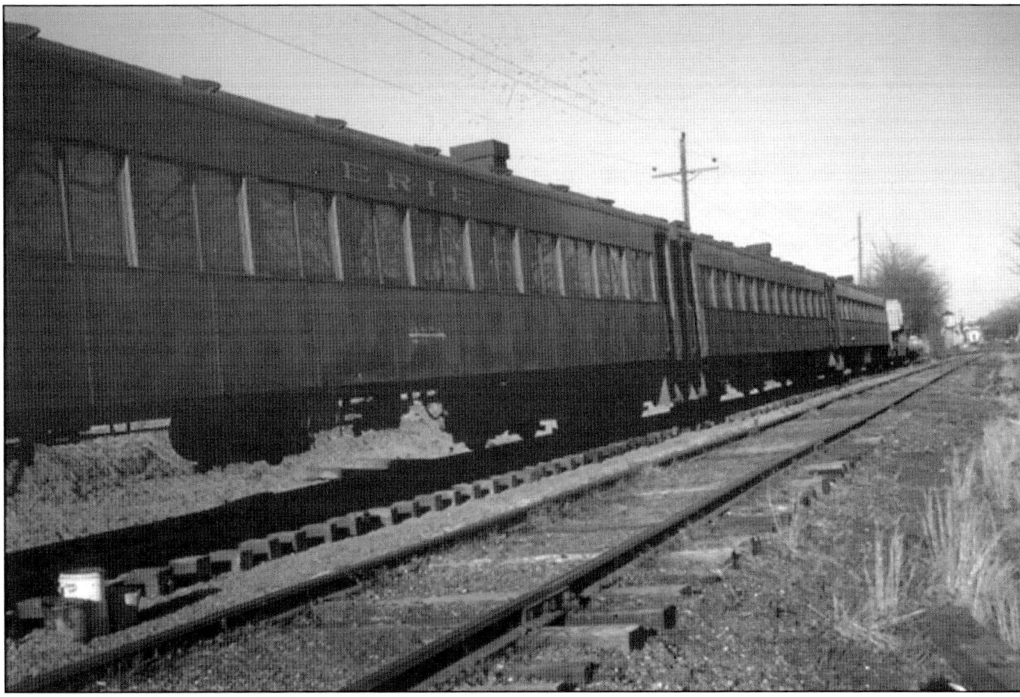

New steel-sided passenger cars began arriving at Black River in late 1965. These ex–Erie Stillwell cars were used for passenger service as Black River & Western Nos. 313, 311, and 312. The steel cars initially supplemented the wooden cars to carry the influx of passengers on weekends. The steel-sided cars eventually replaced the wooden passenger cars. (Nelson Tower.)

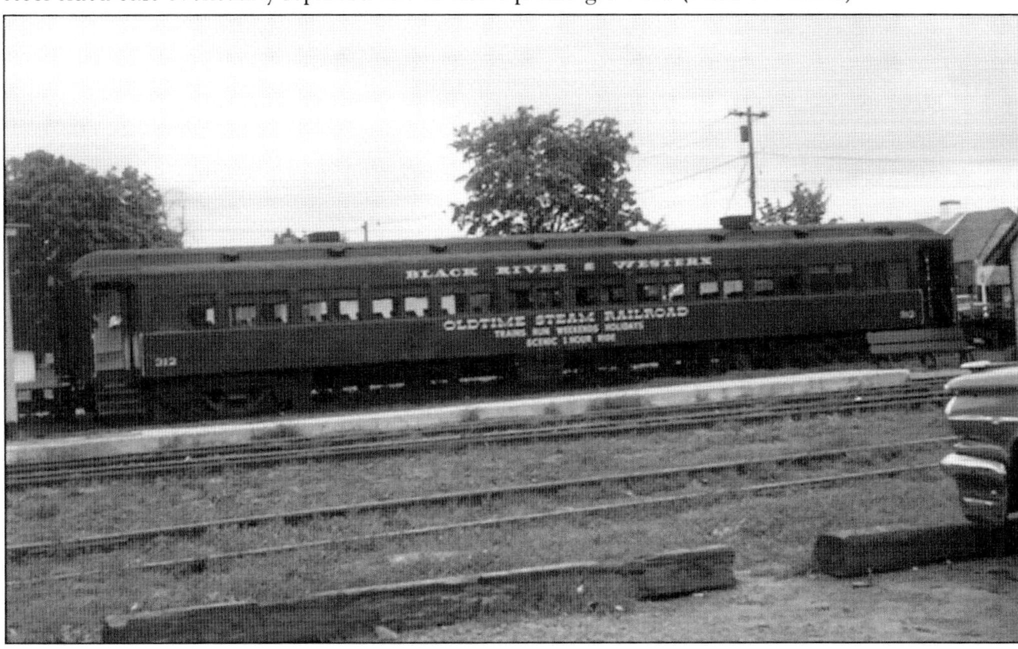

Ex-Erie No. 2558 became Black River & Western No. 312 in 1966. It sported the famous Black River green paint with yellow lettering. Shown here in Flemington, the car became a rolling billboard for the railroad by advertising a scenic one-hour ride on weekends and holidays. (Nelson Tower.)

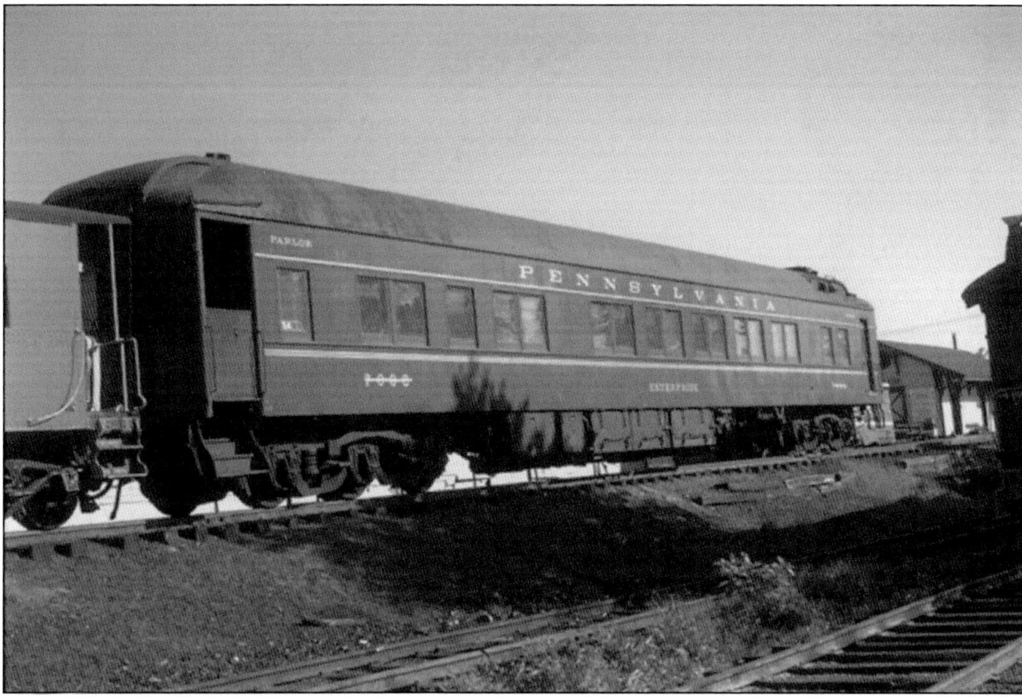

A 1912 parlor car, ex–Pennsylvania Railroad No. 7000 parlor car named *Enterprise*, arrived at the railroad in 1966. The car was renumbered 700 and used for various occasions by the railroad. (Nelson Tower.)

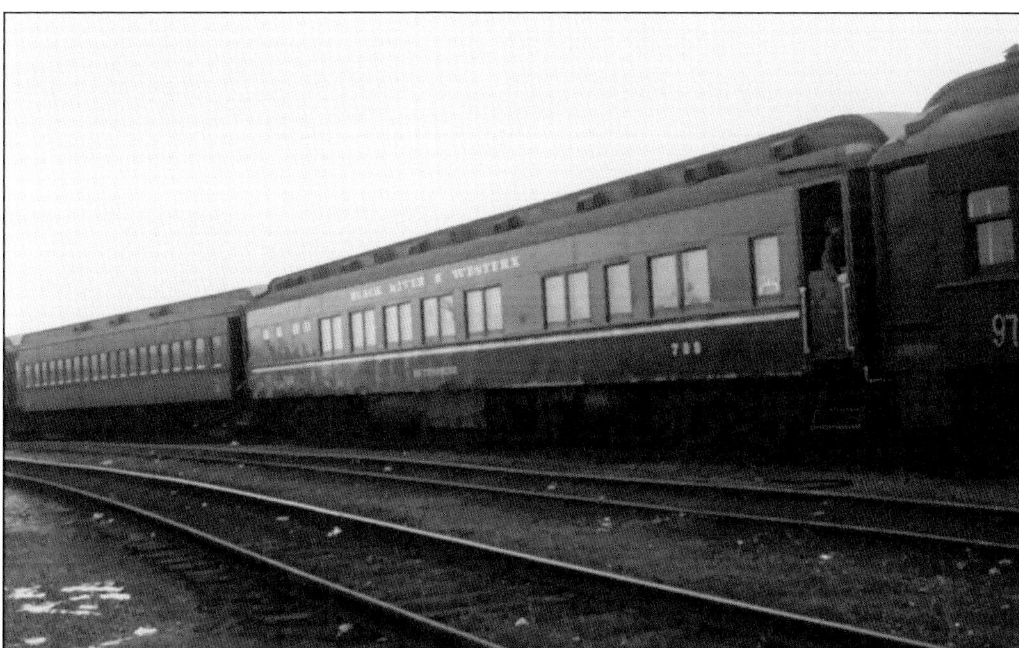

The *Enterprise* No. 700 would make trips off the railroad for special occasions. This passenger car is shown in December 1966 on one of the trips to Bayhead Junction. (Nelson Tower.)

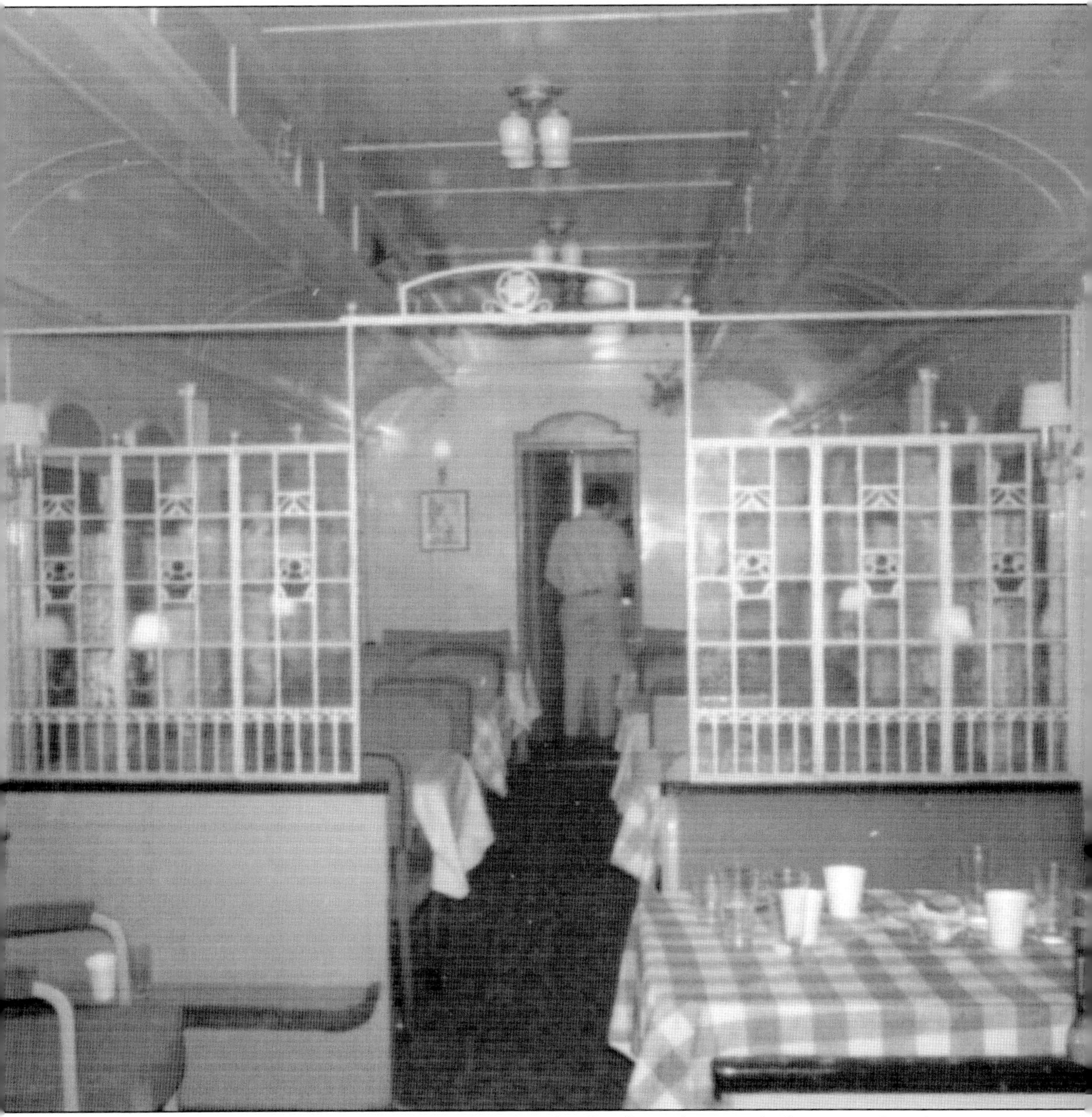

The interior of the *Enterprise* car was fitted with a kitchen along with dining and parlor sections. The car had been used previously on the famous Broadway Limited. The car was renovated and renumbered by volunteers of the Black River & Western as No. 700, the *Enterprise*. It also enjoyed the task of being used for rail trips off the railroad and was in heavy demand for buffet and cocktail parties. (John Bishop collection.)

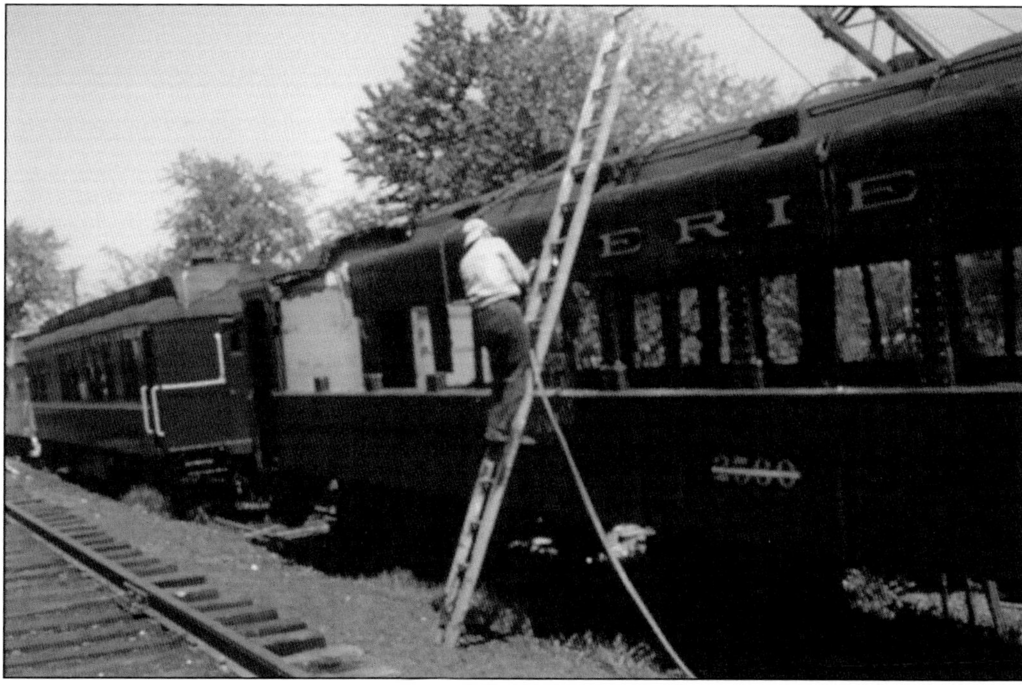

An ex–Erie Stillwell car No. 2560 was received by Black River with a damaged roof, and the decision was made to convert the car into open car No. 311 by cutting off the roof and leaving the vestibules intact. Bench seats were added down the middle of the car. (Nelson Tower.)

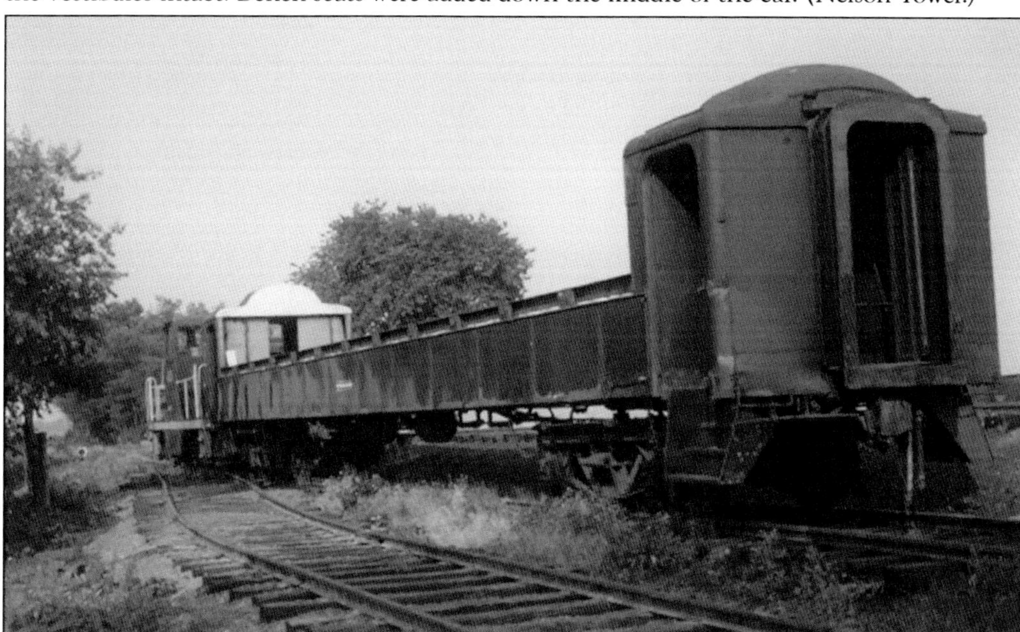

Passenger car No. 311 was used through the 1970s. During its time in service, the car was given a steel-tube frame roof covered by corrugated panels to try to strengthen it. While it was a popular car for the passengers to ride in, the structure became an issue and the car was retired and scrapped. (Nelson Tower.)

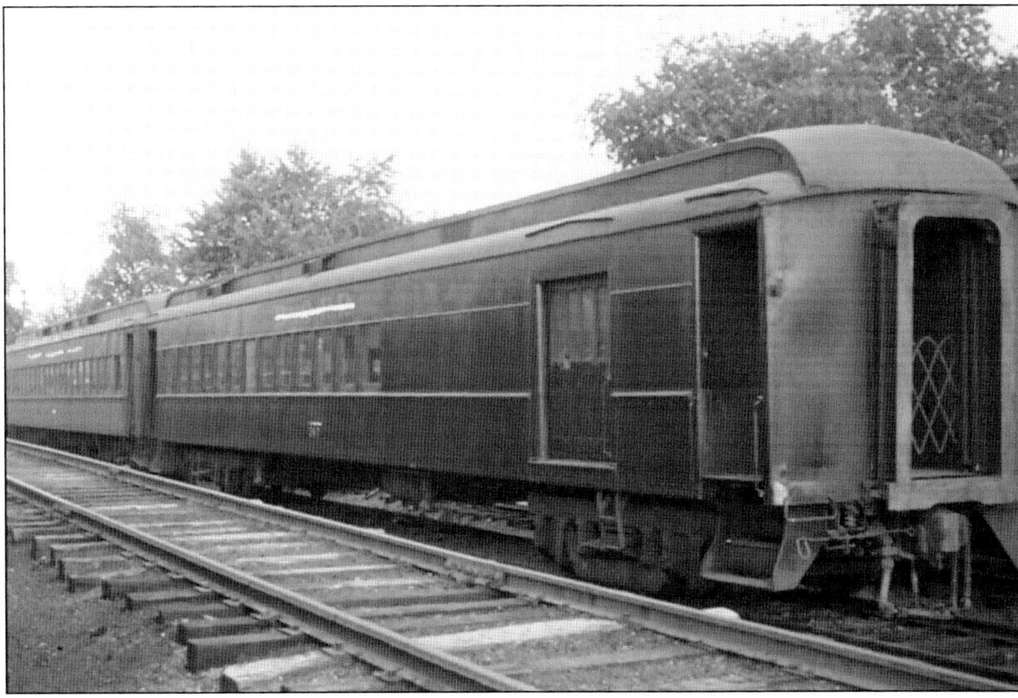

Ex-CNJ cars were obtained in September 1967. This 1923 combine car B&O No. 320 would later become Black River No. 297. The Baltimore and Ohio Railroad (B&O) bought an interest in the Central Railroad of New Jersey and some of the CNJ equipment was re-lettered for the B&O. The second car, a 1923 coach, would become BR&W 322, named the *John L. Bishop*.

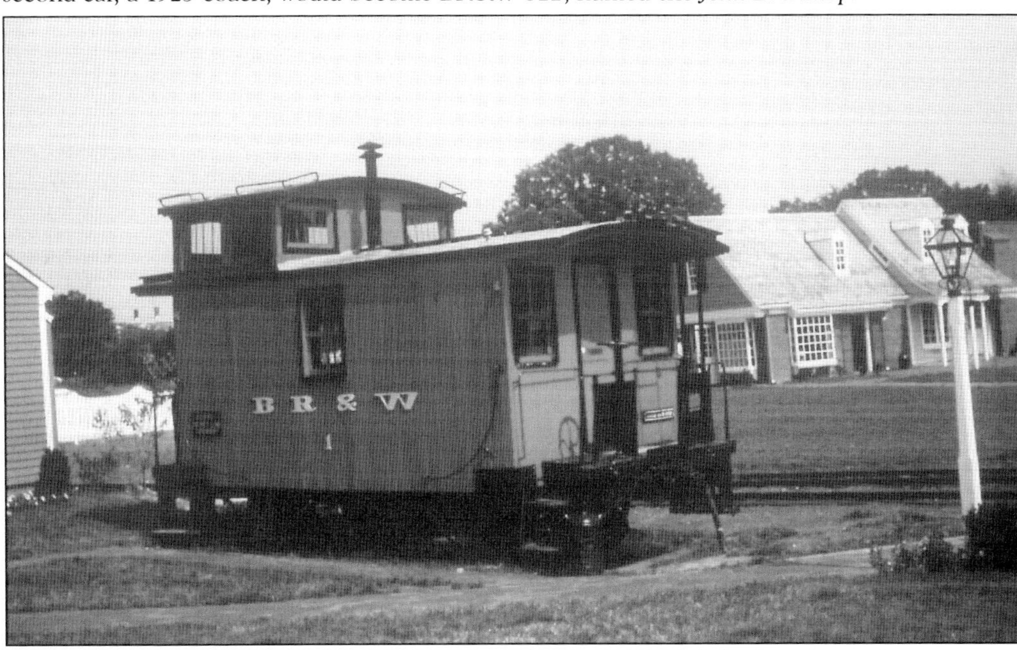

In 1966, the BR&W bobber caboose No. 1 would be moved to and displayed near the area where the turntable was located in Flemington. It would be used as a background display for newly opened Turntable Junction and the BR&Ws Flemington terminal.

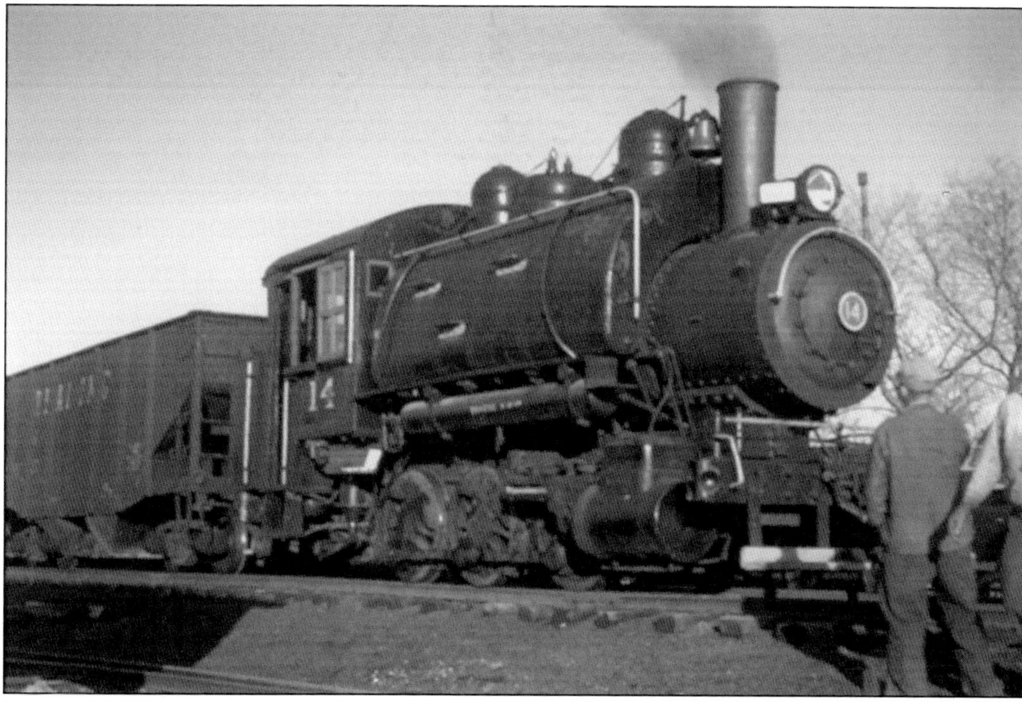

In March 1967, steam engine No. 14 arrived in Ringoes. Owned by George Hart, the 1920 Porter saddle tank engine was leased to the Black River & Western and used during July and August 1967. By the end of 1968 season, the little engine was taken out of service. (Nelson Tower.)

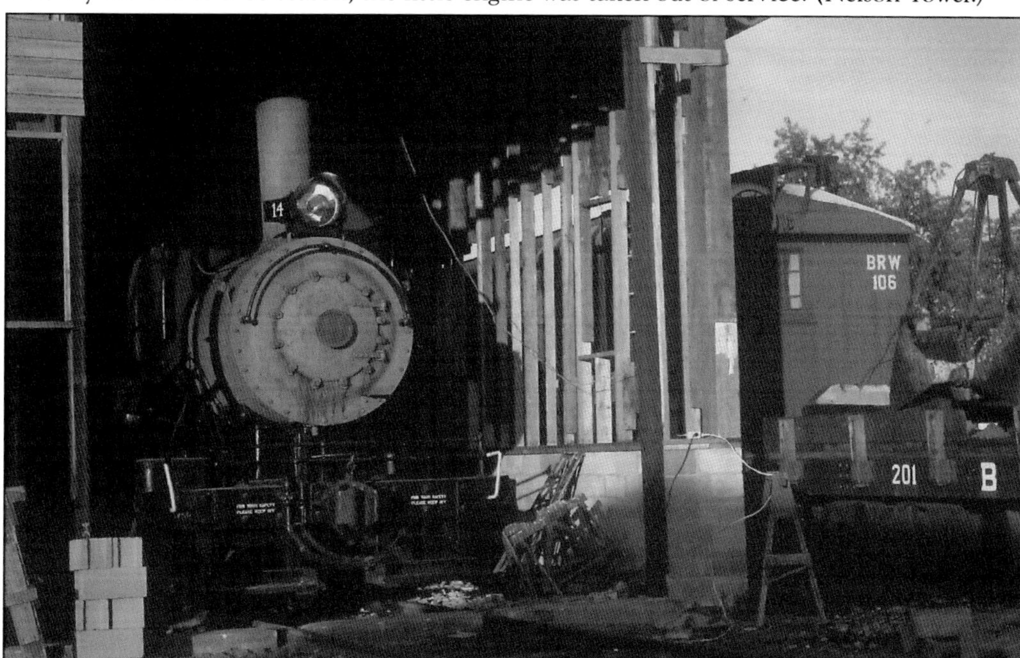

Steam engine No. 14 sits in the engine house, while office car No. 106 and flatcar No. 201 sit on the siding. When this photograph was taken, the engine house was being renovated, with the replacement of siding and a new door.

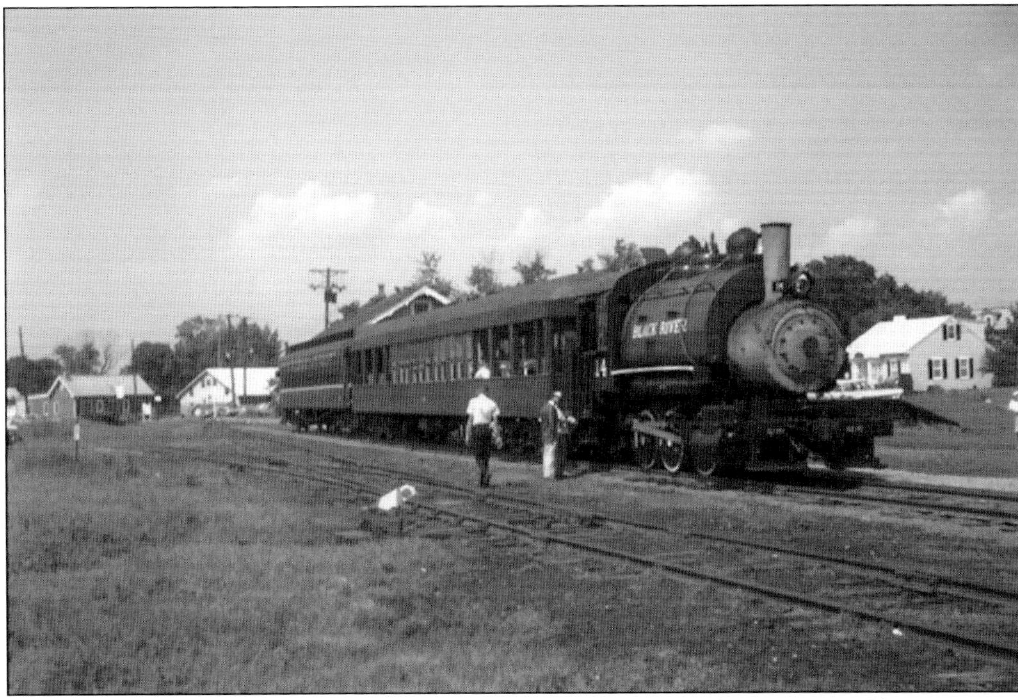

Steam engine No. 14 is shown in Flemington with a Canadian Pacific Mountain Observation car and wooden passenger car No. 103. The observation car was used for only a few months, while the steam engine would only be used for two years. (Nelson Tower.)

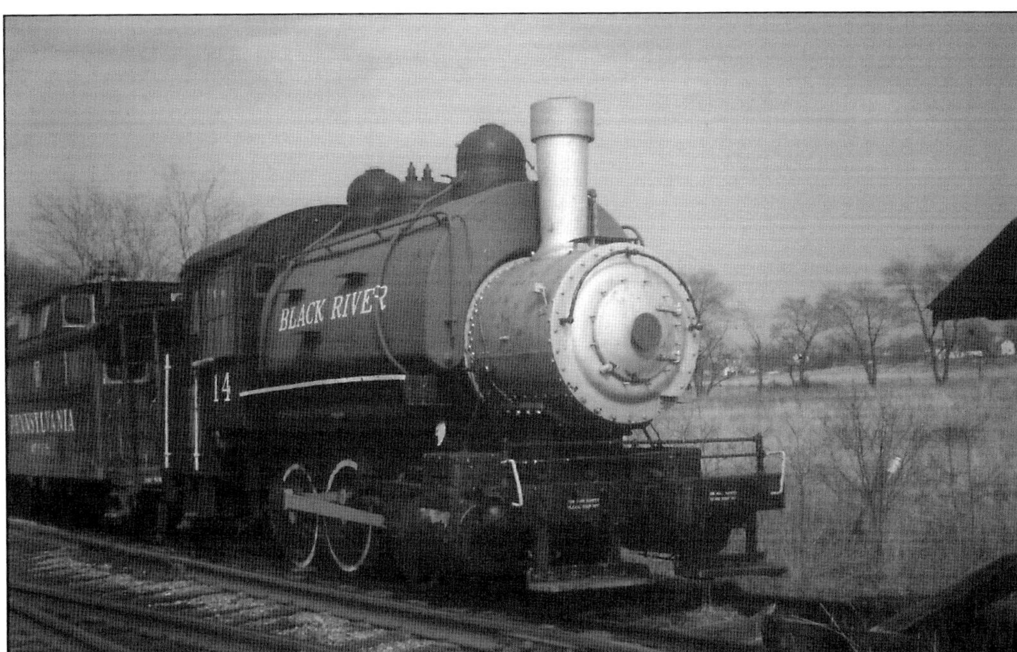

Steam engine No. 14 was retired in 1968. Deemed to be hard on the track and a glutton for fuel, the engine was placed in storage and eventually sold.

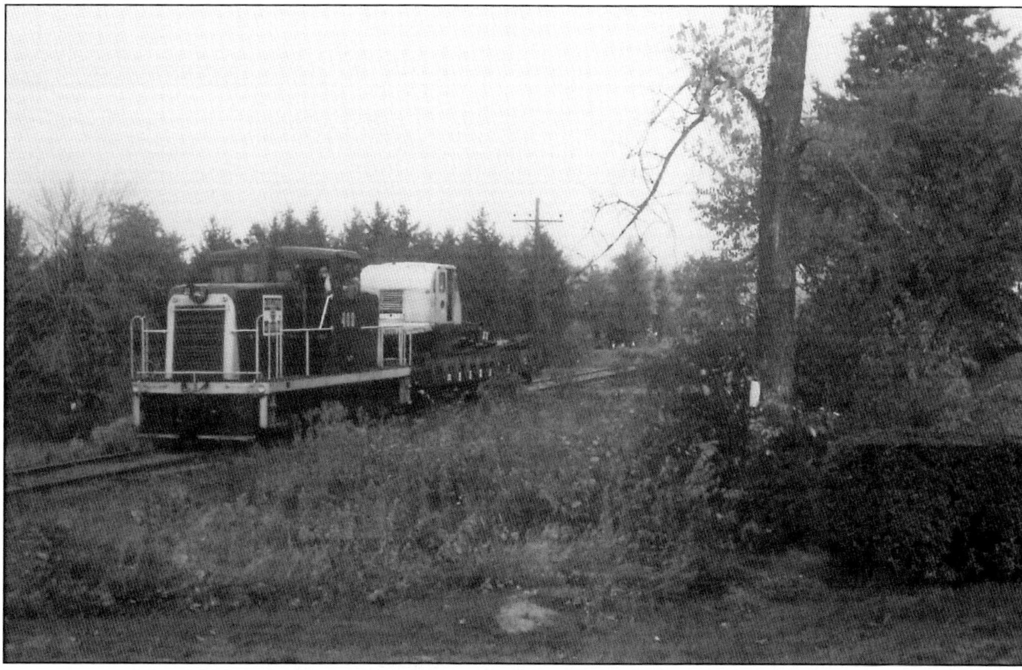

Locomotive No. 400 hauls flatcar No. 201 with the crane in October 1966 while in maintenance-of-way service. Engine No. 400 took over the duties that the little Mack engine had performed. (Nelson Tower.)

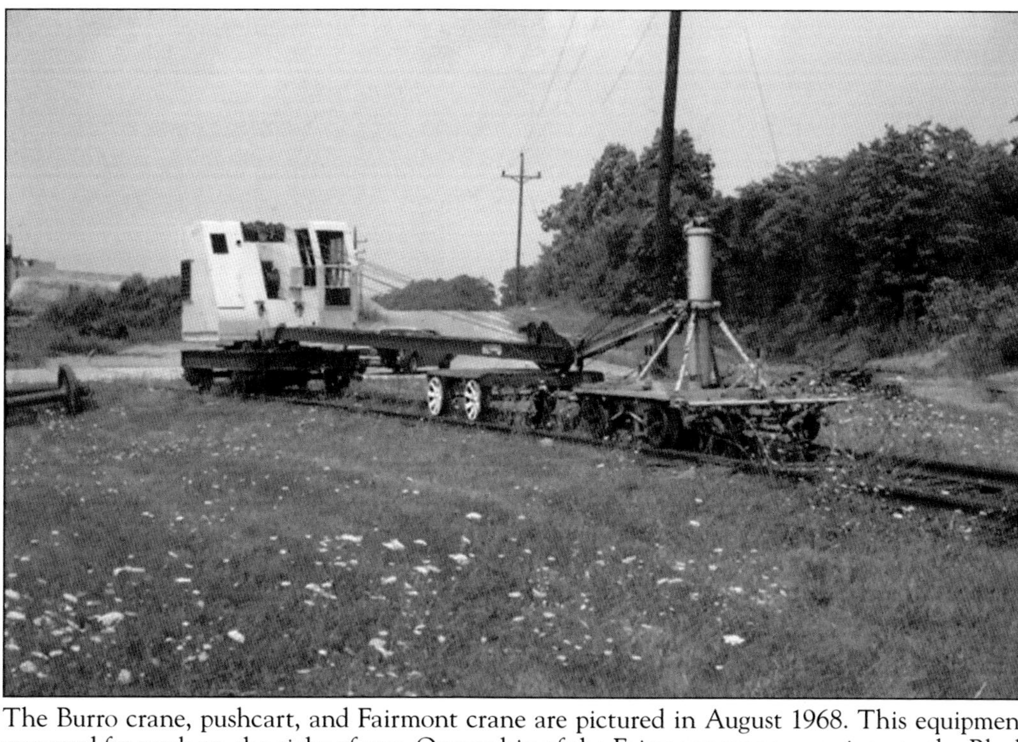

The Burro crane, pushcart, and Fairmont crane are pictured in August 1968. This equipment was used for work on the right-of-way. Ownership of the Fairmont crane was given to the Black River Railroad Historical Trust for restoration and display. (Nelson Tower.)

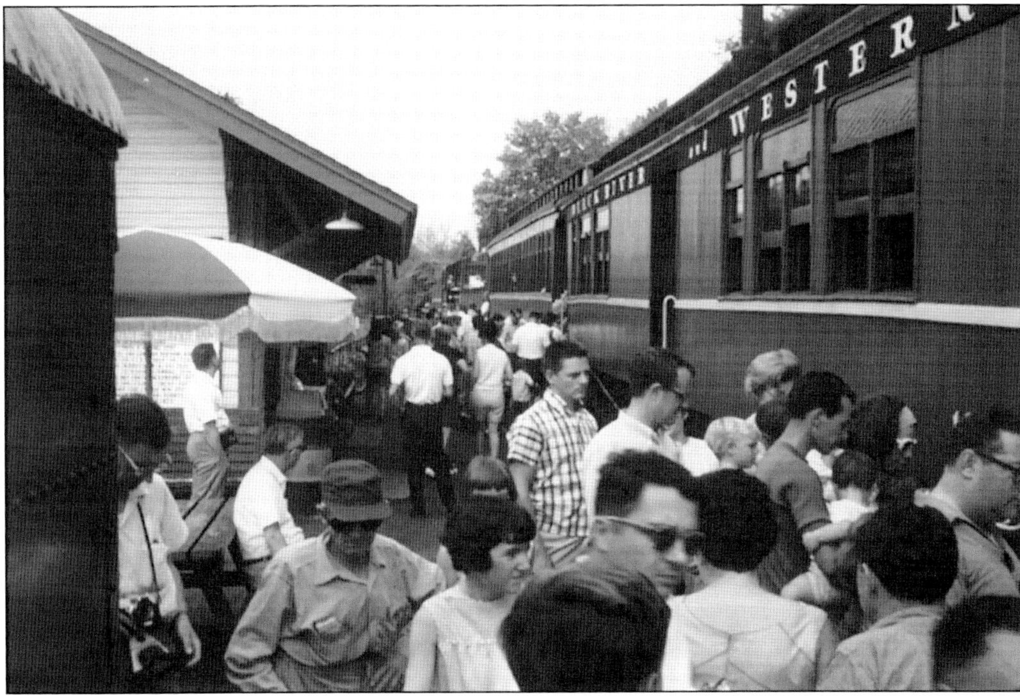

The crowded platform in Ringoes was an indication of the early success of the steam excursion line. Passengers board the train for their return trip to Flemington while steam engine No. 60 waits for the signal top proceed northbound towards Flemington. (Nelson Tower.)

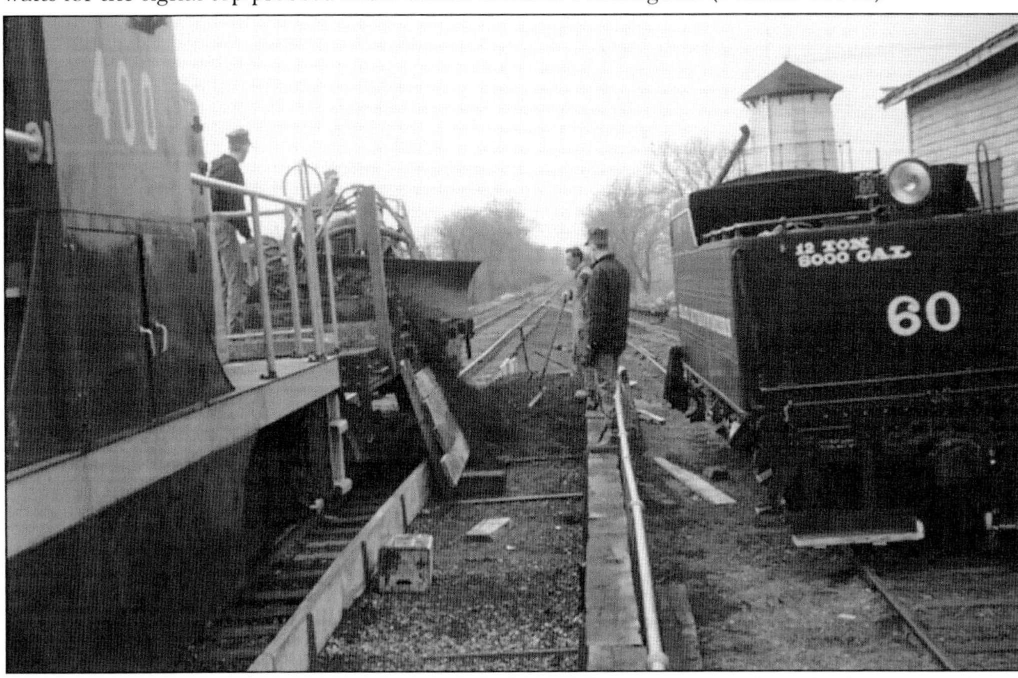

The station platform in Ringoes was extended in 1967 to accommodate the larger number of passengers riding the weekend excursions. Volunteers use a bulldozer to move material from the flatcar to fill in the base of what would become the new platform. (Nelson Tower.)

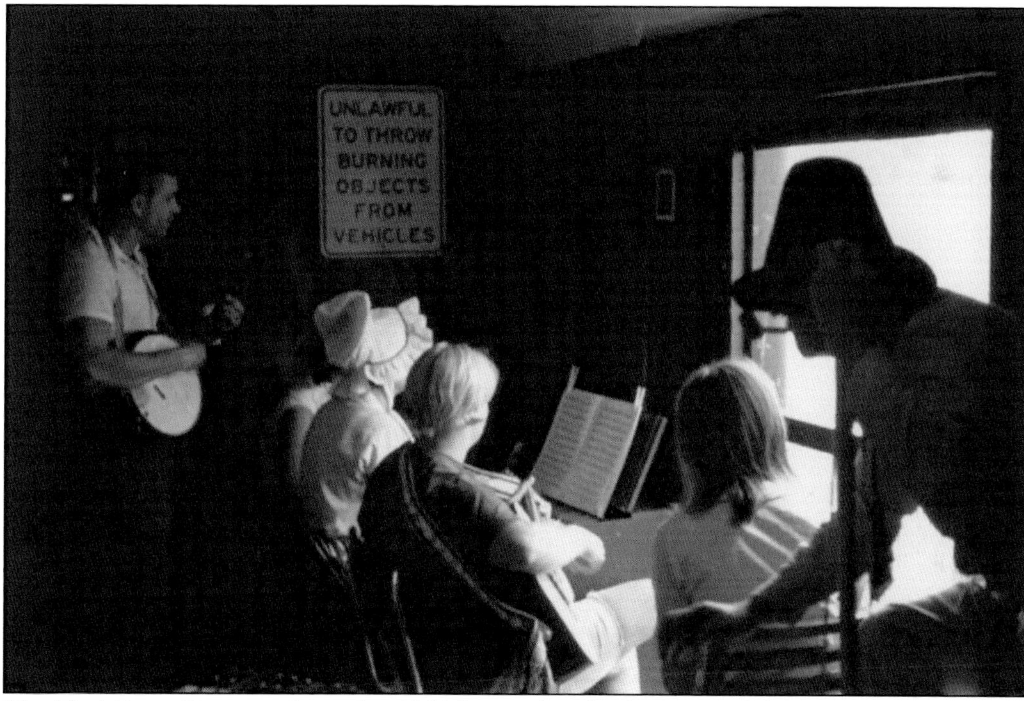

The Black River Gang was formed in 1966 from railroad volunteers to fill the void when Diamond Paul Jones left. The ragtime band included musical instruments such as an accordion, trumpet, flutes, piano, drums, and a jug, as well as other instruments. Some performers wore 19th-century -style dress while the band played tunes such as "Roll Out the Barrel" and "Has Anybody Seen My Gal?" (Nelson Tower.)

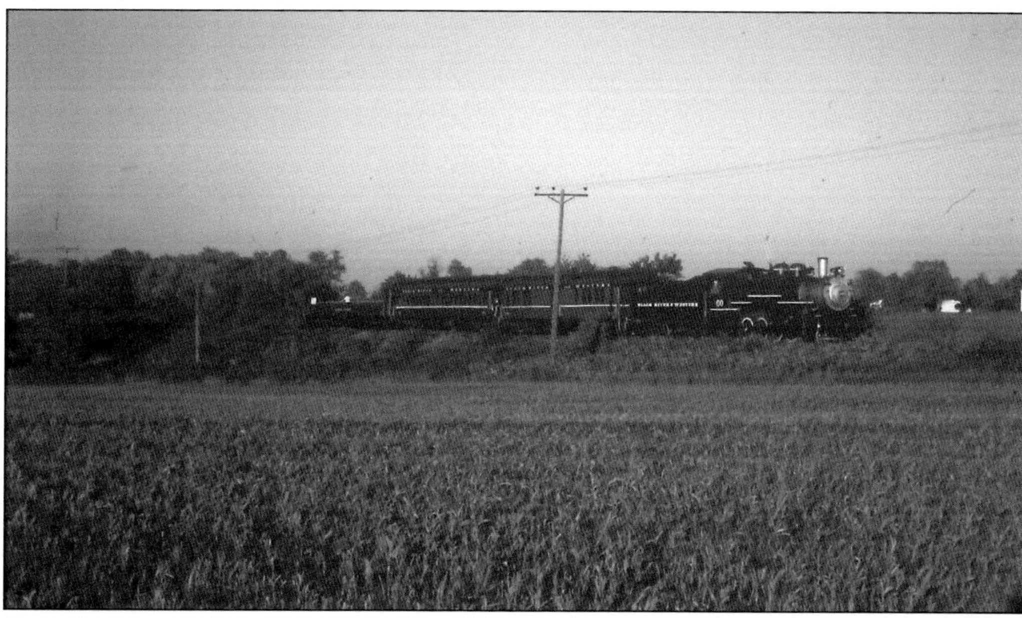

On a nice summer day, steam engine No. 60 has combine No. 102, coach No. 103, and the open car No. 311 in tow during one of the weekend excursions heading south near the Muirhead crossing on the way to the Ringoes station.

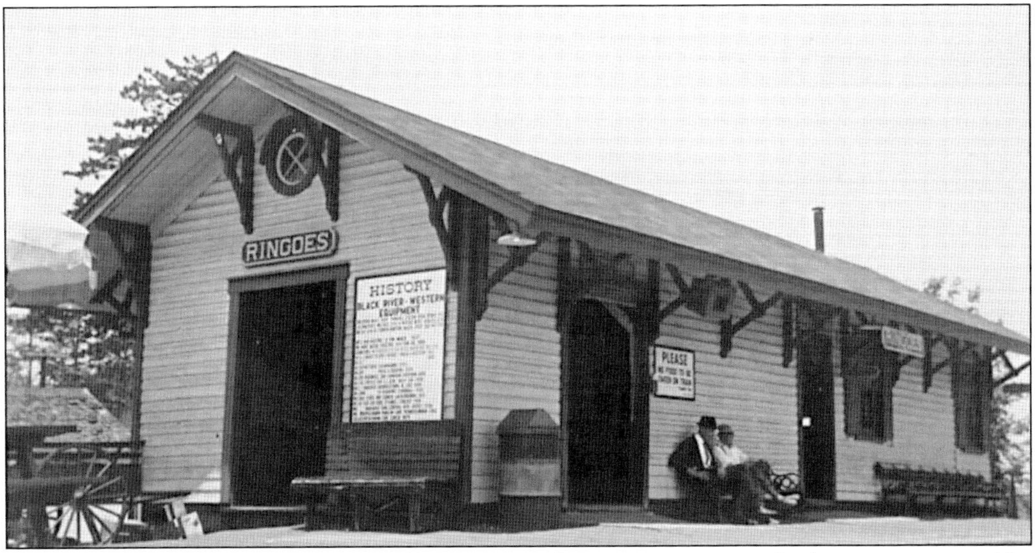

By 1967, the Ringoes station, in its yellow paint with green trim, sported a large sign painted by Harold Alpaugh of Clinton. The sign summarized the history of the railroads equipment. The sign was later moved and mounted across the tracks opposite the station.

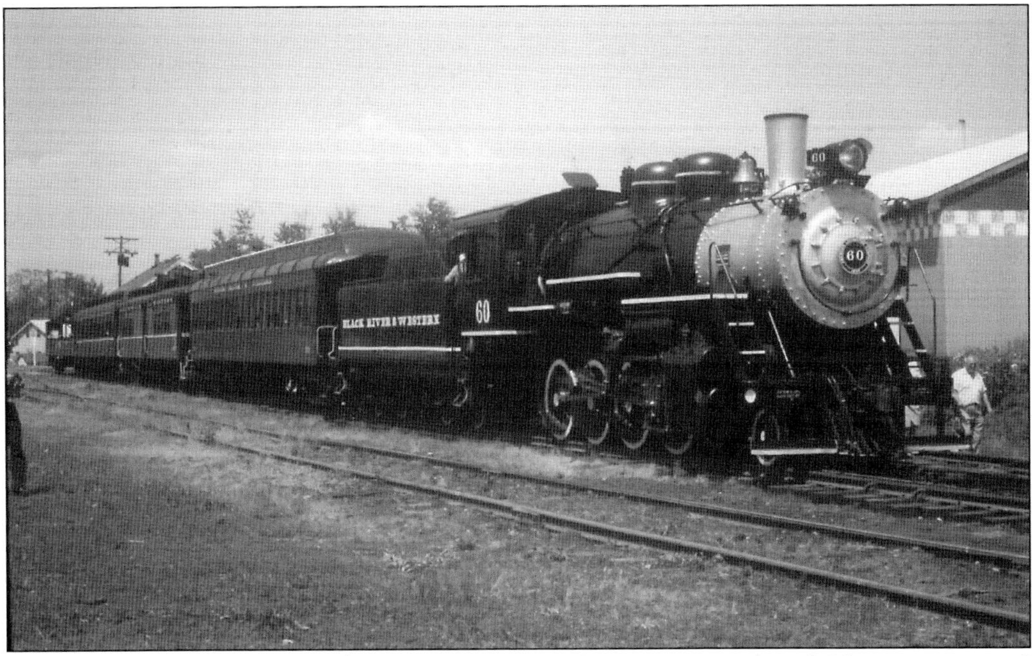

Steam engine No. 60 waits in Flemington in June 1967 for passengers to board. The train consisted of passenger car No. 301 and wooden passenger cars No. 102 and No. 103, and the end car was the converted open passenger car No. 311.

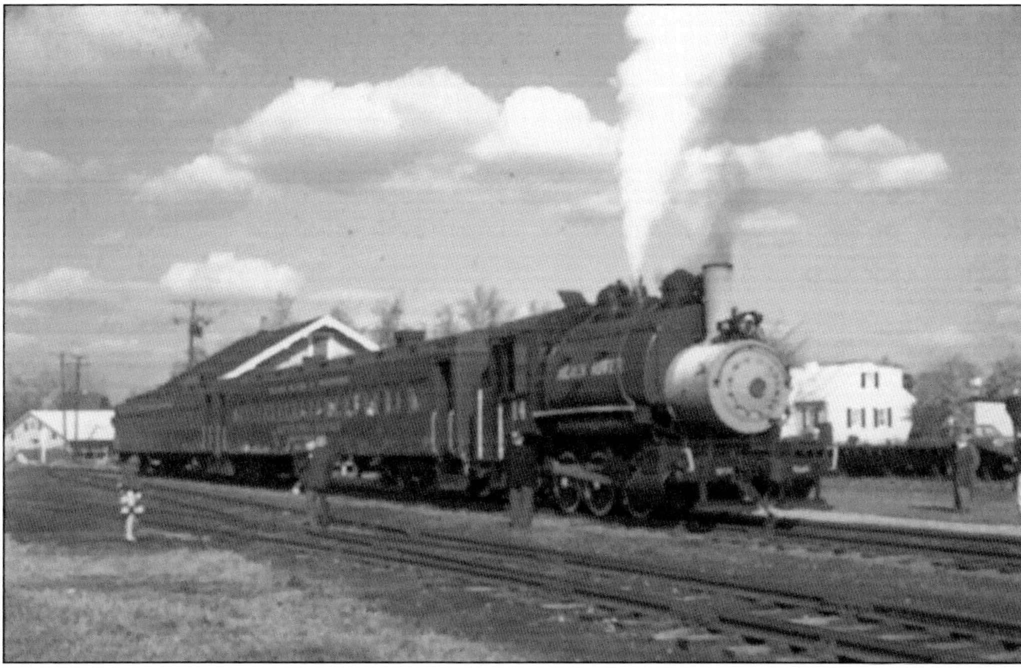

In November 1967, the first steam-heated train was run from Flemington using steam engine No. 14 to heat passenger cars No. 312 and No. 313. Steel-sided passenger cars utilized steam pipes through the car, which were much more efficient and safer than the coal stoves used in the wooden coaches. (Nelson Tower.)

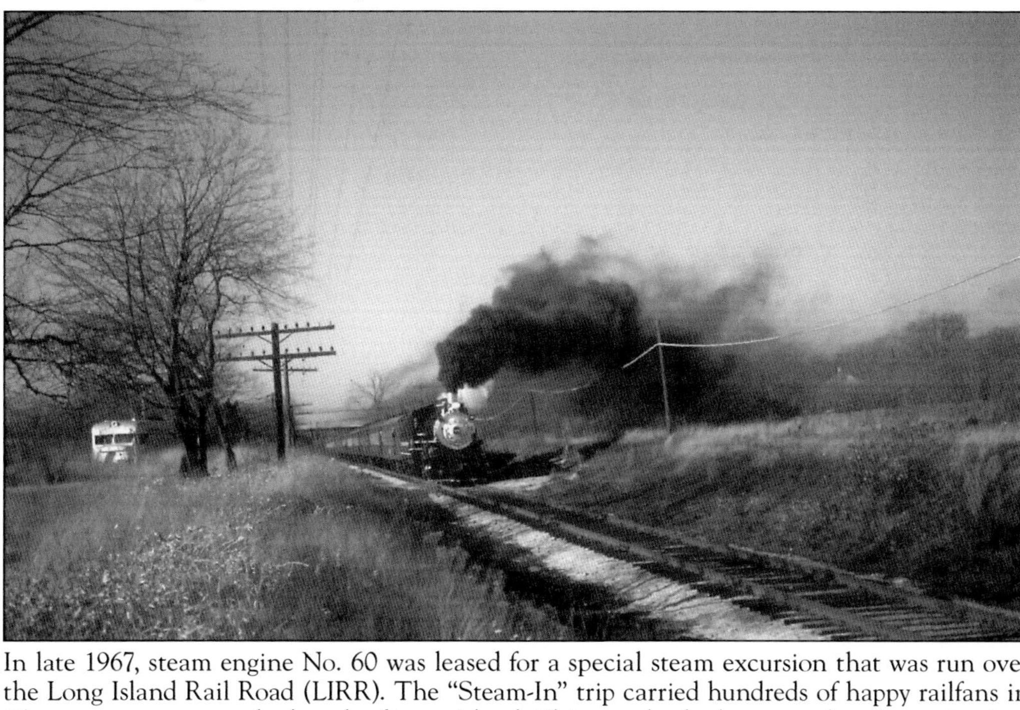

In late 1967, steam engine No. 60 was leased for a special steam excursion that was run over the Long Island Rail Road (LIRR). The "Steam-In" trip carried hundreds of happy railfans in 15 passenger cars over the length of Long Island. This was the farthest east that the engine had ever been.

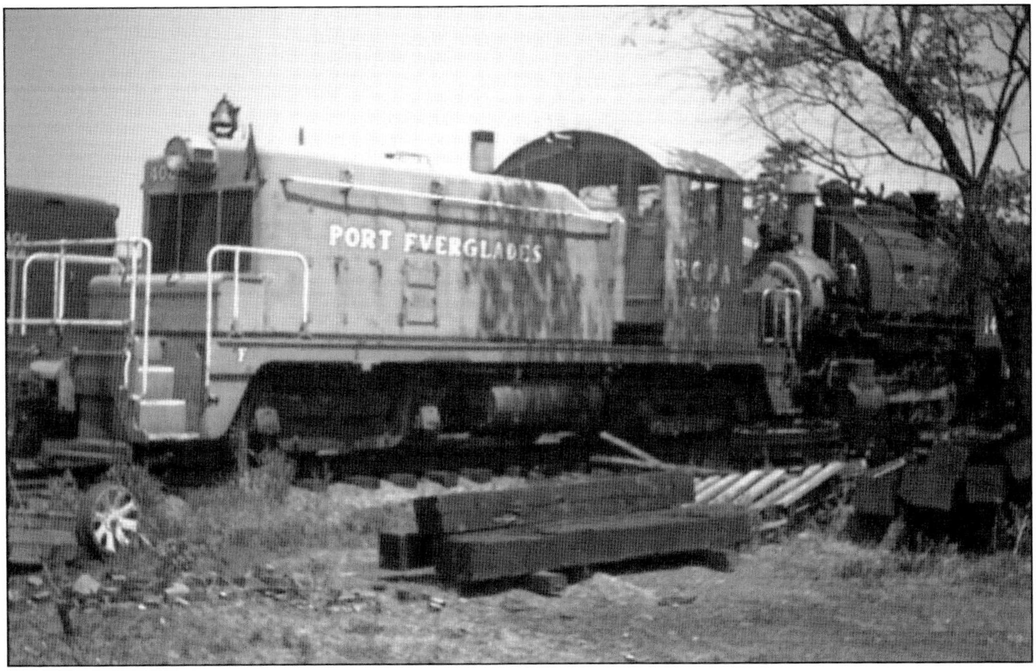

In May 1968, a new locomotive EMD model SW-1 No. 400 was leased by the railroad to replace the smaller GE 44-ton locomotive. The two No. 400 locomotives on the railroad became known as "Little 400" and "Big 400." This unit temporarily became No. 401 with the use of masking tape until the smaller GE unit was sold.

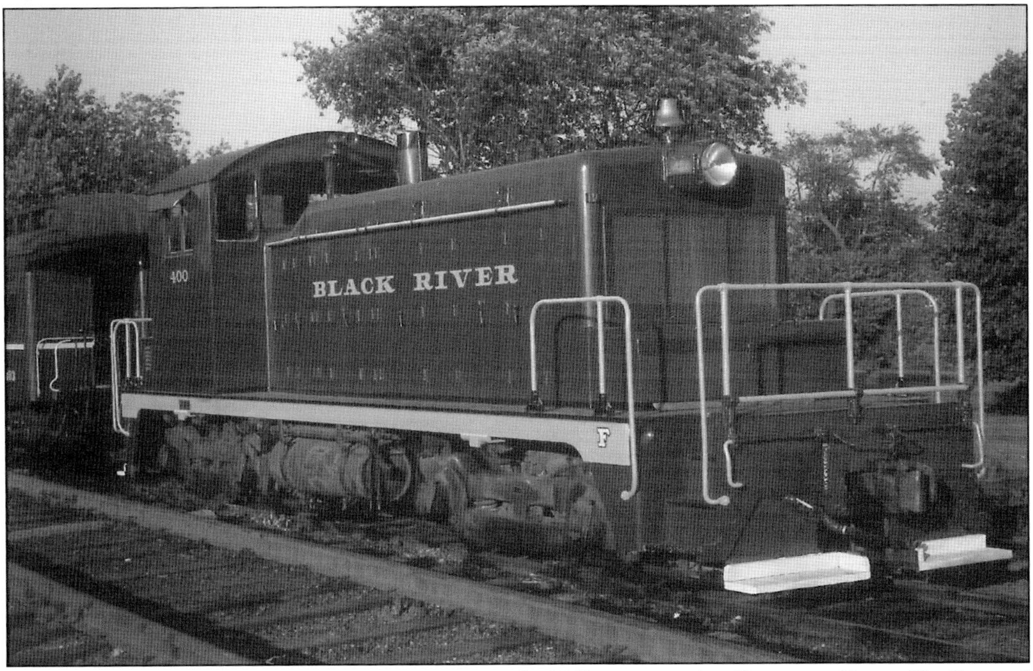

Locomotive No. 400, called "Big 400" or "Second 400," is pictured in Ringoes. Owned by Samuel Freeman, the engine was leased to the railroad and used for both freight and passenger service. The engine would take over the duties that the smaller No. 400 engine had performed.

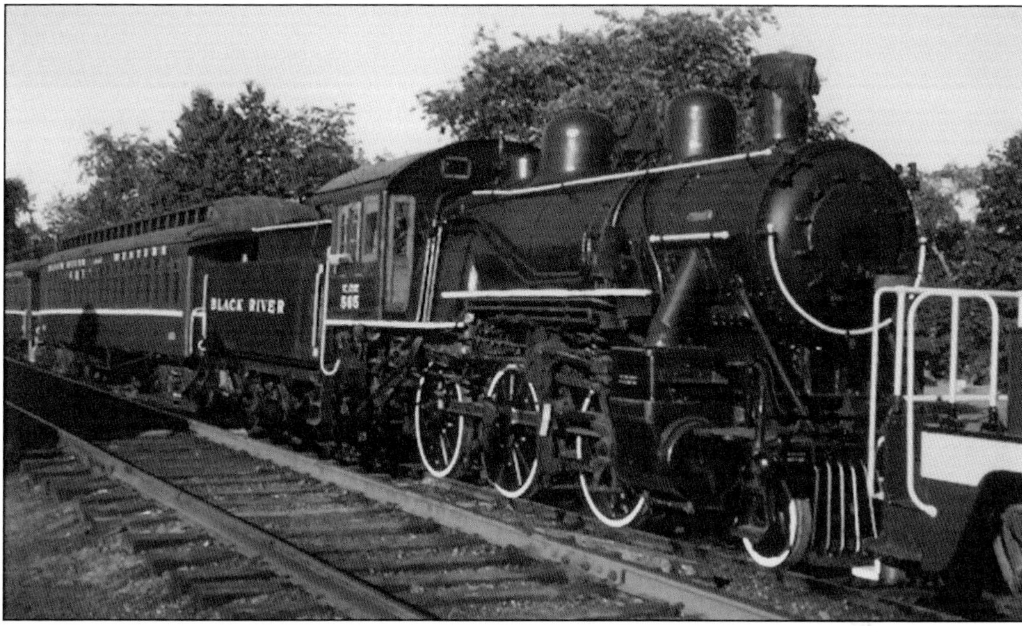

Steam engine No. 565 was sold in 1968 and readied for shipment. The engine spent a number of years in various locations; it most notably displayed at Citro's Restaurant in Wayne, New Jersey, before ending in its final location in the collection at Steamtown.

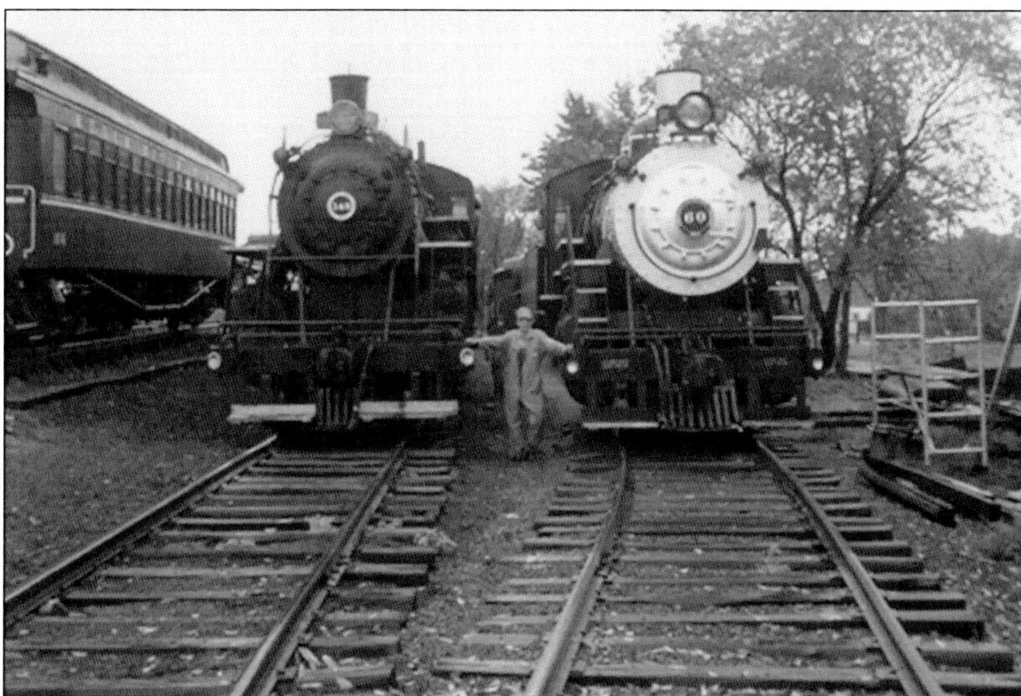

While one steam engine left, another arrived. Nelson Tower, vice president of the BR&W, stands between steam engine No. 148 and steam engine No. 60 in Ringoes. Steam engine No. 60 continued with excursion trips, while newly arrive steam engine No. 148 was worked on for eventual service on the railroad. (Nelson Tower.)

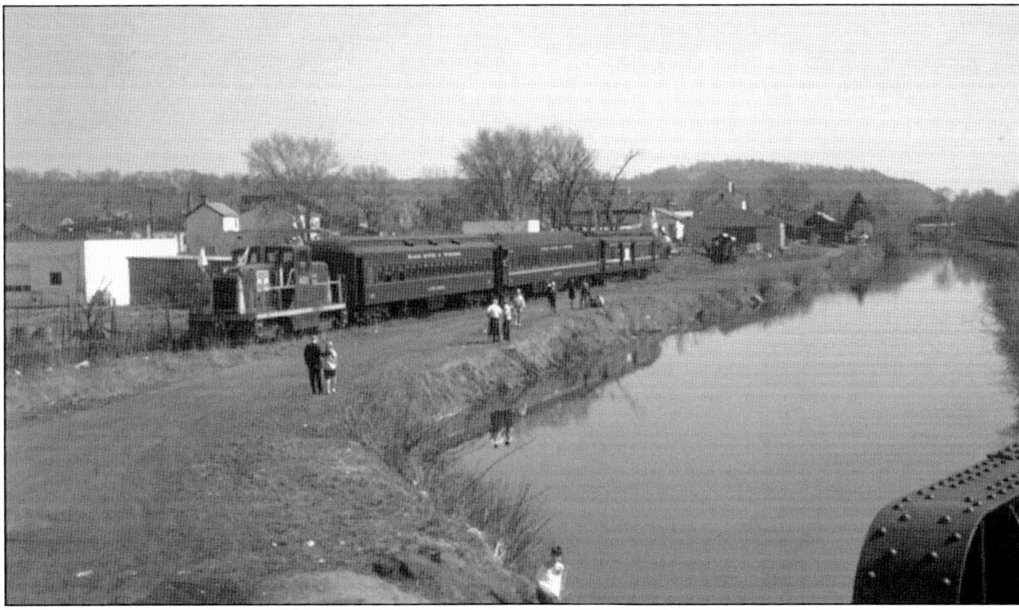

The first "Thank You Express" for the volunteers and families occurred in April 1968. The trip ran from Flemington to Lambertville, pulled by locomotive No. 400 with the assistance of the little Mack engine consisted of car No. 322 *John L. Bishop*, car No. 700 *Enterprise* and the Railway Post Office (RPO) car No. 100. The little Mack engine is seen in the background of this photograph taken in Lambertville. (Nelson Tower.)

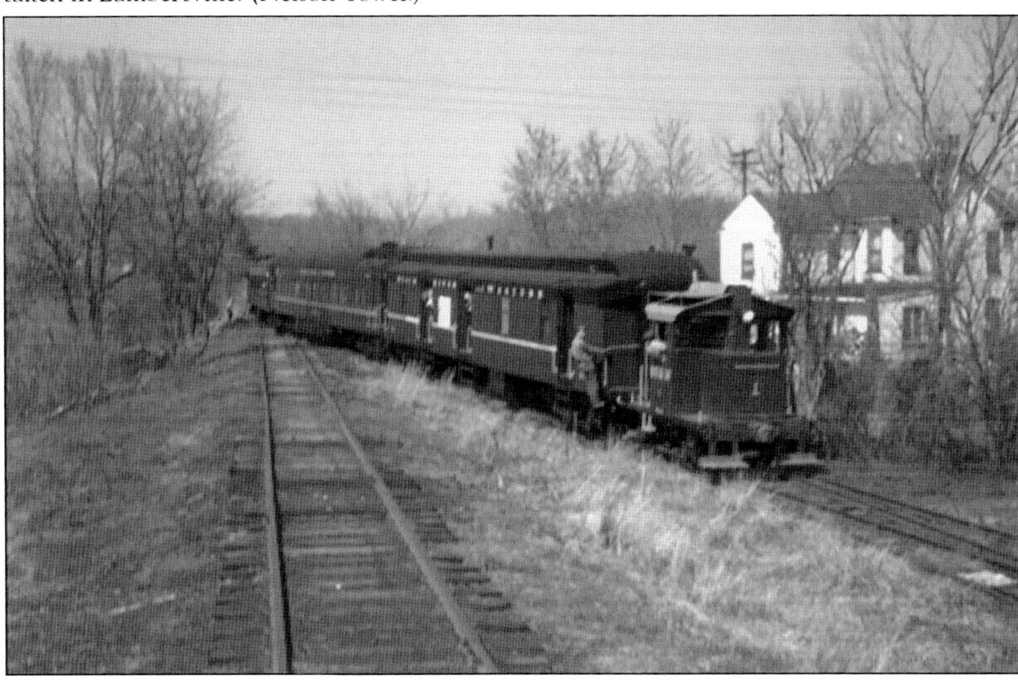

The little Mack engine assisted the Thank You Express with RPO car No. 100, car No. 700 *Enterprise*, and car No. 322 *John L. Bishop*, with locomotive No. 400 following. The appreciation trip ran along the line from Flemington toward Lambertville for the volunteers and families. (Nelson Tower.)

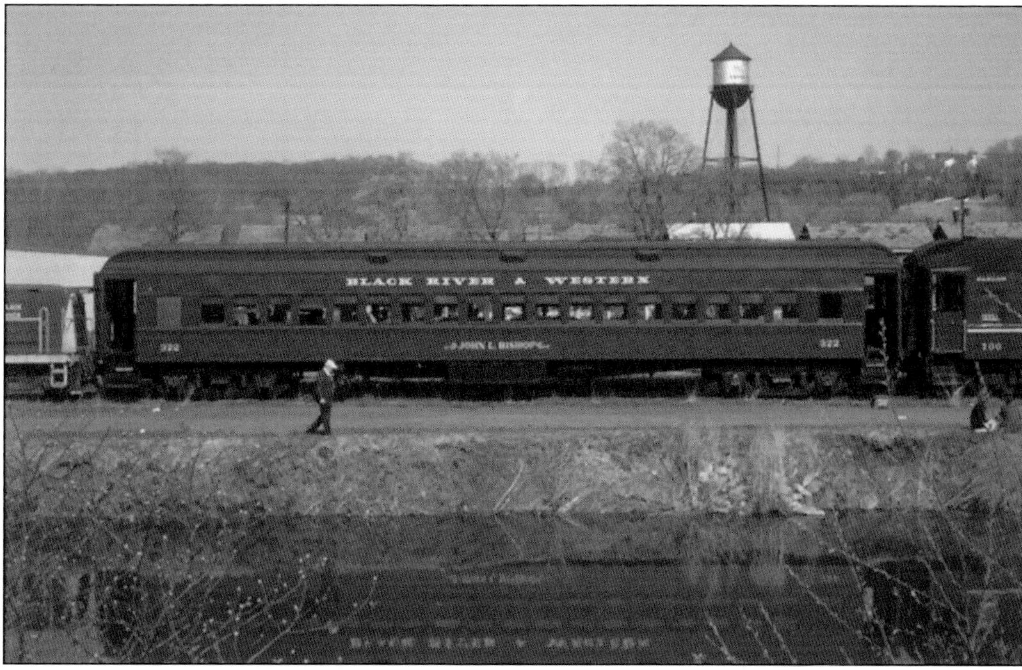

Passenger car No. 322 *John L Bishop* on the Thank You Express in 1968. The coach had previously been used in the filming of a scene in the movie *Funny Girl.* The car is named for the second president of the railroad—a man who spent countless hours at the railroad working on the equipment and the facilities and as the weekend conductor on the train. (Nelson Tower.)

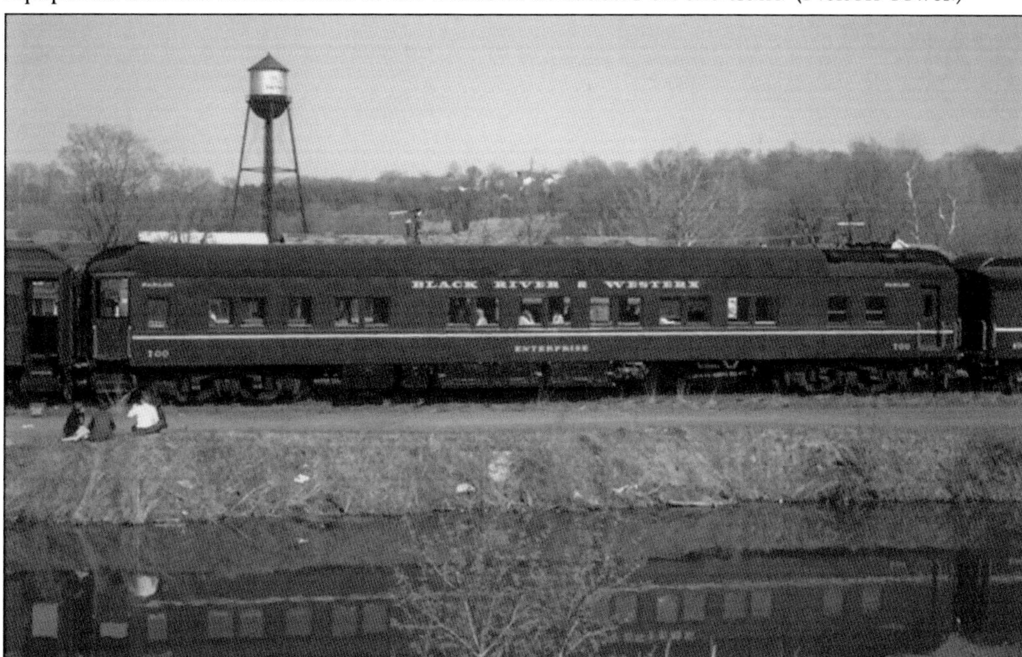

Shown here is passenger car No. 700 *Enterprise* on the Thank You Express on April 13, 1968, as it is parked on a siding in Lambertville. Many of the volunteers enjoyed the luxury of the parlor car, one of three cars used during the trip. (Nelson Tower.)

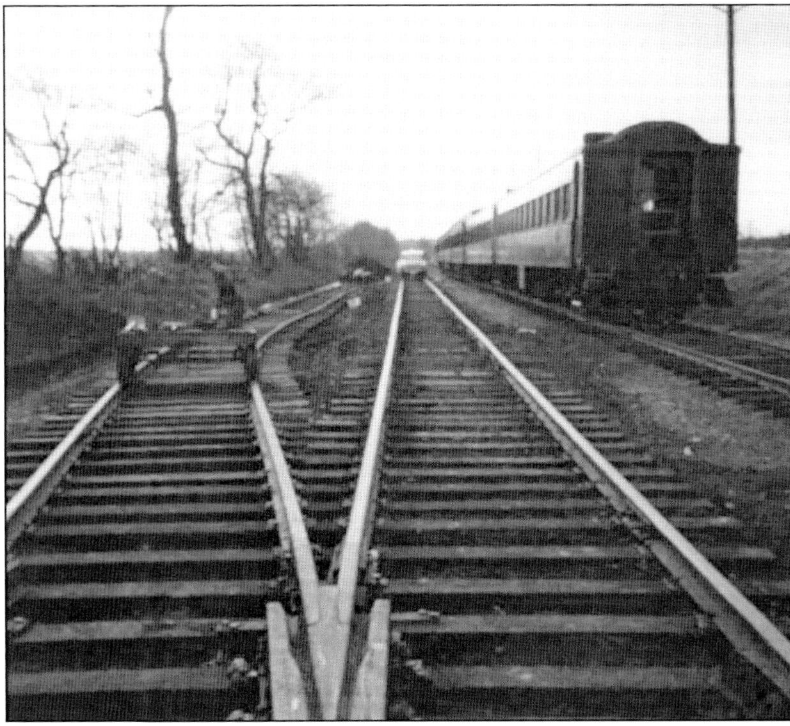

With the arrival of additional passenger cars, more storage space was required, so work on a second storage siding began in South Ringoes in February 1968. The siding was completed with a few months, and equipment was moved onto the siding for storage. (Nelson Tower.)

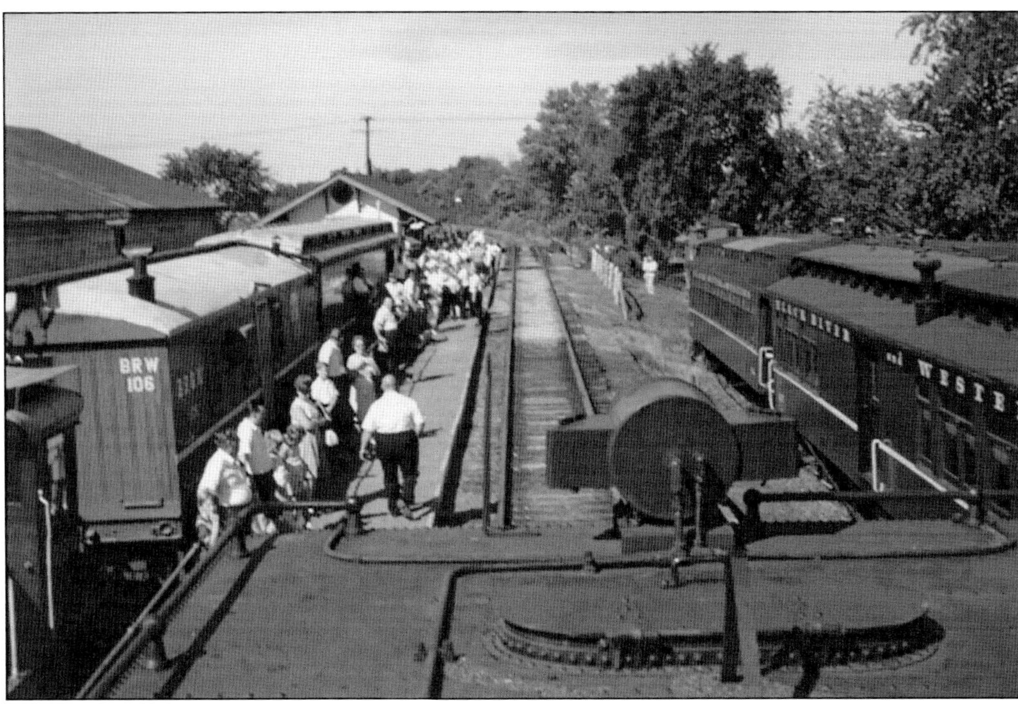

This is a view from the tender of steam engine No. 60 as the engine approaches the Ringoes station platform while passengers wait to board the train. On the left are, from front to back, the Mack engine, car No. 106, and baggage car No. 420, which was used as a museum/souvenir shop. On the right are passenger cars No. 103 (back) and 102. (Nelson Tower.)

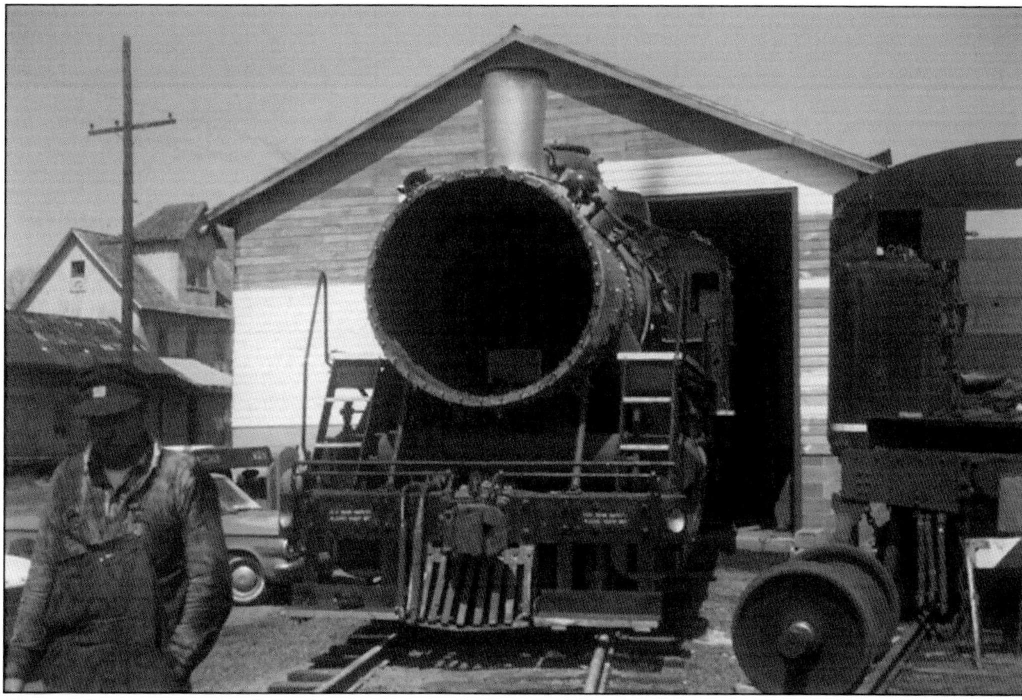

Shown here in front of the Ringoes engine house, steam engine No. 60 required re-tubing of its boiler in early 1968. The tender had been separated and is shown on the right. The engine returned to service later in that year. (Nelson Tower.)

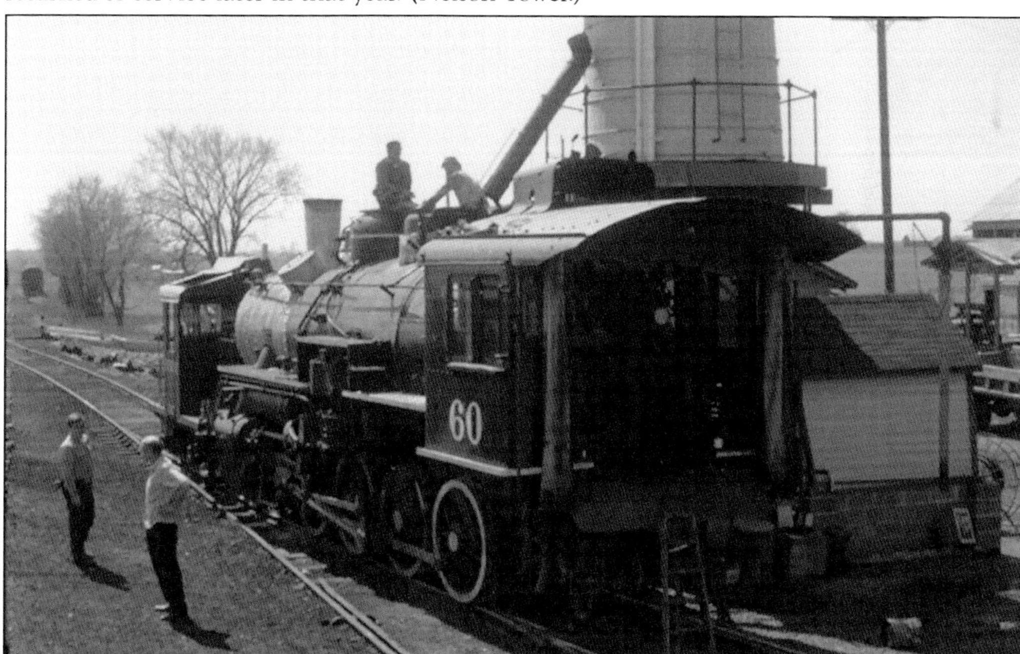

The little Mack engine was pressed into service to move steam engine No. 60 in and out of the engine house during its overhaul in 1968. Volunteers worked feverously to get the engine back in service by the fall for passenger excursion service. (Nelson Tower.)

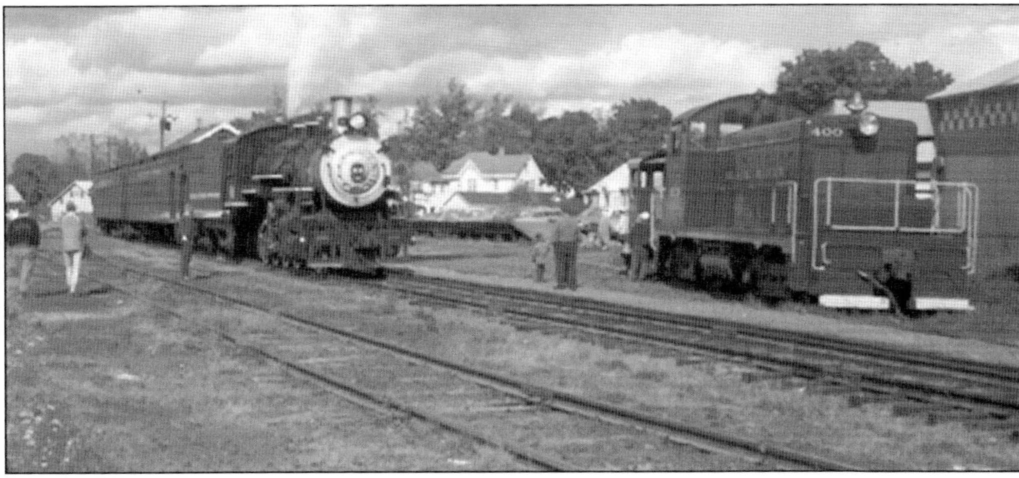

Steam engine No. 60, with passenger cars No. 297 and No. 322, waits at the Flemington station in the fall of 1968 as locomotives No. 1 (back) and No. 400 are shown on the siding to the right. These are three of the railroad's operating locomotives during this time period. (Nelson Tower.)

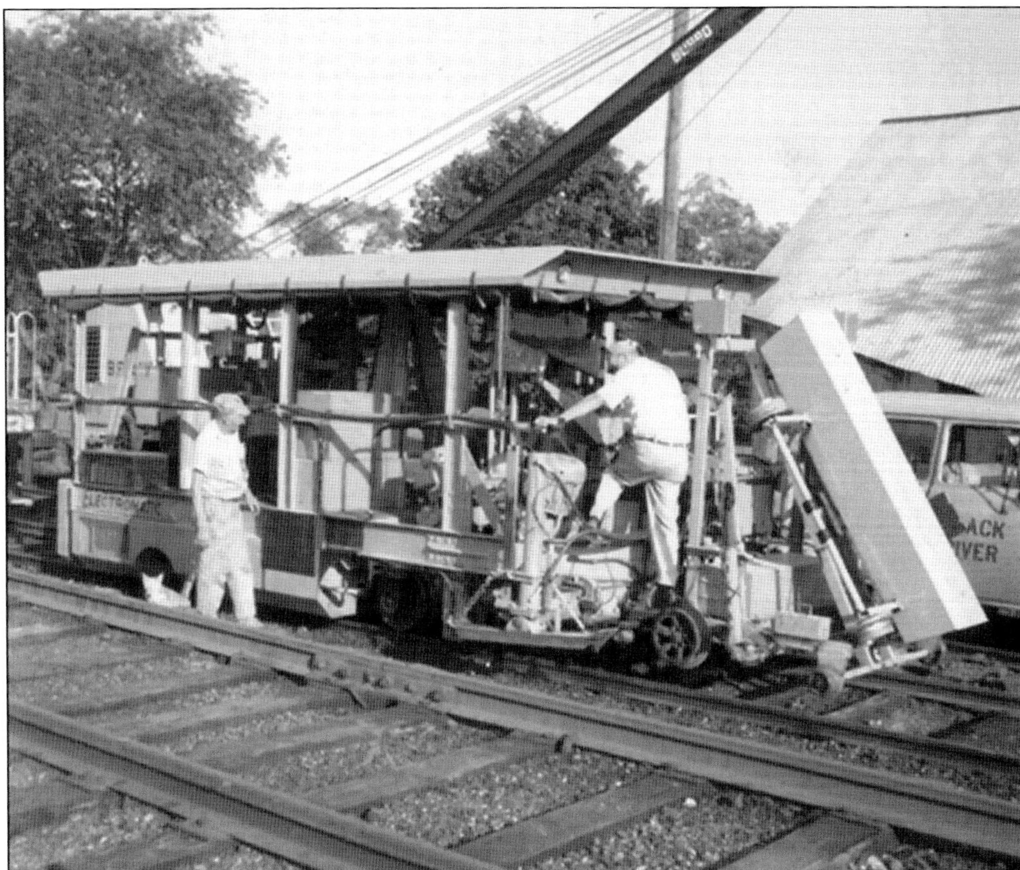

An Electromatic tamper was used by the railroad along the right-of-way to tamp the ballast. Behind the tamper are the Burro crane and the railroad's pick-up truck. This was just one of several pieces of track equipment the railroad used. (Nelson Tower.)

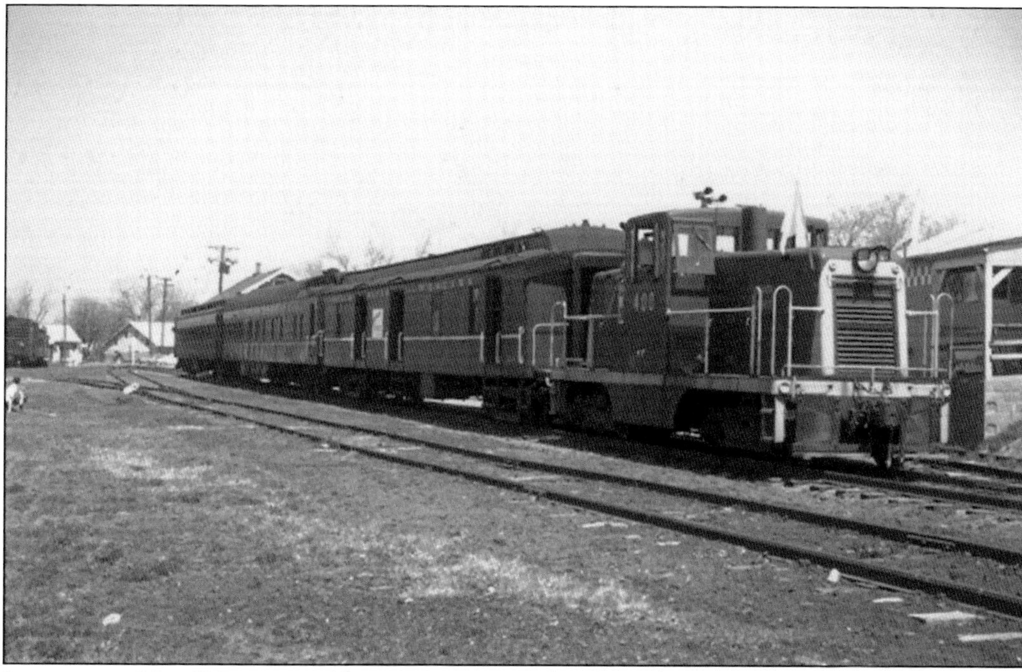

Locomotive No. 400 waits in Flemington in April 1968 with passenger cars No. 100, No. 700 *Enterprise*, and No. 322 *John L. Bishop*. The Thank You Express would treat the volunteers and their families to a trip over the line between Flemington and Lambertville.

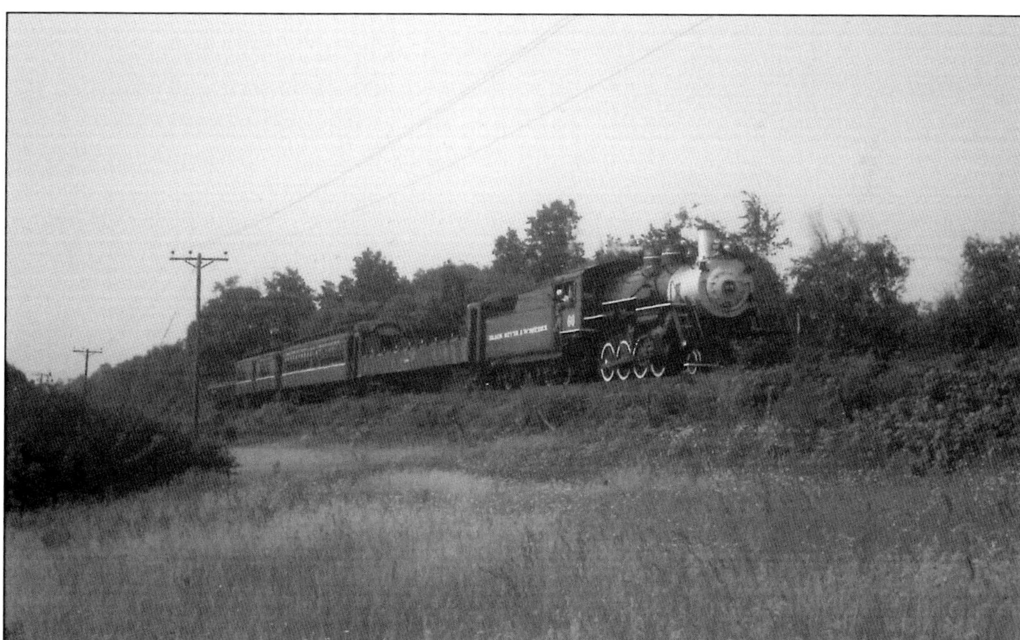

The year 1968 saw passenger excursion runs still using steam engine No. 60 along with two wooden passenger cars and two open cars, the converted Stillwell coach No. 311, and at the end of the train, the converted ex–Lehigh & New England gondola.

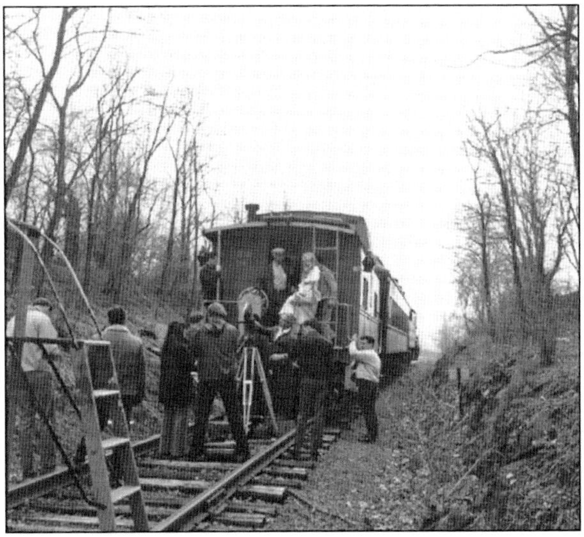

In 1969, a film shoot for a segment for the show *Big Blue Marble* occurred on the Black River & Western Railroad using the steam engine, a wooden coach, and the No. 200 caboose. During the 1960s, the railroad and its equipment were used for a number of commercial backdrops and short films. (Nelson Tower.)

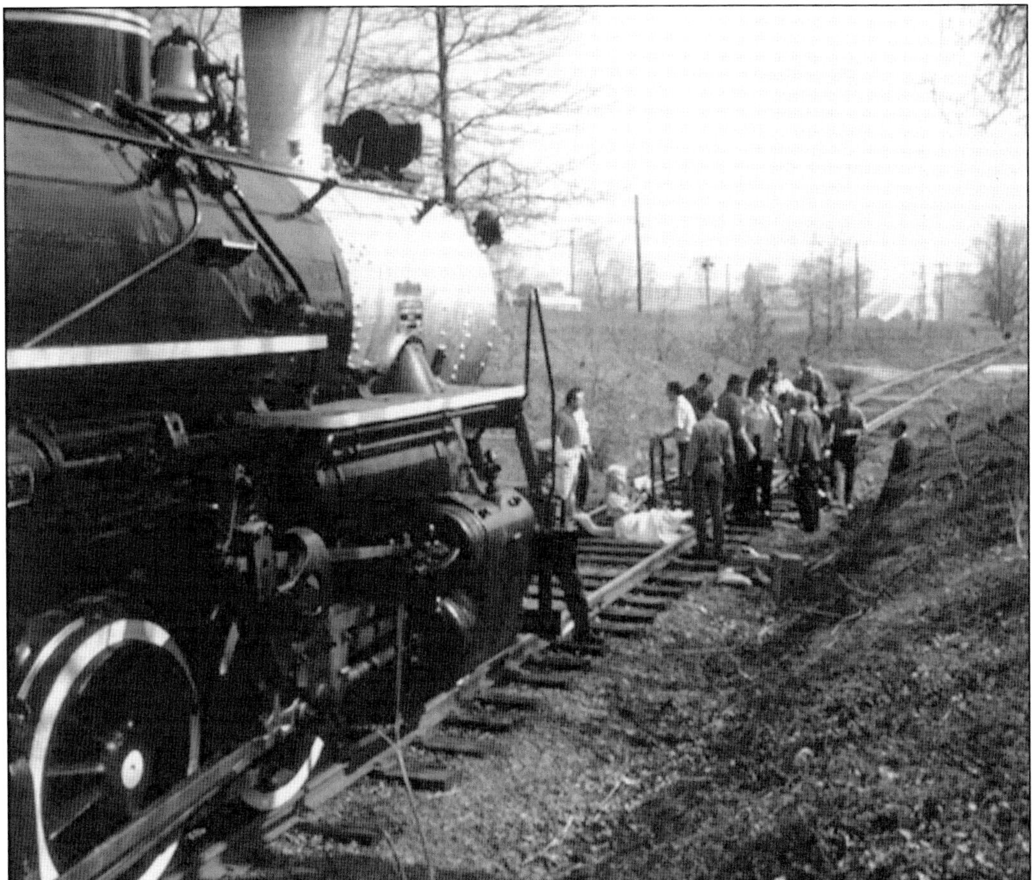

Steam engine No. 60 and other equipment were used during the filming of a scene from "My Seventeenth Summer," a segment from the series *Big Blue Marble*. This was one of several scenes shot along the railroad. (Nelson Tower.)

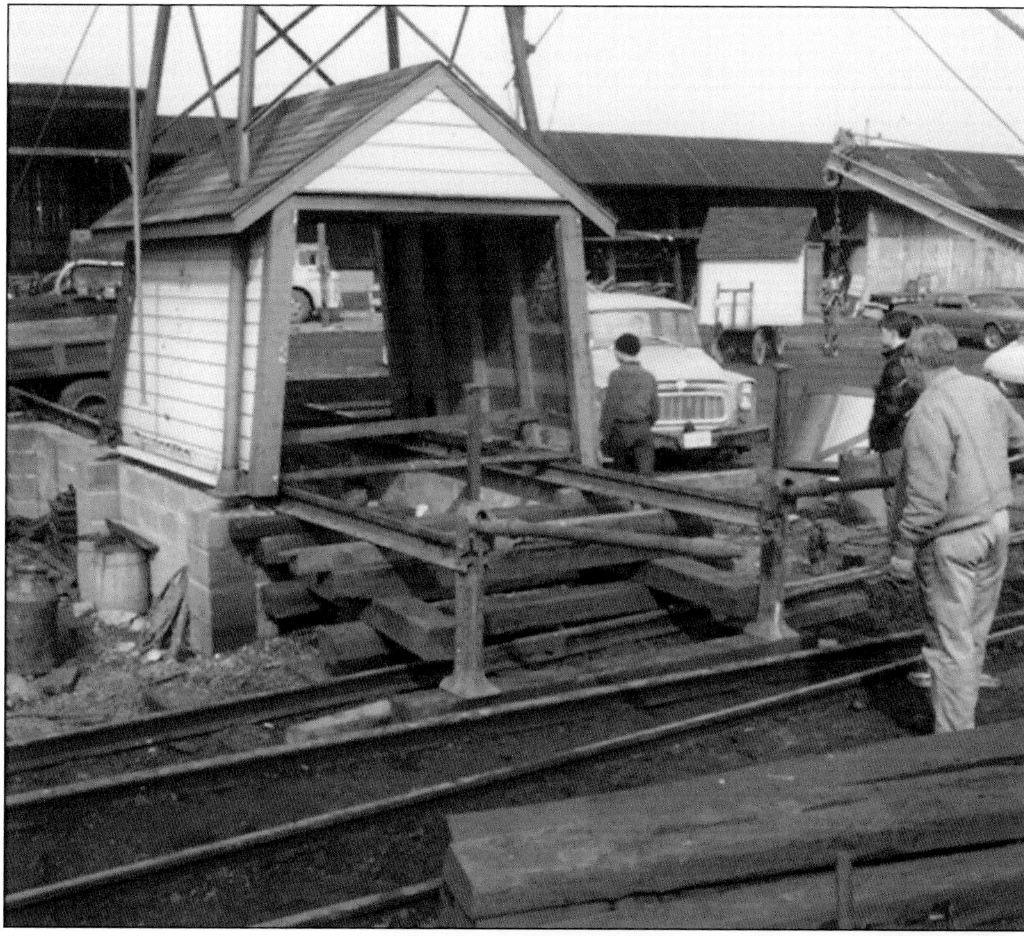

In March 1969, the water tank and shed were moved by the volunteers using a series of rail, jacks, and hard work. The move allowed the track to be realigned for easier access to the engine house. (Nelson Tower.)

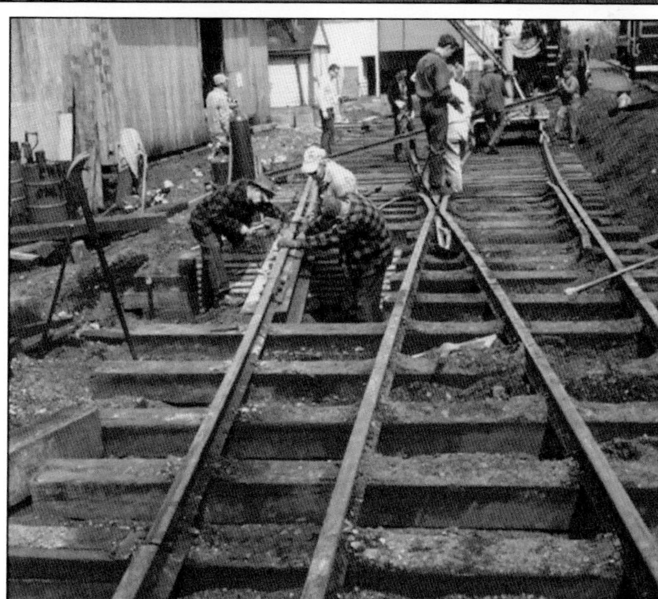

After the water tank and shed were moved, the track into the engine house was realigned by the volunteers. New ties had to be installed to accommodate the realignment of the track. (Nelson Tower.)

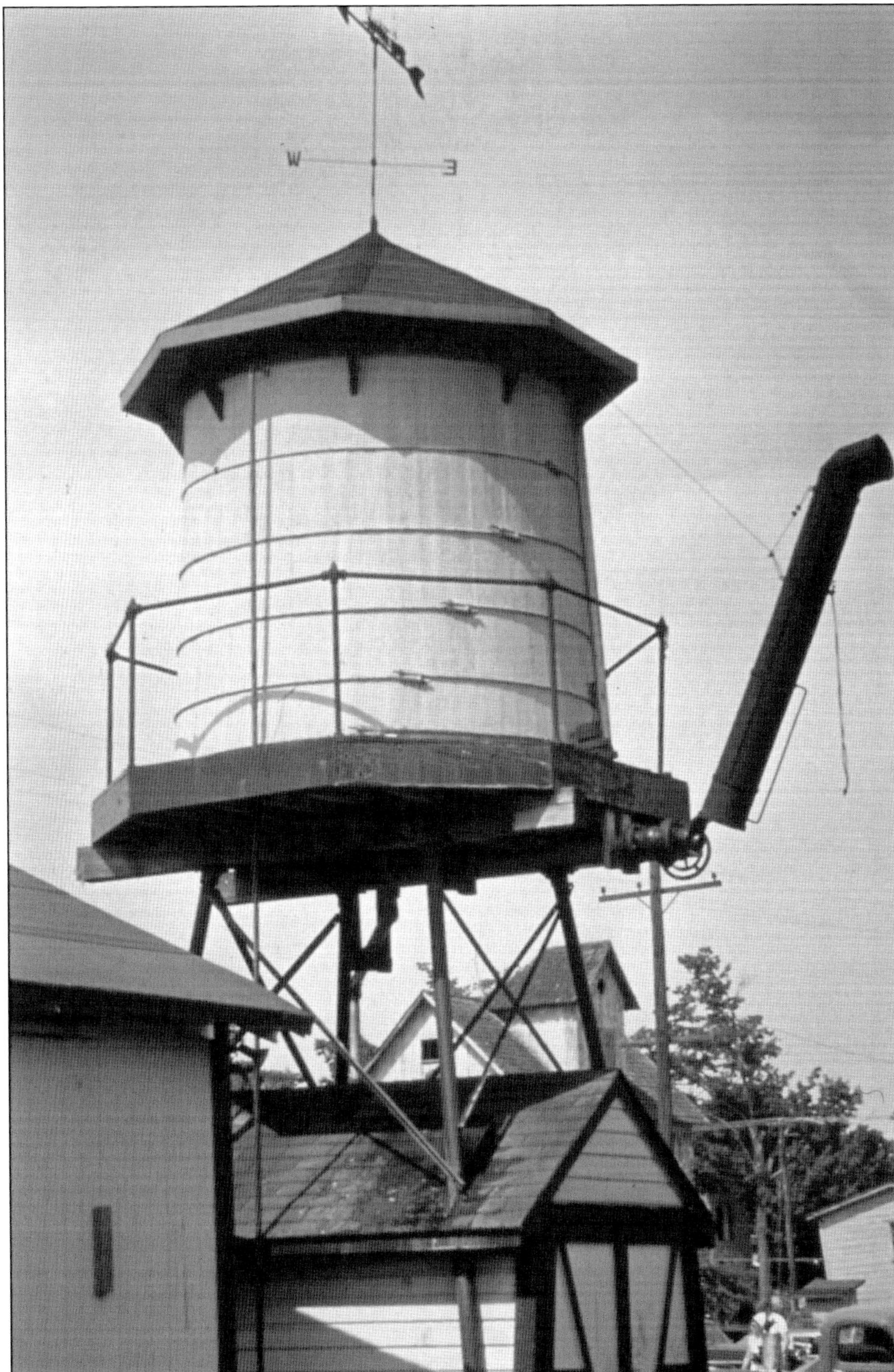

The water tower in Ringoes sits atop a storage shed and sports a weather vane with a train on top. The wooden tank was used until a water plug near the main track was installed. The water tank was eventually torn down.

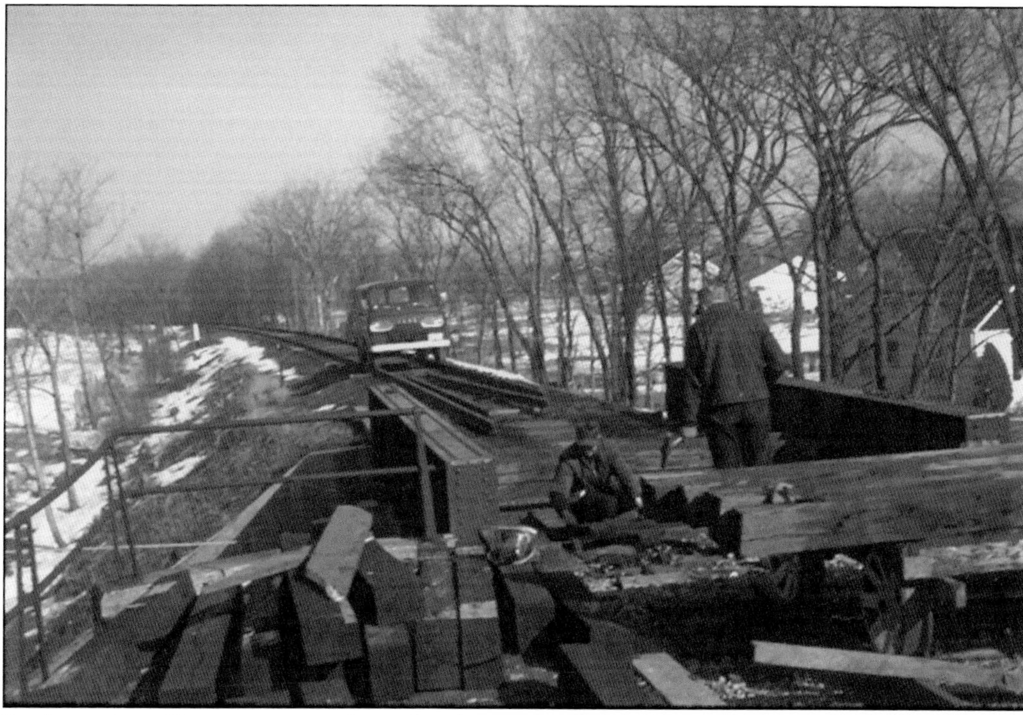

Bridge work in Ringoes was performed in January 1967. Rails were removed, and ties across the bridge were replaced by volunteers. The railroad's track van is shown just north of the bridge. Track upkeep and repair has remained a constant effort for the railroad. (Nelson Tower.)

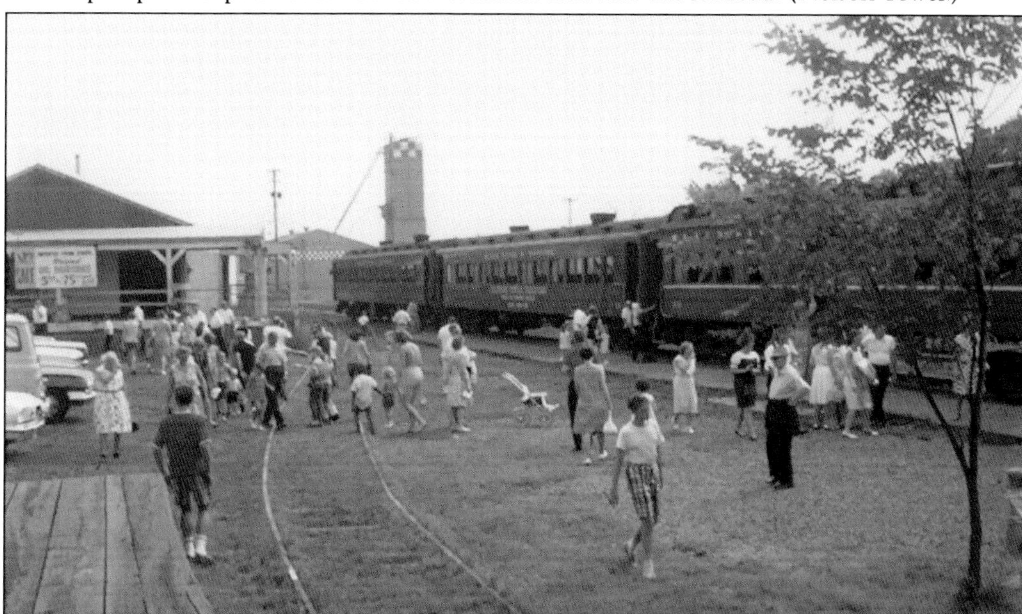

Seen here are passenger cars No. 313, No. 312, and No. 102 as visitors gather in Flemington during one of the excursion trains in 1967. The small ticket office was located just out of view on the right. (Nelson Tower.)

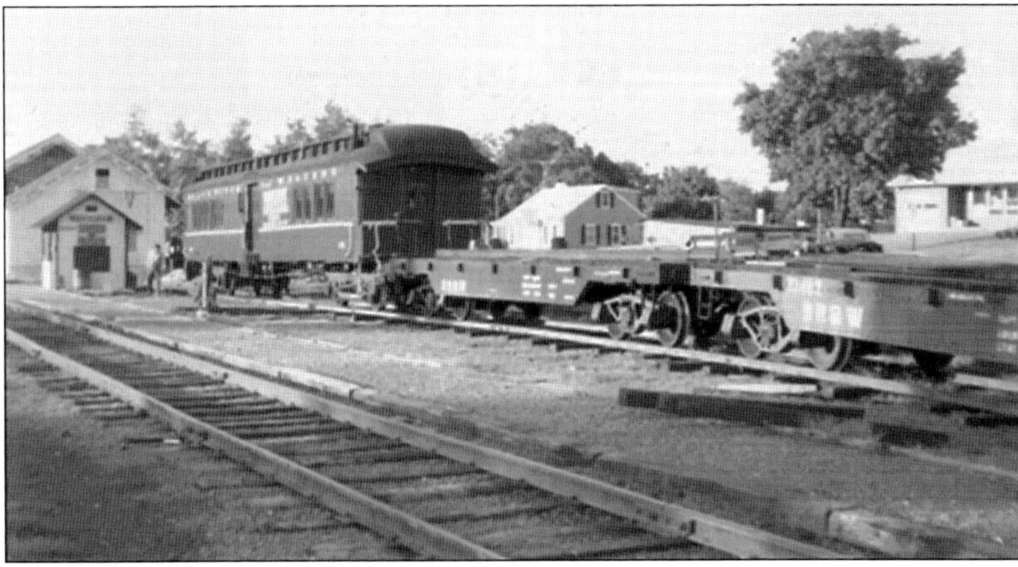

The small ticket office in Flemington was replaced in May 1969 by wooden coach No. 101, put in place by using a temporary track and flatcars to push the coach into position. The temporary tracks were then taken up for use elsewhere along the railroad. (Nelson Tower.)

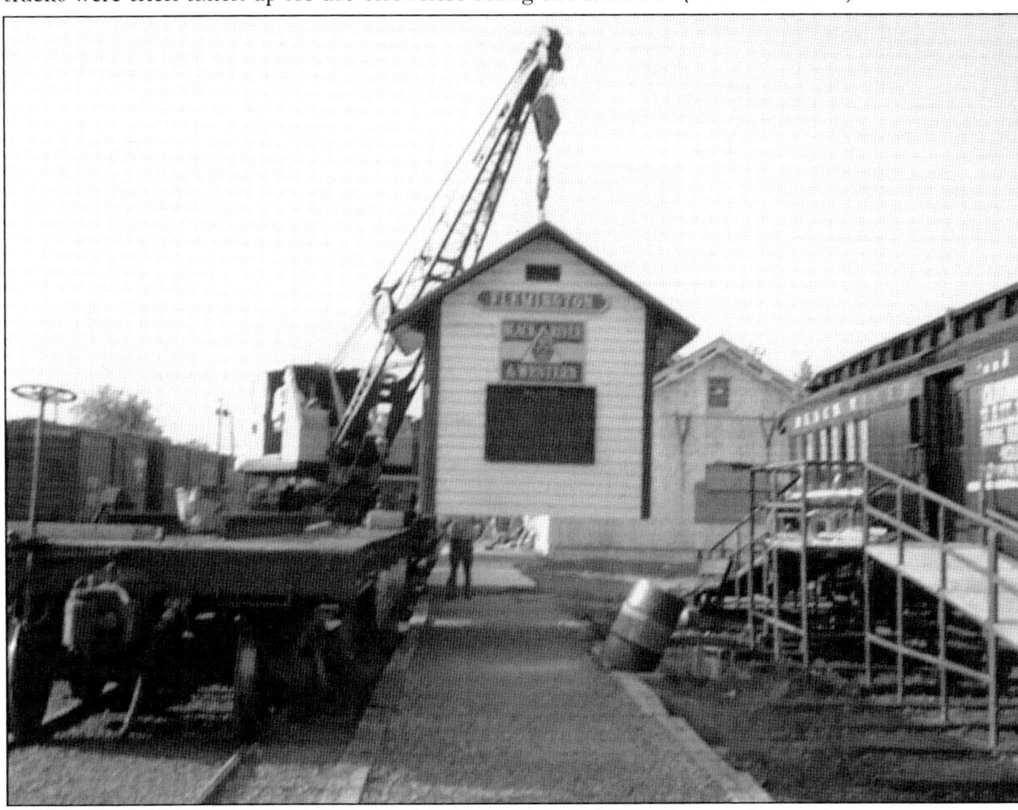

The original Flemington ticket office was removed and loaded on a flatcar for storage. Brought back to Ringoes and stored on the end of track in the south Ringoes yard, the building would eventually be utilized as a storage shed. (Nelson Tower.)

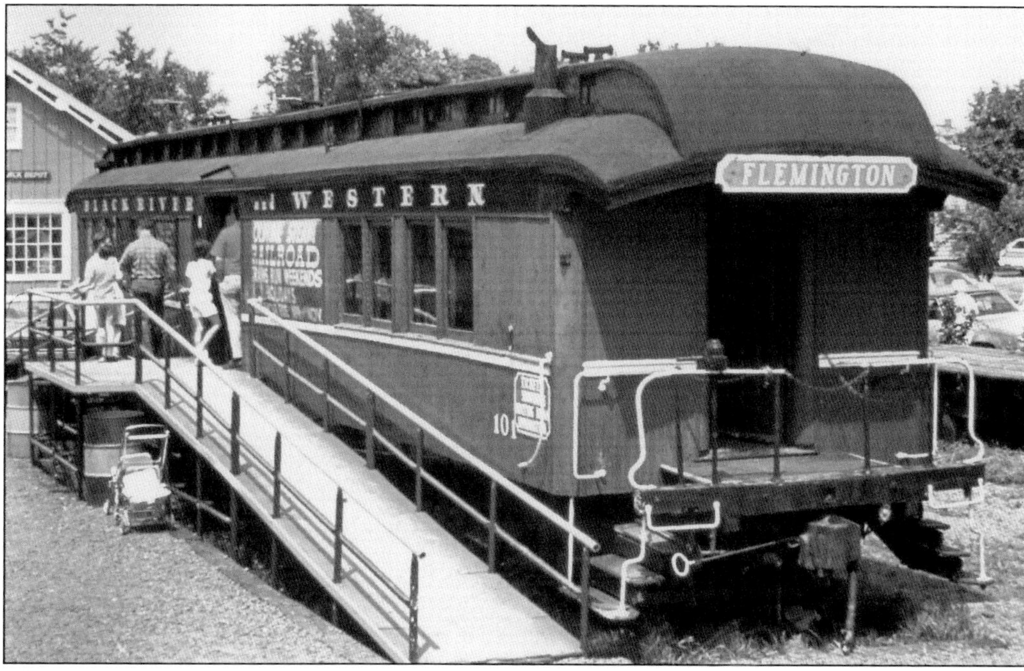

The second Flemington ticket office, the converted combine car No. 101, served as the ticket office and waiting area for a number of years. A ramp and stairs were added outside the car to allow access, and the car retained the original Black River colors of green with yellow lettering.

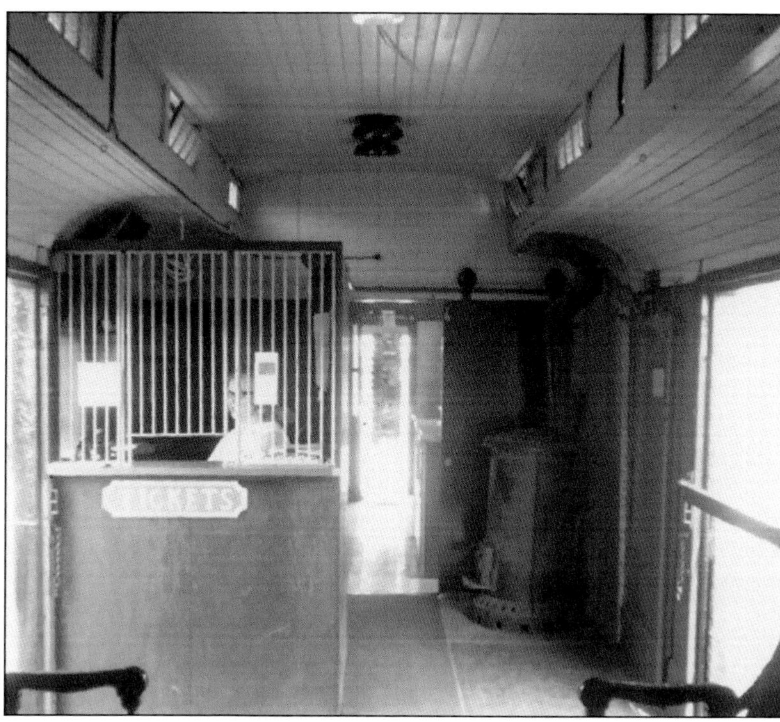

This image of the inside of the converted combine car No. 101 in Flemington shows how the wooden car was renovated with a coal stove to provide heat and wooden benches for passengers to sit on while waiting for the next excursion train. (Nelson Tower.)

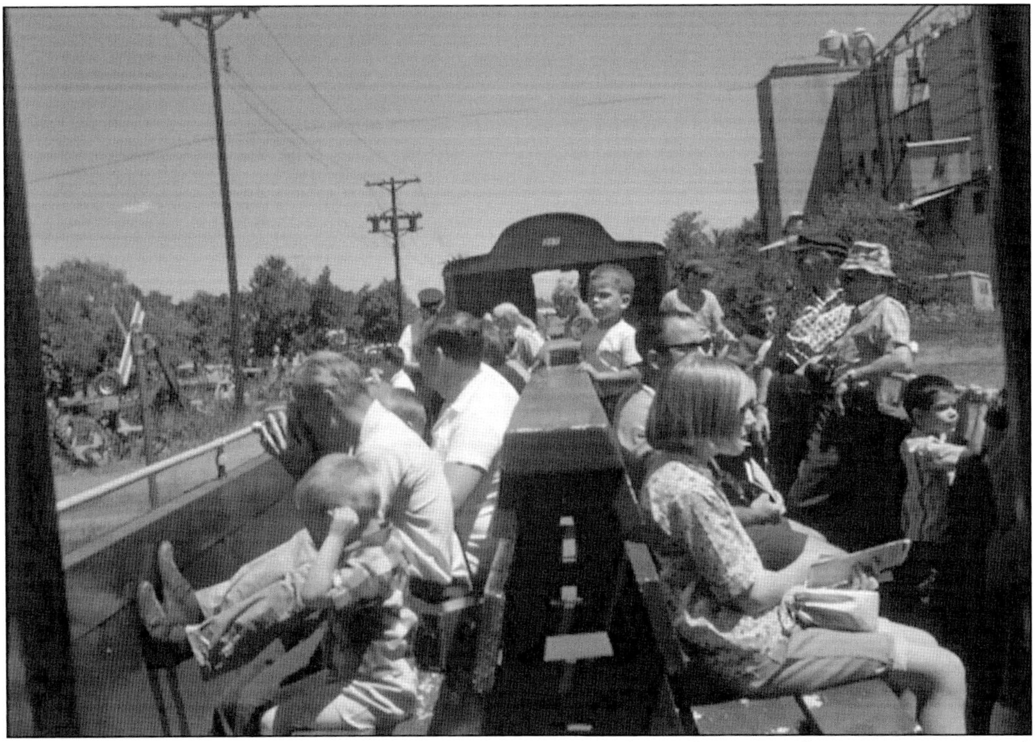

Passenger car No. 311, the converted Stillwell car, was popular with tourists for its open-air appeal. However, the car had structural problems, forcing the railroad to later add a pipe-and-corrugated roof structure in an effort to strengthen the car. (Nelson Tower.)

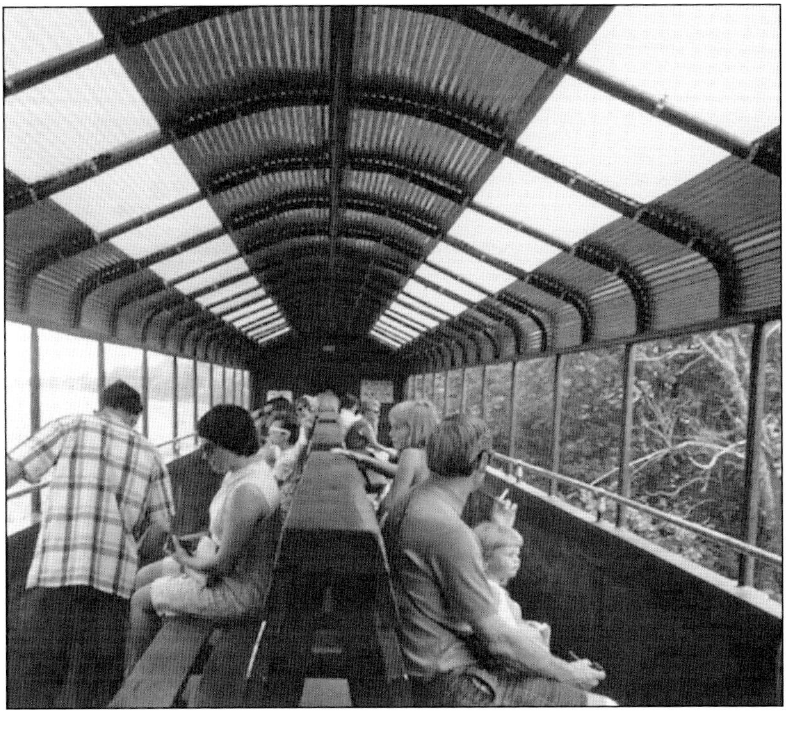

With the newly installed roof, No. 311 ran for a few more years before being scrapped. While in service, the car remained a popular place for the passengers to ride, so they could enjoy the open air while gazing at the countryside. (Nelson Tower.)

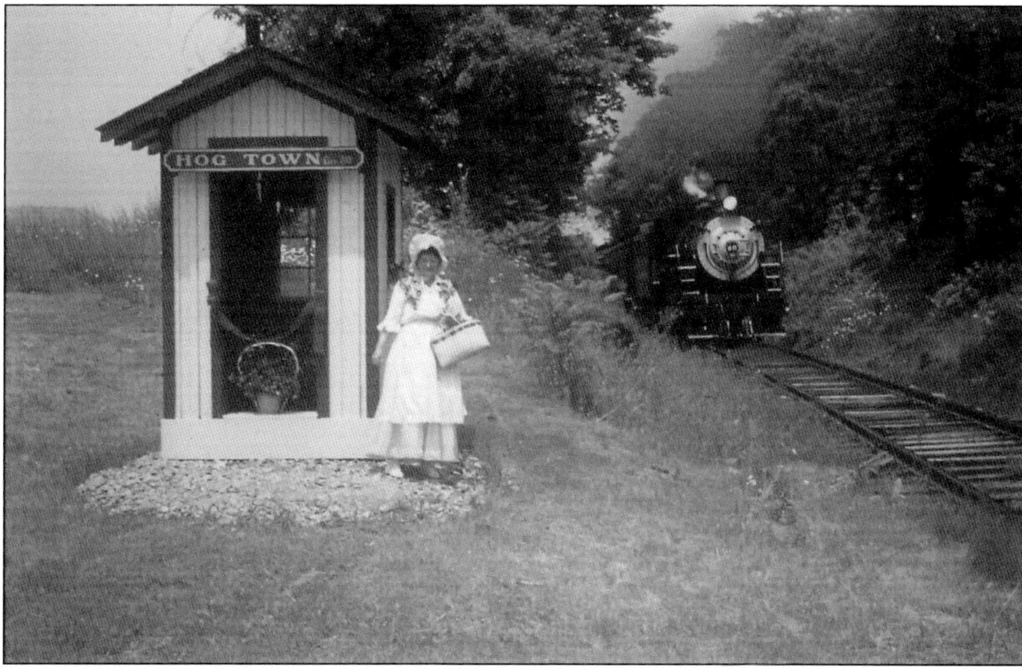

On June 8, 1969, Bea Quick, a regular BR&W volunteer, poses by the newly dedicated Hogtown station as steam engine No. 60 approaches the small station. The old telephone shed was found in a dump and brought to Hogtown to be restored by Joe Adda. (Nelson Tower.)

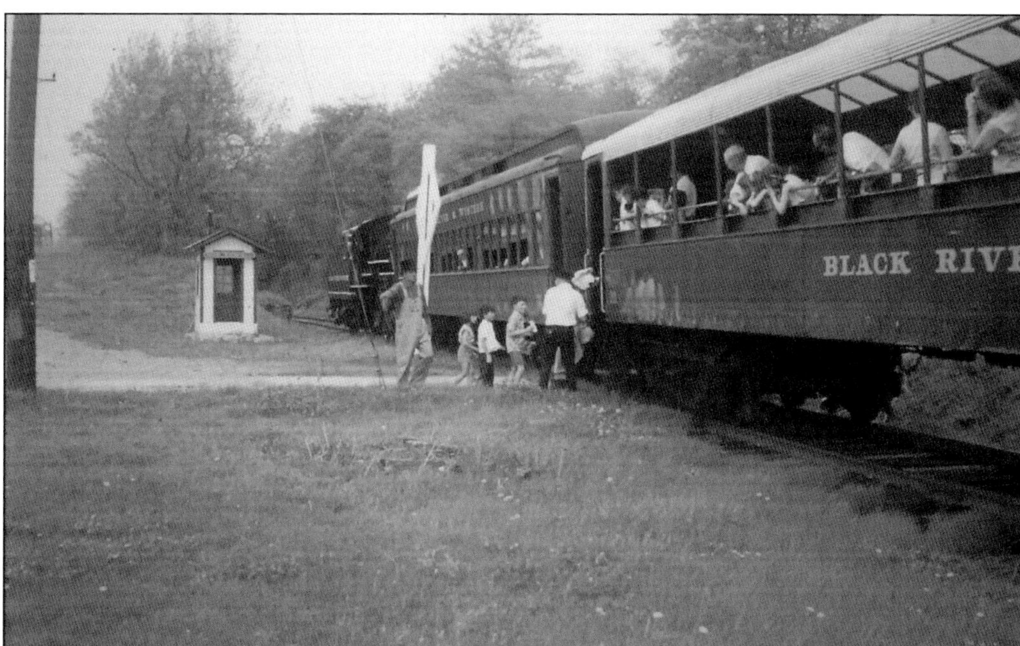

Northbound trips stopped at Hogtown and were greeted by the unofficial mayor of Hogtown, Joe Adda. Adda would wear his overalls and top hat to greet the passengers to the station and try to entice them to vote for him for mayor.

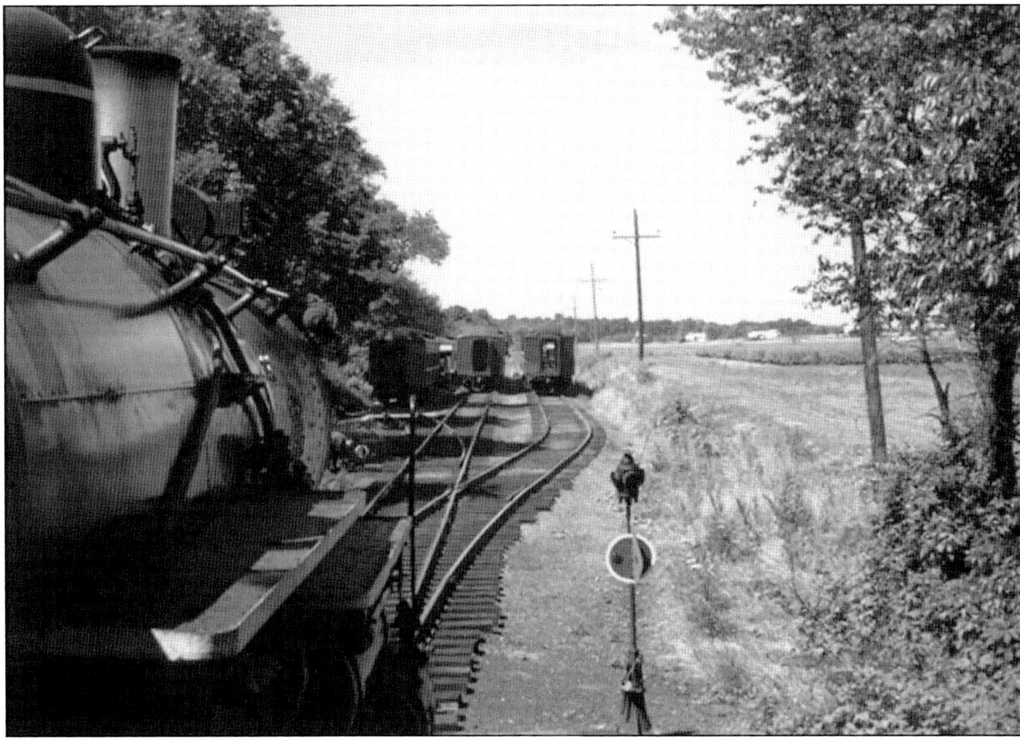

This 1968 view from the engineer's side of the cab of steam engine No. 60 shows the yard in South Ringoes filled with passenger cars. More than a dozen cars were stored in the yard during this time period, as the railroad continued to purchase surplus equipment. (Nelson Tower.)

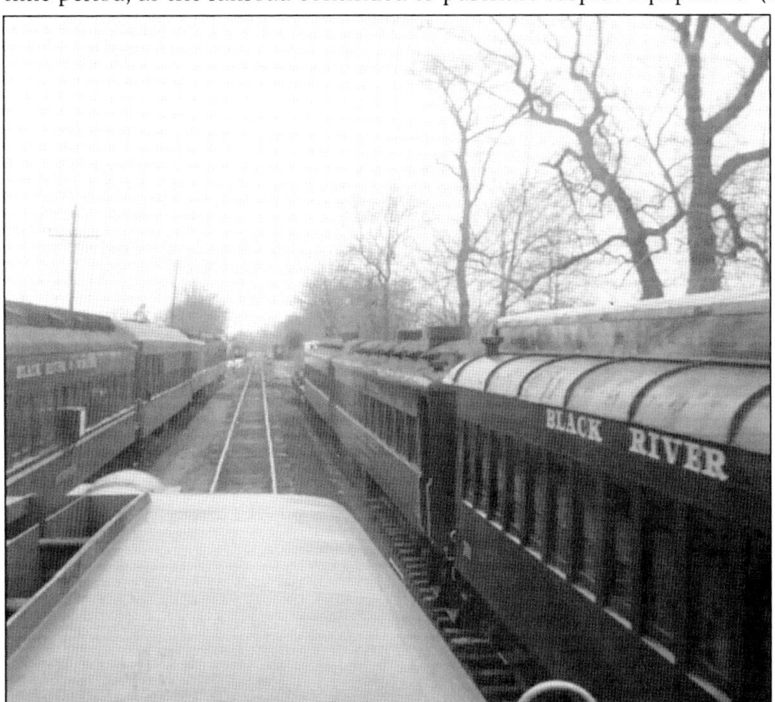

Here is another 1968 view of the Ringoes yard from the cab of locomotive No. 400. Looking north toward the Ringoes station, it shows many of the passenger cars owned by the railroad. The car on the left with the air conditioner is No. 700 Enterprise. (Nelson Tower.)

One of two ex–Pennsylvania Railroad flanger cars sits on the engine house siding with locomotive No. 400 and the small Fairmont crane in December 1969. The flanger was used in maintenance-of-way service along the right-of-way. (Nelson Tower.)

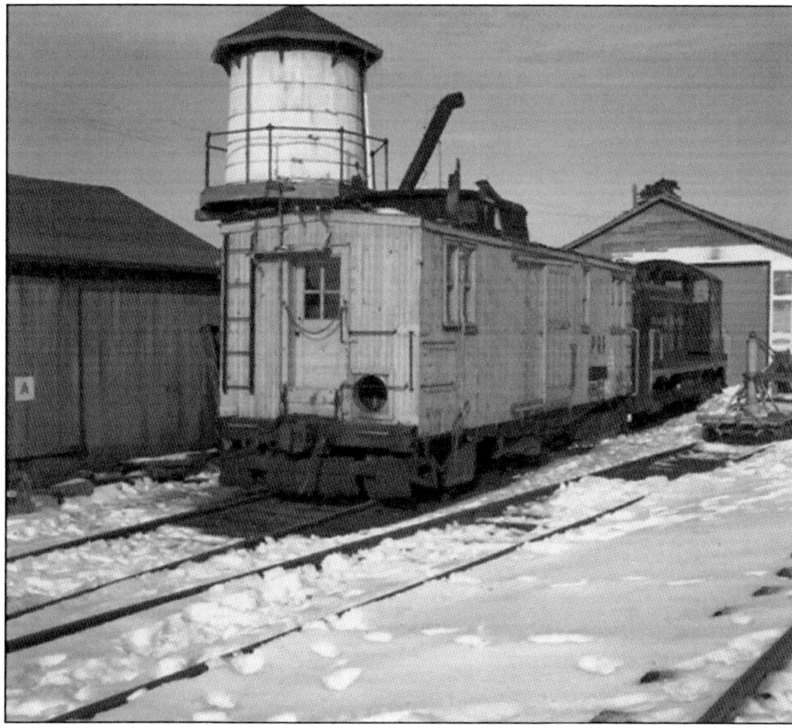

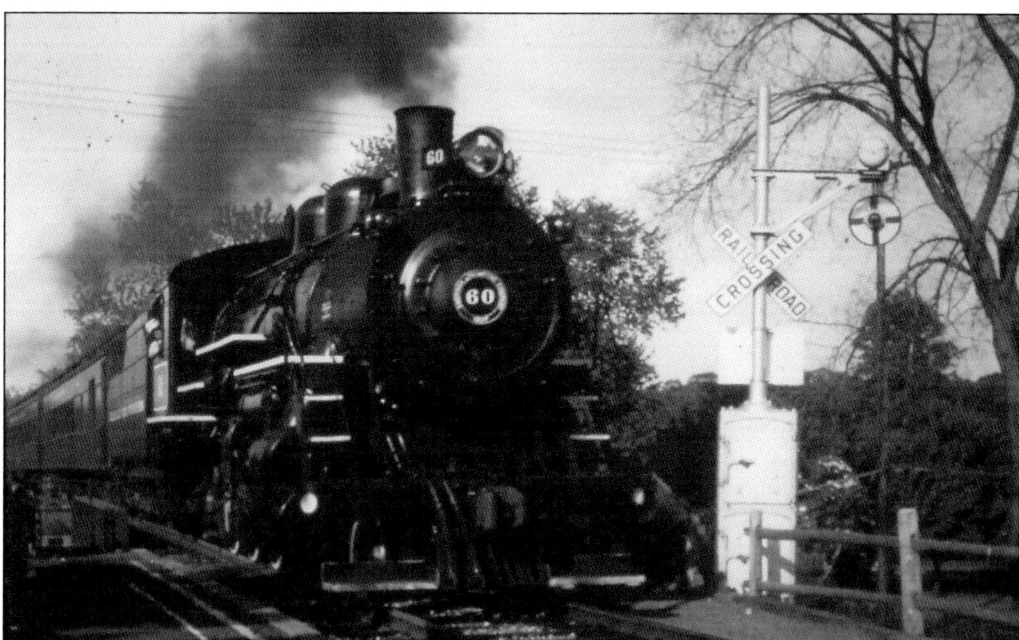

Steam engine No. 60 arrives at the Ringoes station on a fall day in 1969. Note the wig-wag signal on the right side of the main track that was used as a display. The two cars behind the steam engine are the combine No. 297 and No. 322 *John L. Bishop*. (Norman Cole.)

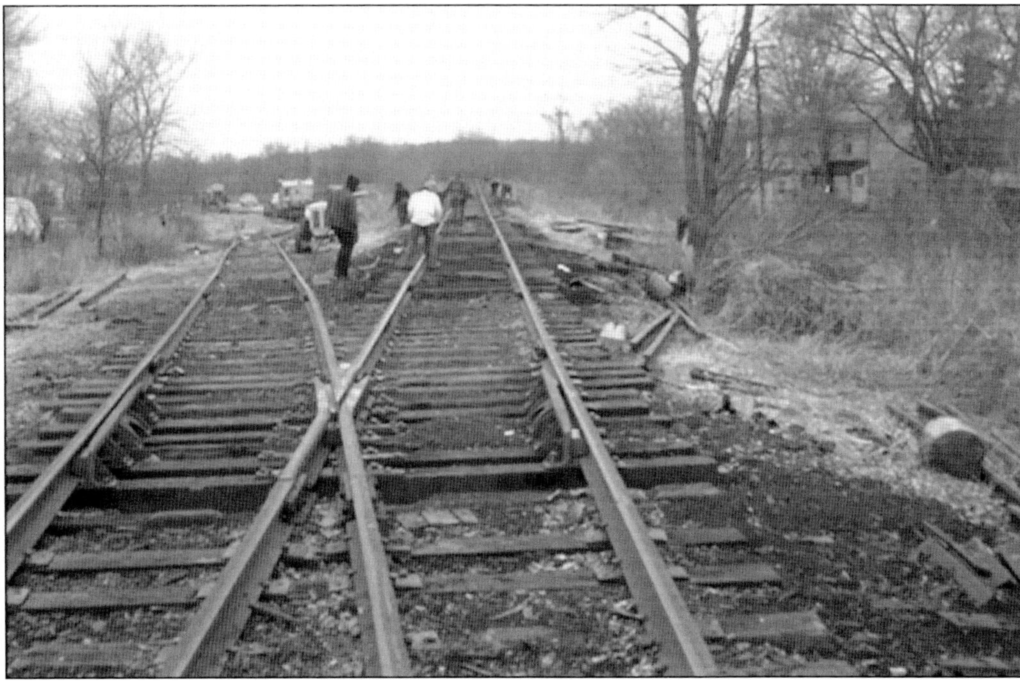

A new 10-car interchange to be used for freight car service was built between December 1969 and March 1970 in Lambertville, for connection with the Penn-Central Railroad. Freight was delivered here and taken by the Black River North to customers along the line. (Nelson Tower.)

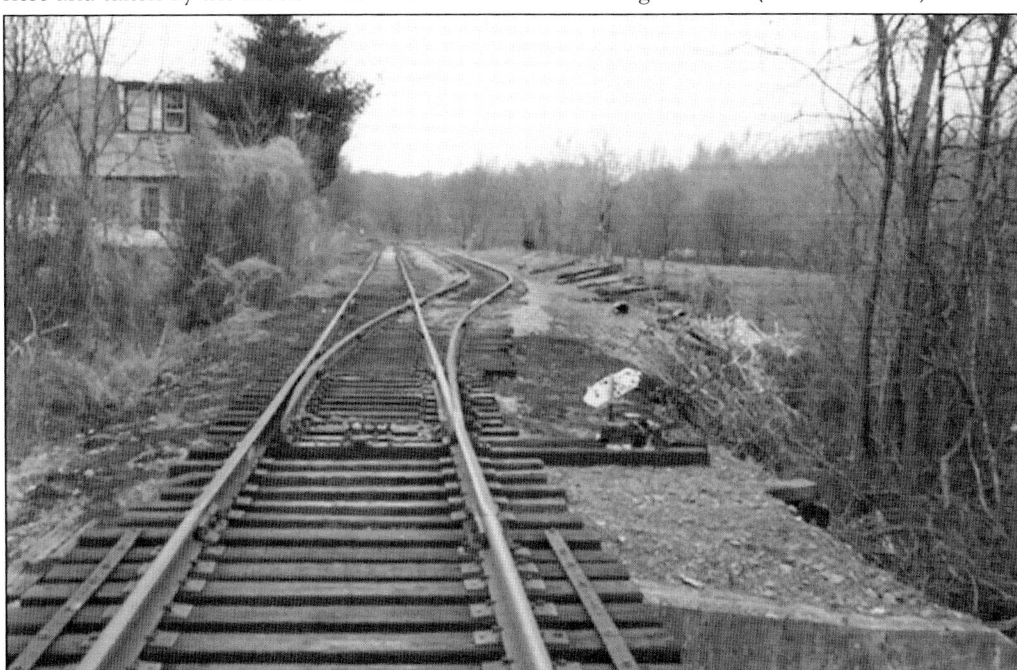

By March 1970, the Black River & Western Railroad officially assumed control of freight movement over its line from Lambertville to Flemington, utilizing the new interchange track that had been built in Lambertville. (Nelson Tower.)

Two

GROWTH INTO A SHORT LINE

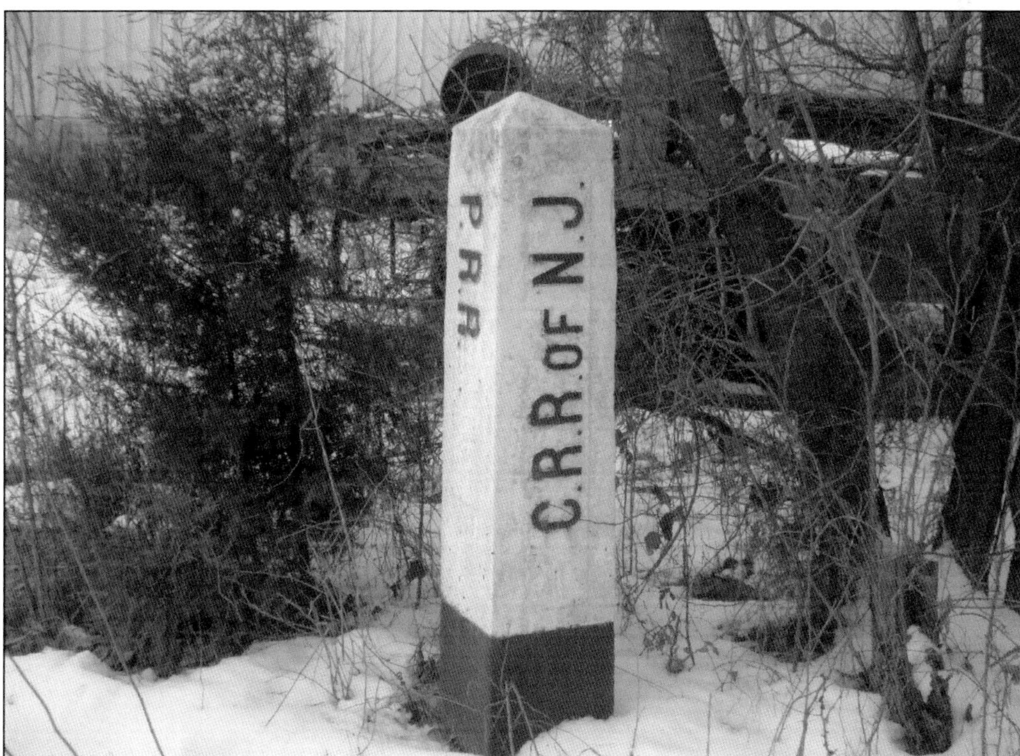

Shown here is the marker post in Flemington that indicates where the Pennsylvania Railroad and the Central Railroad of New Jersey met. Black River & Western would first lease and then purchase the Pennsylvania Flemington branch between Flemington and Lambertville and later purchase a portion of the South Branch line of the Central Railroad of New Jersey from Flemington to Three Bridges.

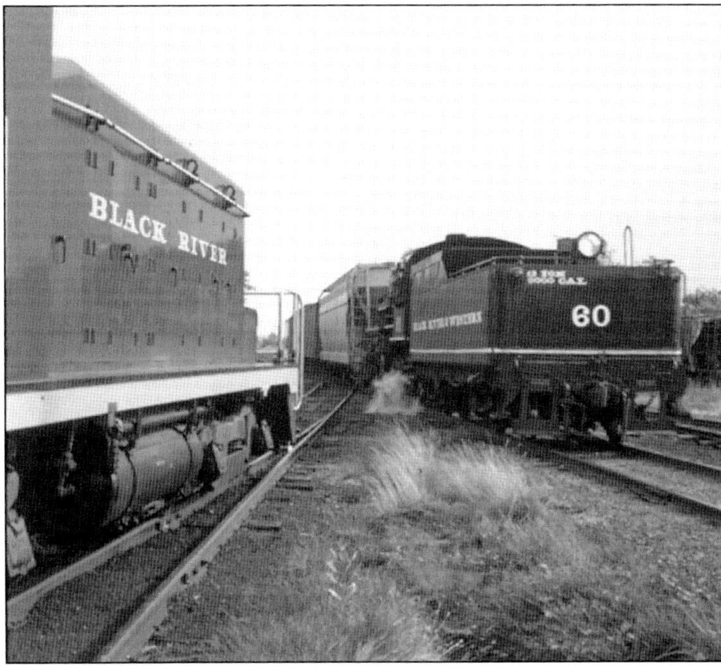

Locomotive No. 400 waits on a siding while steam engine No. 60 passes by to help switch freight cars locally in Flemington. The two engines were used to jockey the freight cars into their correct siding positions. (Nelson Tower.)

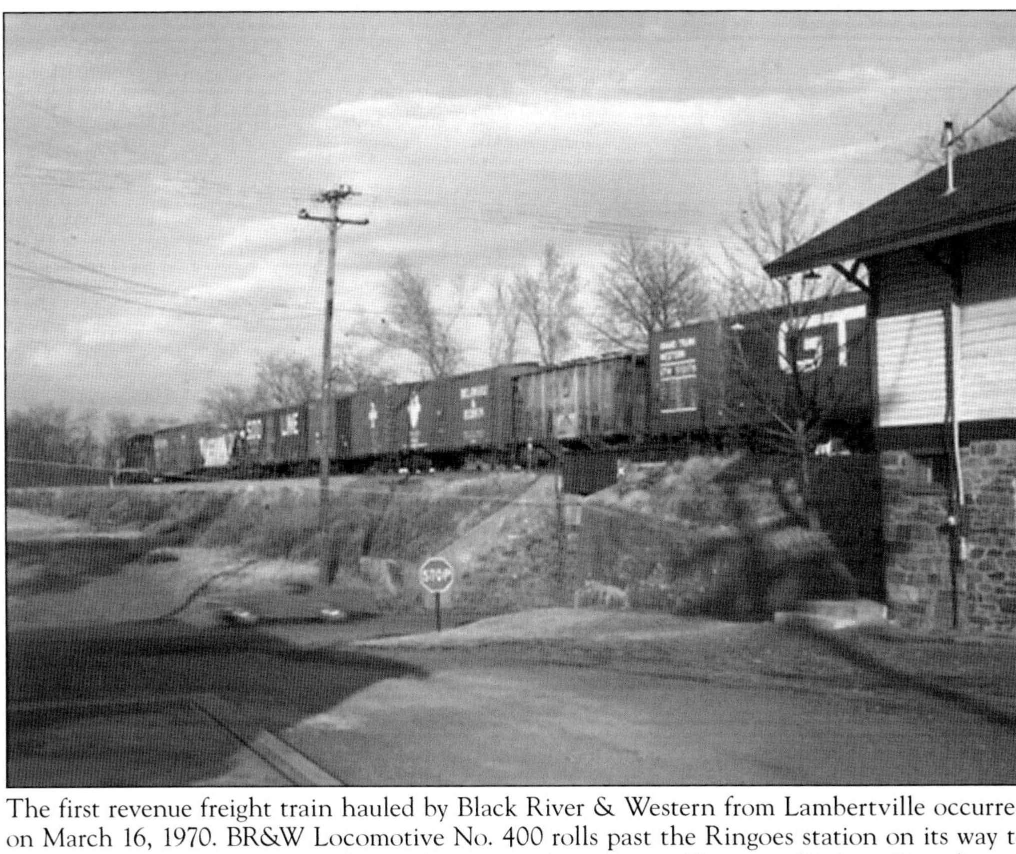

The first revenue freight train hauled by Black River & Western from Lambertville occurred on March 16, 1970. BR&W Locomotive No. 400 rolls past the Ringoes station on its way to Flemington. The train consisted of six boxcars and two covered hoppers. (Nelson Tower.)

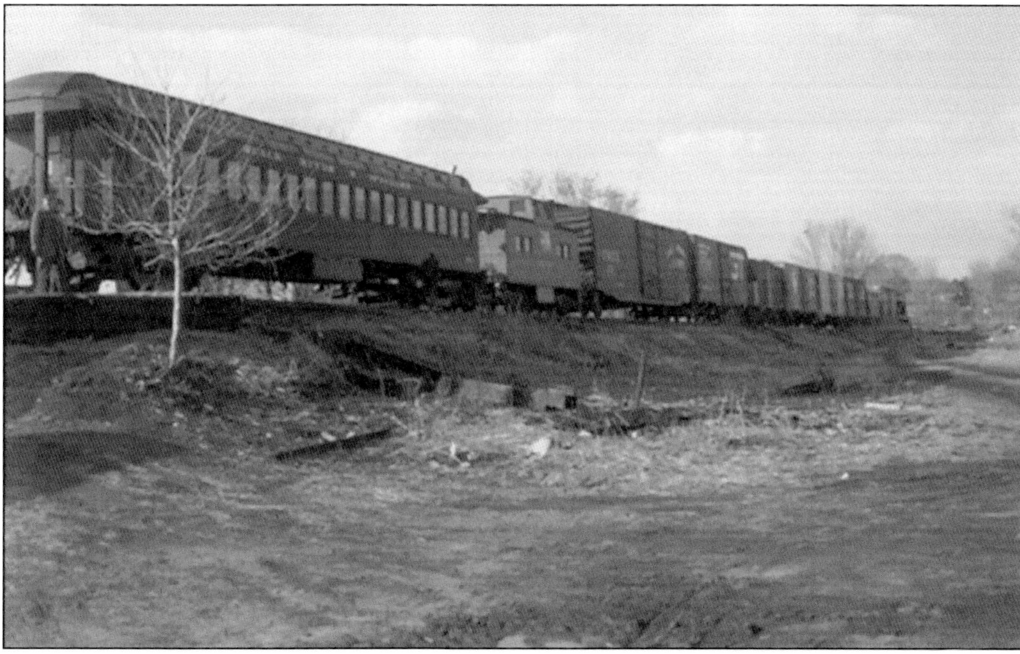

The first freight train to run by the Black River & Western on the line traveled north from Lambertville and included passenger car No. 301 and the No. 200 caboose. Volunteers rode in the coach for the historic trip from Lambertville to Flemington and return. (Nelson Tower.)

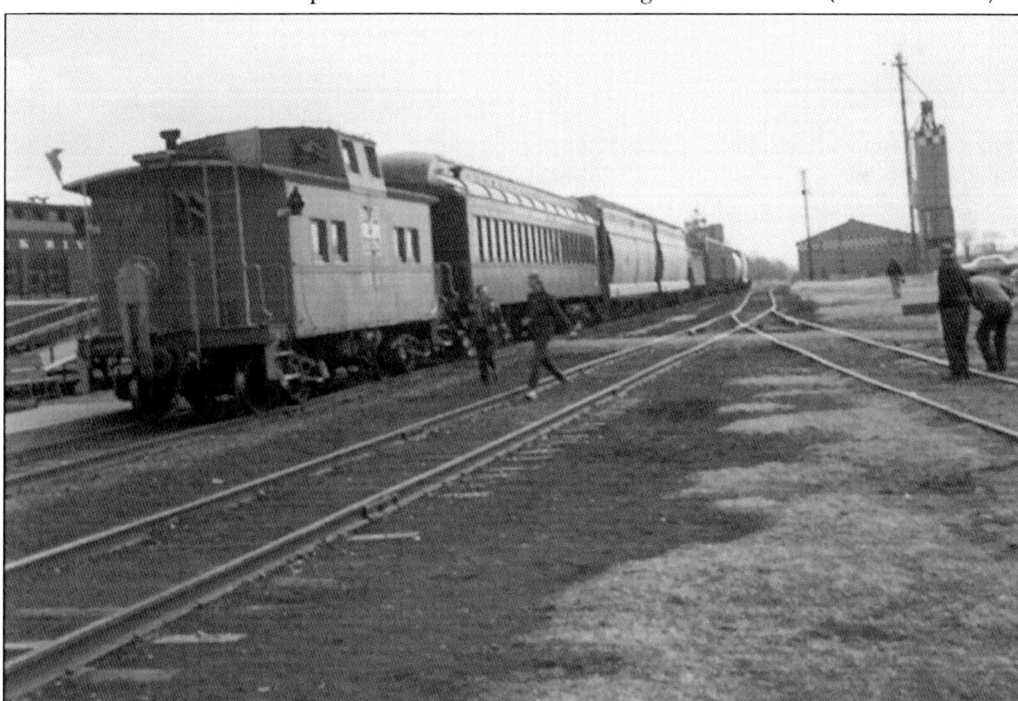

During the first freight run by the railroad on March 16, 1970, the train of empty freight cars is readied in Flemington for its return trip to Lambertville for delivery to the Penn-Central Railroad at the new interchange. (Nelson Tower.)

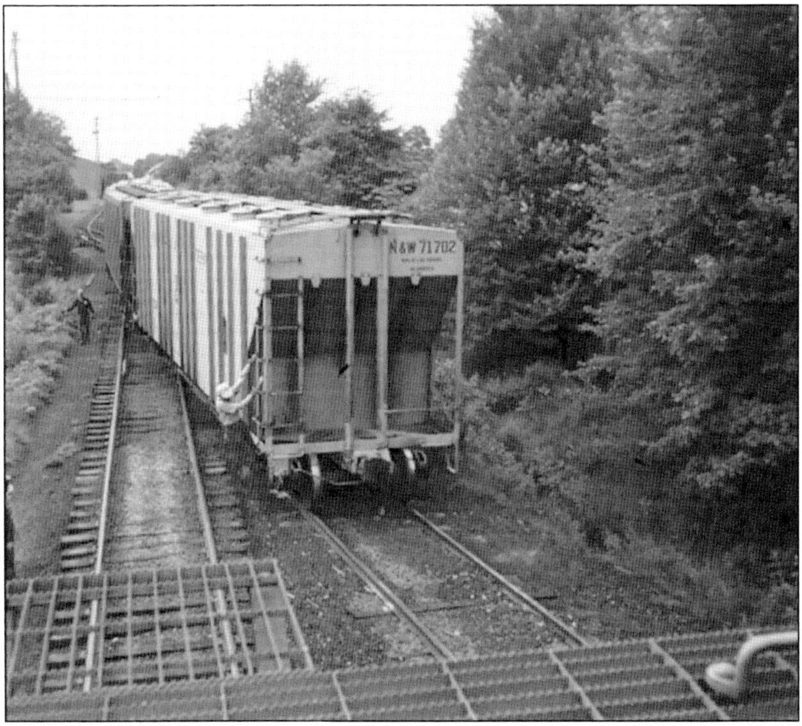

Freight moves would continue throughout the 1970s. Pictured is a shoving move with brakeman Bill Kitner on board. A second brakeman, Nelson Tower, is shown on the left, able to relay hand signals to the engineer, who would not be able to see the rear-most brakeman. (Nelson Tower.)

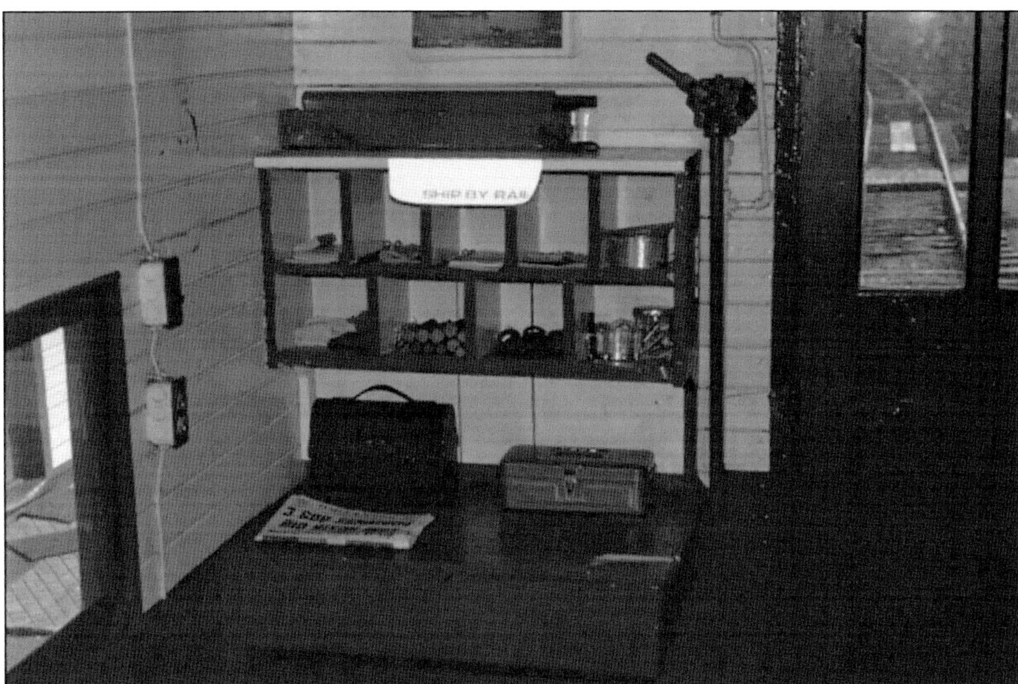

The inside work area of caboose No. 200 would be used in freight service. This area is where the freight conductor prepared his reports and conducted other railroad business. The caboose also served as an area to relax and enjoy a meal. (Nelson Tower.)

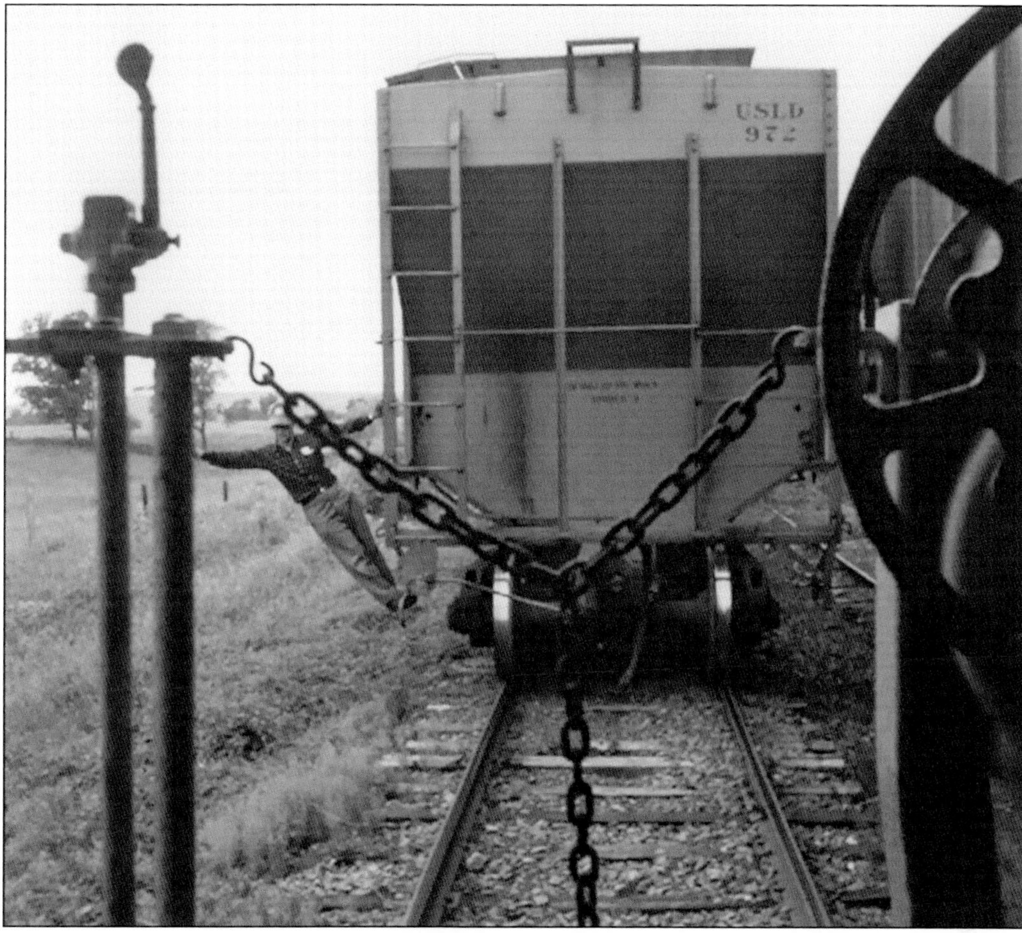

The brakeman riding the side of a covered hopper car gets ready to signal the engineer for a stop prior to coupling the freight car to the caboose. The caboose's brake wheel is on the right, and the emergency air dump valve and caboose whistle are shown on the left. (Nelson Tower.)

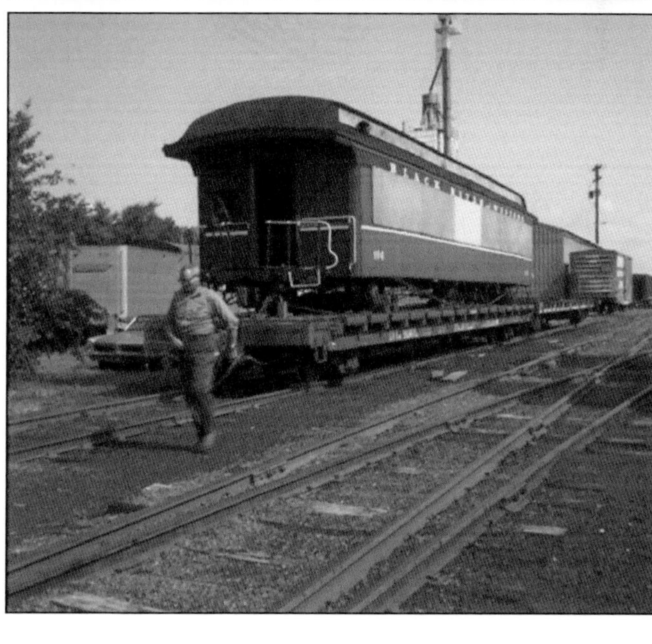

In August 1970, passenger car No. 104 was sold and loaded onto a flatcar for its last trip northbound. The wooden coach was sold to the Yankee Silversmith Inn in Wallingford, Connecticut. (Nelson Tower.)

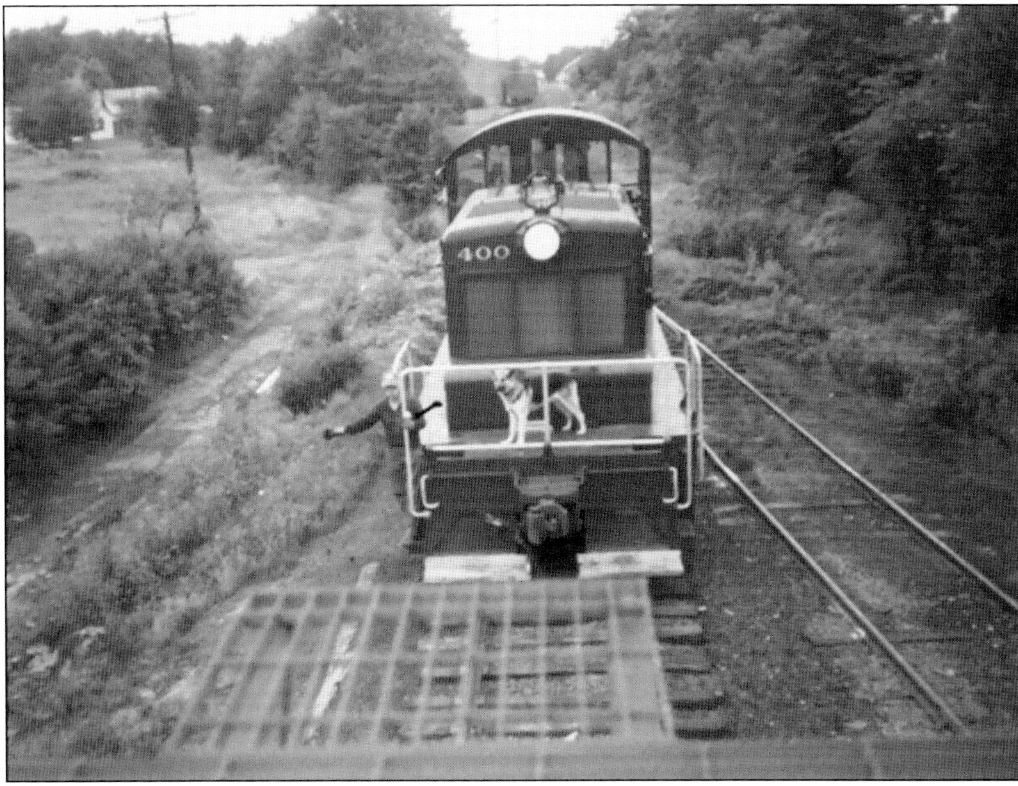

The German Shepard mascot of the railroad, Rintzi, rides the locomotive while brakeman Bill Kitner stands ready to couple up to the freight cars. Rintzi would often ride the regular freight trips between Ringoes and Flemington. (Nelson Tower.)

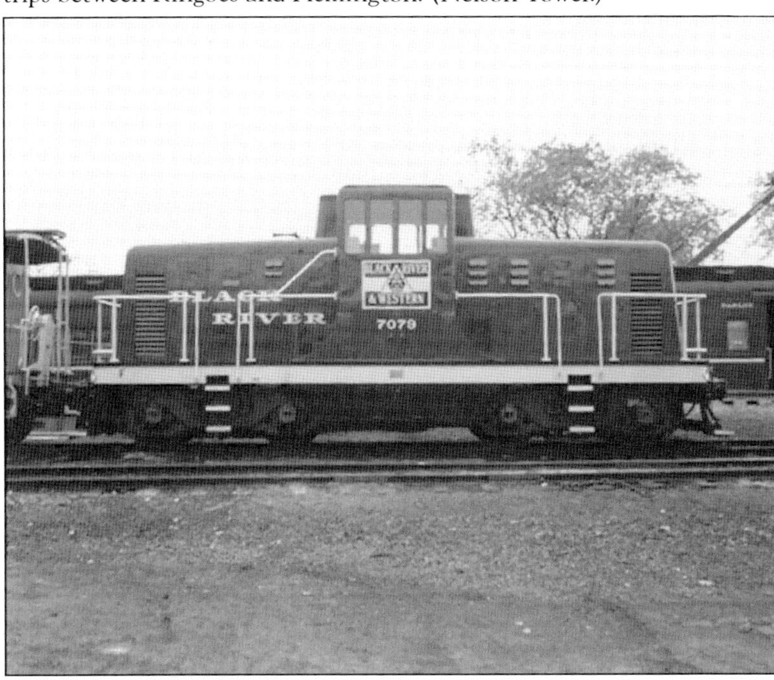

A new "school" engine arrive in 1970. Owned by North Hunterdon High School, the 1941 General Electric locomotive was used as a rolling vocational diesel shop. The engine would be used by the railroad until 1979, when it was sold and removed from the property.

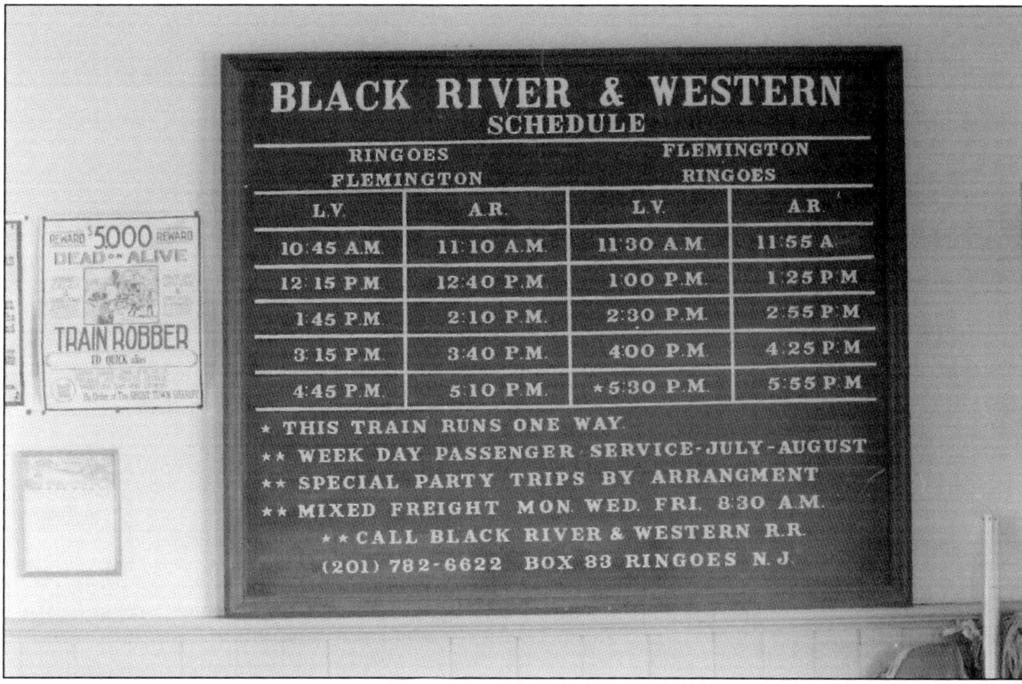

The schedule board from the 1970s that hung in the Ringoes station shows departure and arrival times for passenger trains between Ringoes and Flemington. The sign displays both weekday and weekend times departures and arrivals. A sign hanging on the left advertises one of the early train robbery events.

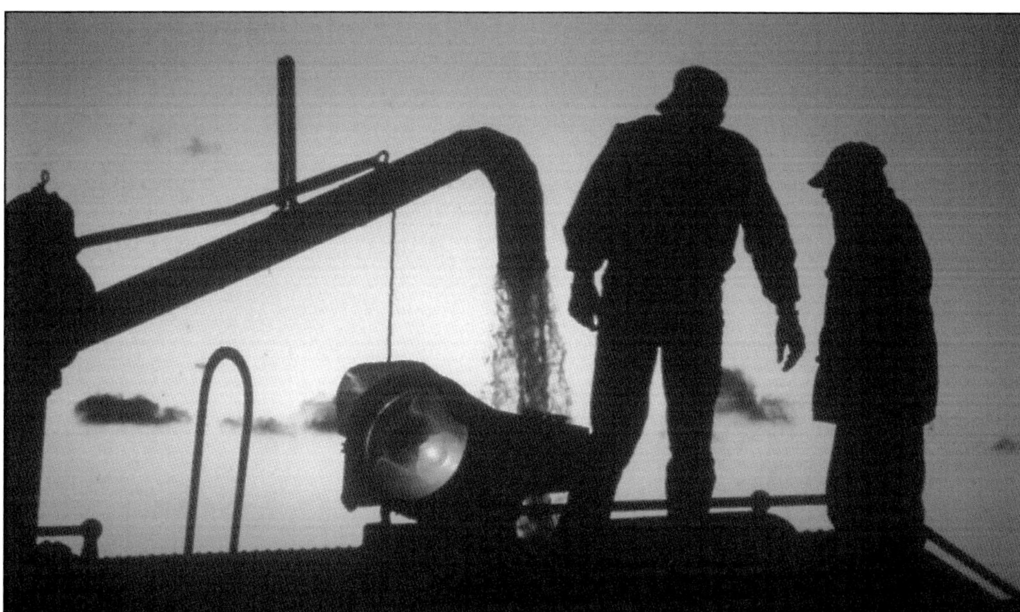

A beautiful summer sunset scene is the backdrop as two crewmen on the steam engine are seen loading water into the tender from the water pipe prior to the end of the day's excursion service. Loading water at night saved time during the morning preparation of the engine.

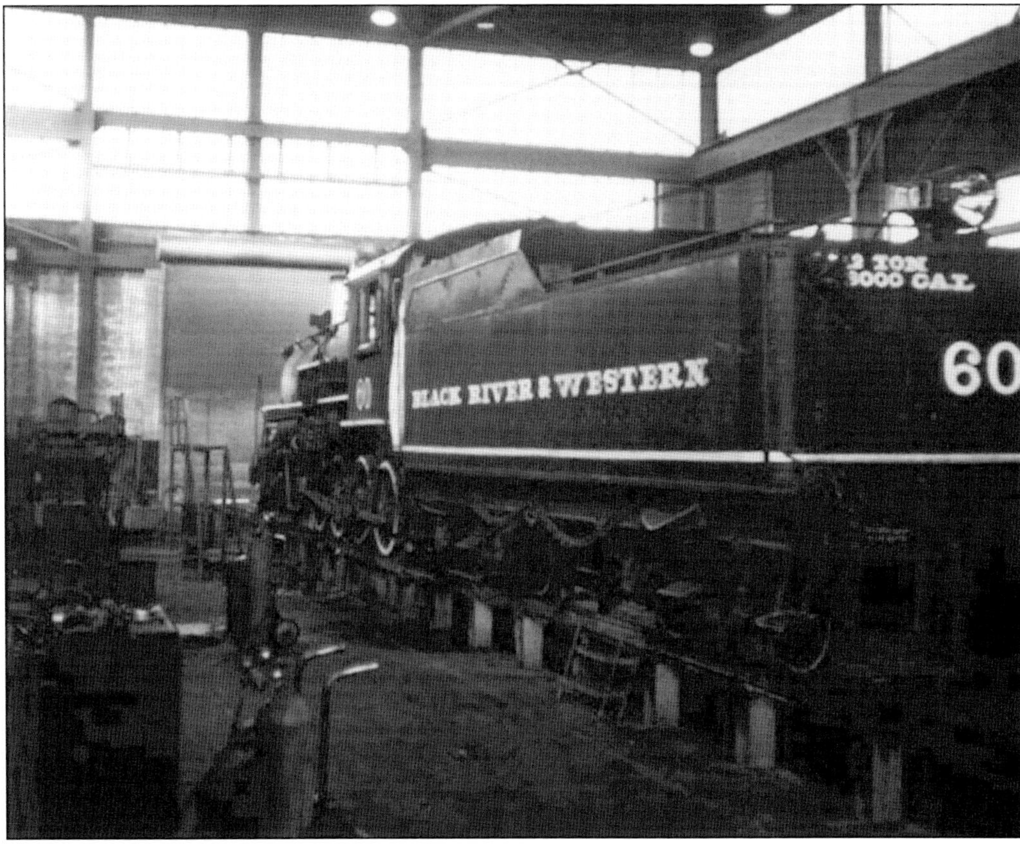

In December 1970, steam engine No. 60 was taken to the Penn-Central Railroad's repair shop in Morrisville, Pennsylvania, for necessary spring hanger repairs. The Pennsylvania Railroad and, later, the Penn-Central Railroad were always willing to assist when possible. (Nelson Tower.)

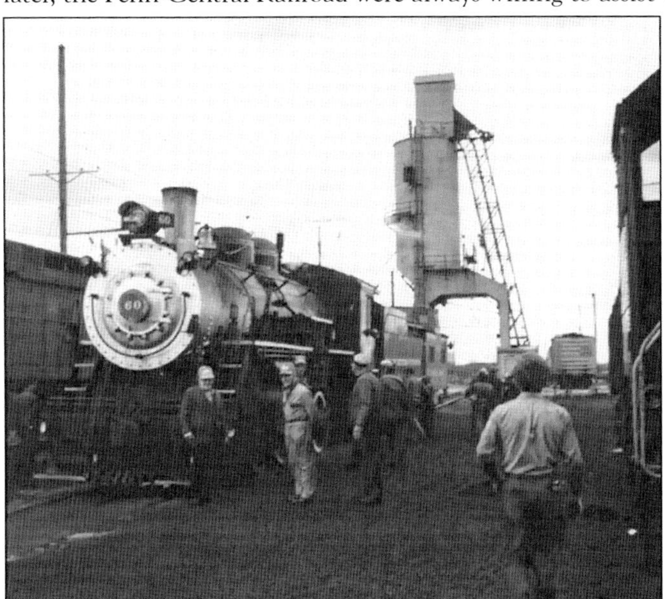

Some of the volunteers accompanied the steam engine to Morrisville, Pennsylvania, by riding in caboose No. 200. The route took them from their home base in Ringoes to Lambertville, then south to Trenton and over the bridge into the repair shops at Morrisville. (Nelson Tower.)

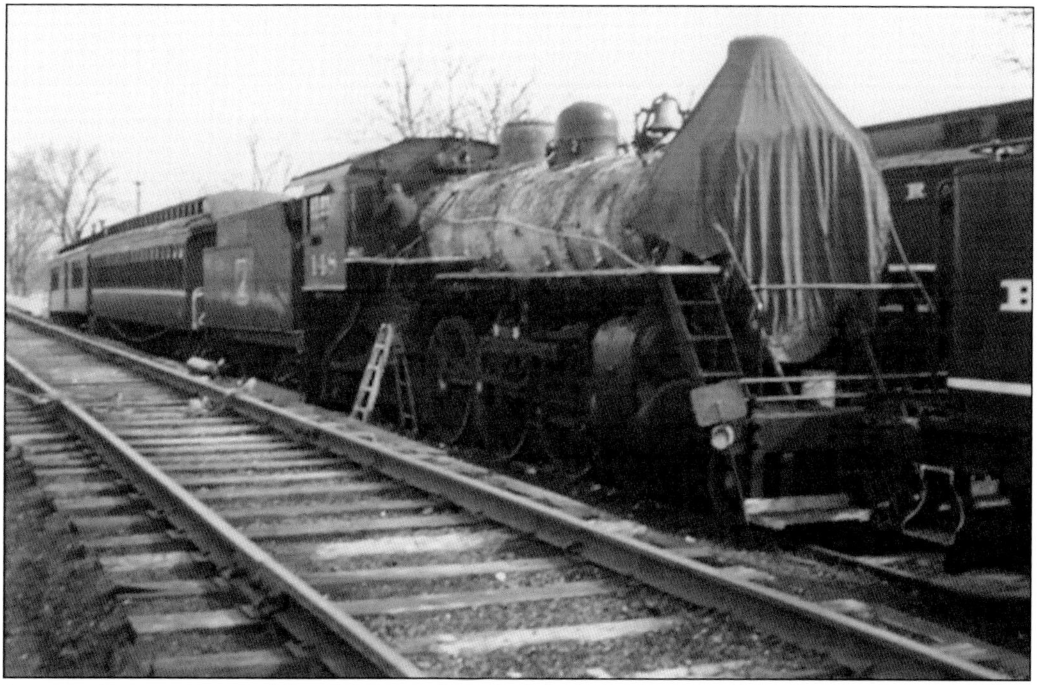

A second steam engine, No. 148, arrived at the Black River & Western Railroad in 1968. The engine was purchased by Samuel Freeman and was leased to the BR&W. Built in June 1920 by the American Locomotive Company as a Pacific-type locomotive, it had been converted to an oil-burning engine. (Nelson Tower.)

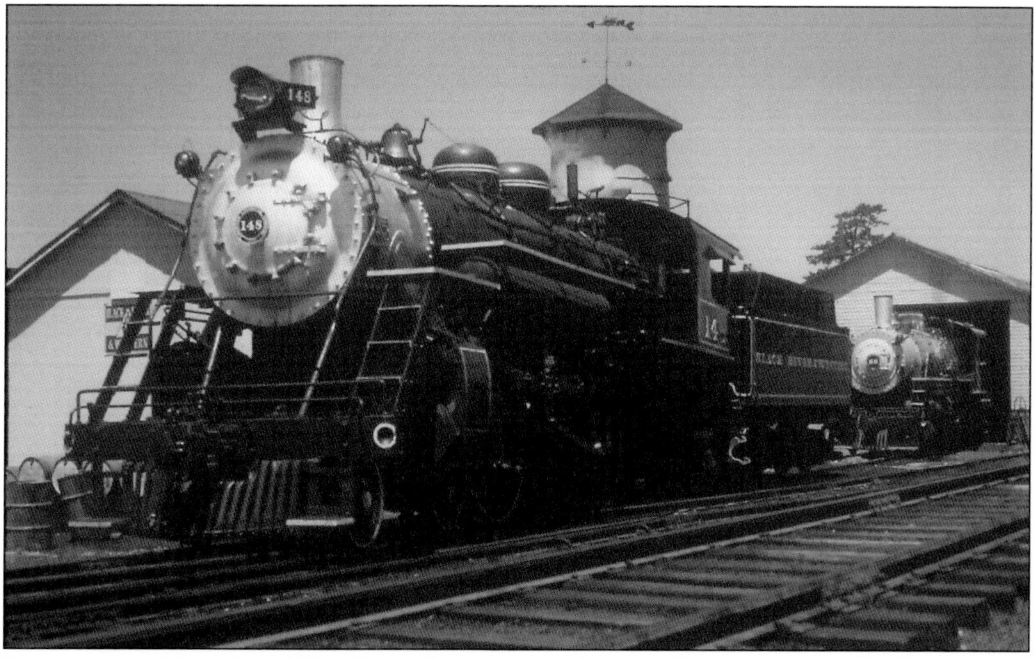

Steam engines No. 148 and No. 60 pose by the engine house in Ringoes in July 1971. Locomotive No. 148 first operated on the Black River & Western Railroad in 1971 and ran until 1974. During this time period, two steam engines ran between Flemington and Ringoes.

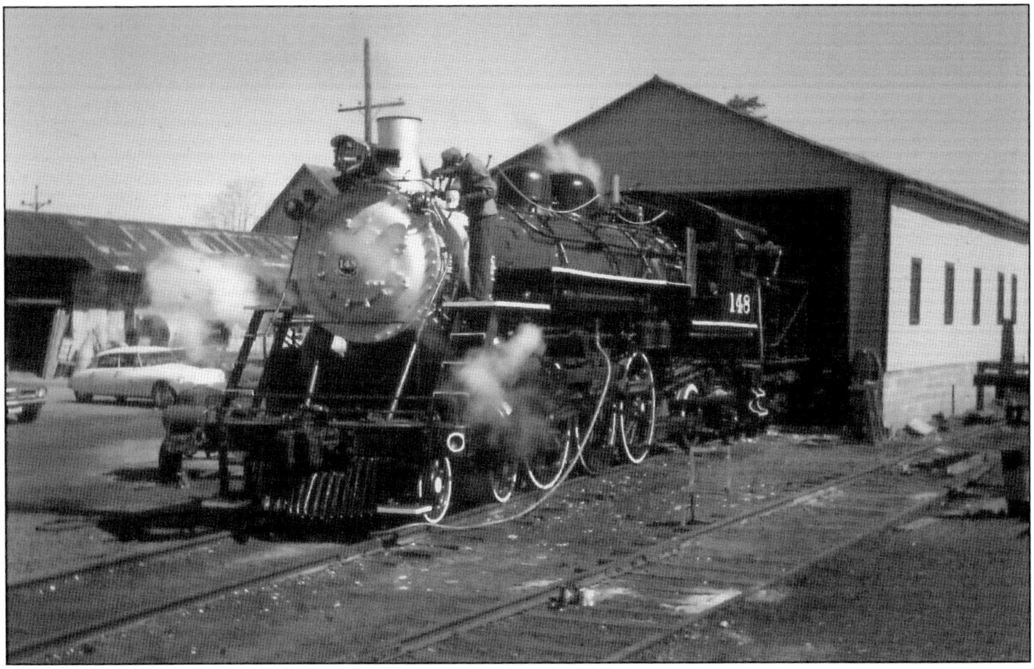

Steam engine No. 148 is readied for service by the engine house in Ringoes. Freshly painted and looking ready for service, the engine was used to pull passenger excursion trips.

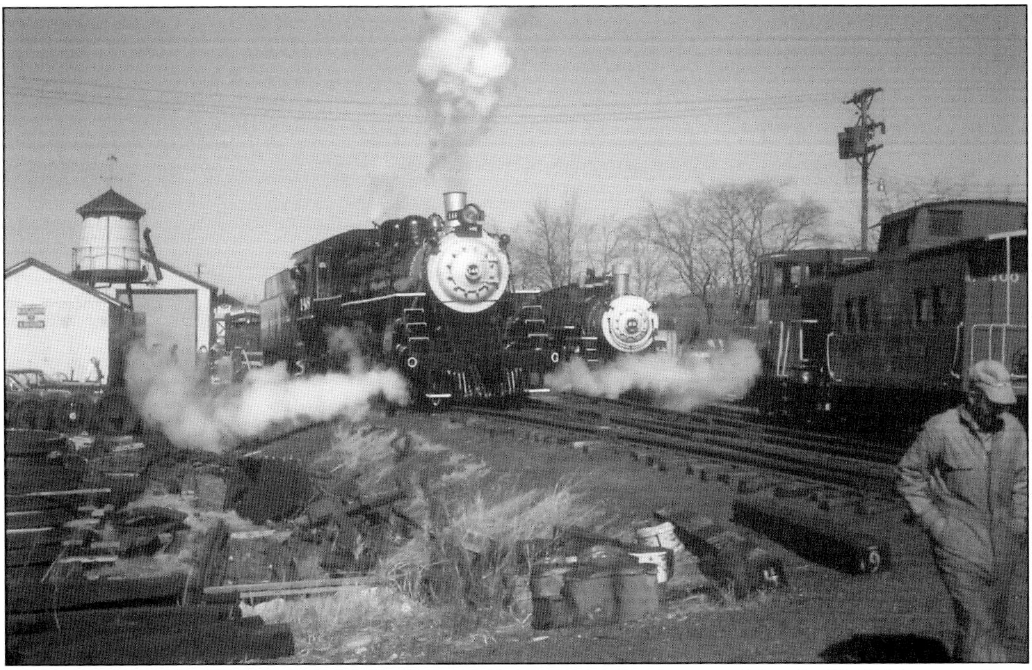

Steam engine No. 148, shown during her maiden run in Ringoes on March 27, 1971, is ready to enter the main track. Behind the steam engine is the little Mack engine, and to the right are steam engine No. 60, locomotive No. 7079, and caboose No. 200.

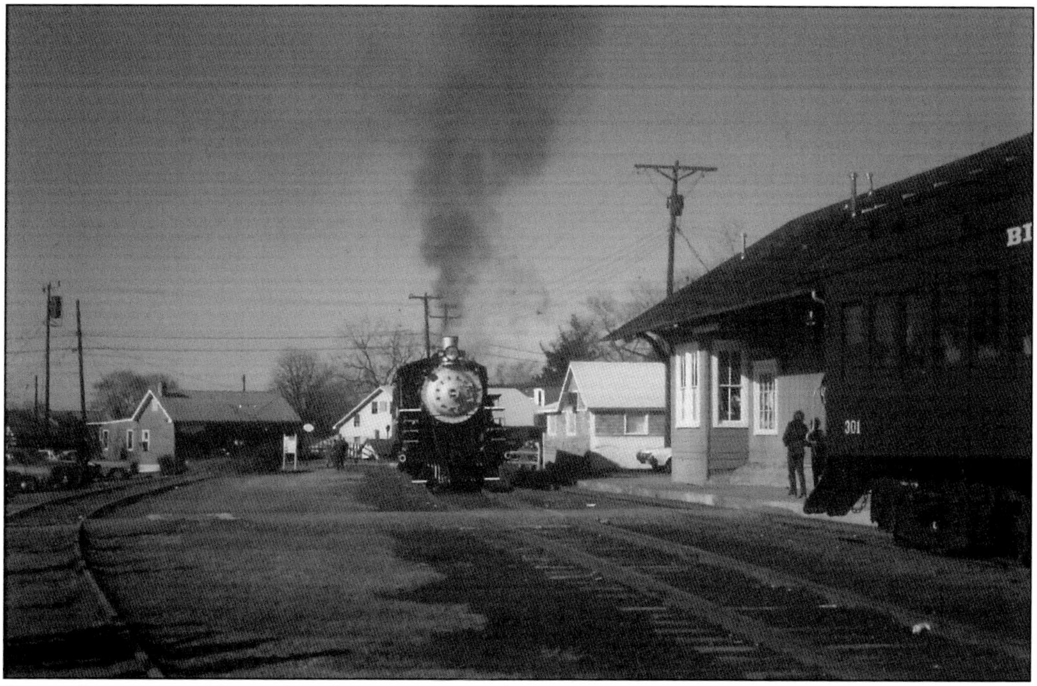

Steam locomotive No. 148 makes a runaround move past passenger car No. 301 in Flemington during her first passenger excursion trip. The engine was oil-fired, and the cab was amazingly clean compared to the other coal-fired engines on the railroad.

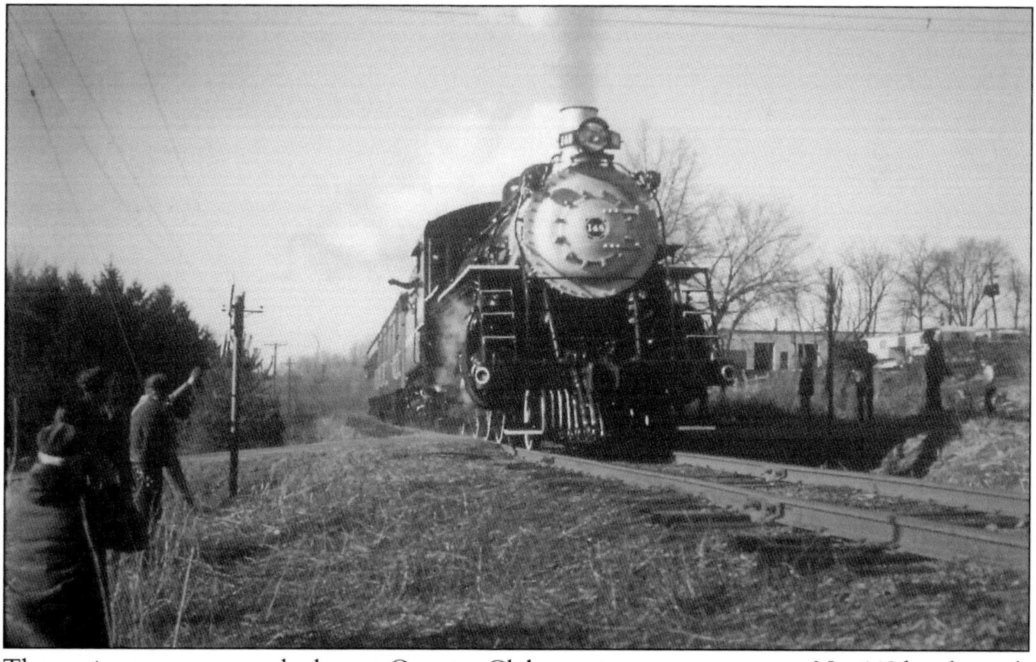

The engineer waves to onlookers at Country Club crossing as steam engine No. 148 heads south towards Ringoes on her maiden run, much to the enjoyment of railfans. The engine first ran in 1970 and continued until 1974. She was removed from the railroad in 1975.

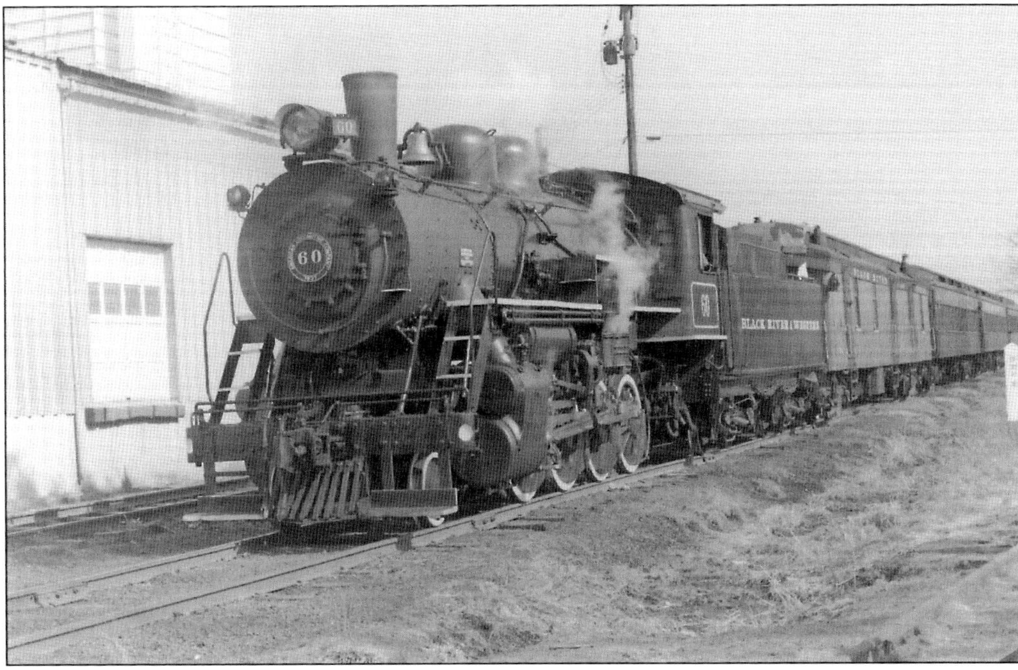

Steam engine No. 60, with a string of passenger cars in Flemington in 1971, waits for a southbound departure. The steam engine sported a rectangular outline over the No. 60 on the side of her cab. The marker post on the right reads "BR&W," which had been painted over the original Pennsylvania Railroad marking.

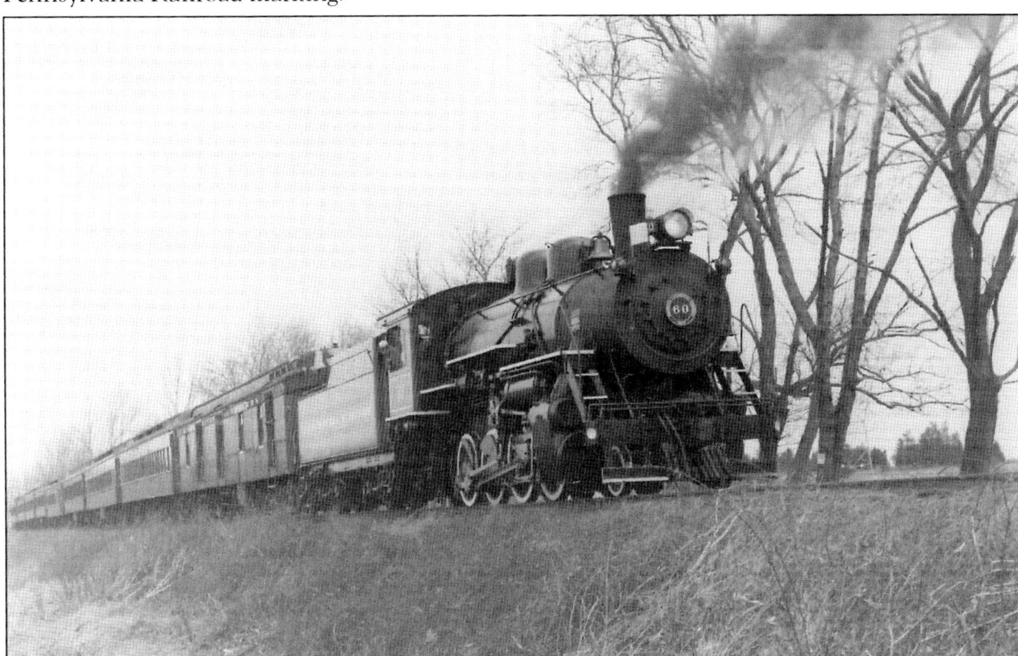

Steam engine No. 60 heads south with a string of nine passenger cars. Behind the steam engine is the Railroad Post Office car No. 100. During the early years of operation, the railroad's passenger base supported the use of these long trains.

A makeshift snowplow is shown off by Nicholas Burenga in the fall of 1971. BR&W hopper MW 12 had a V-shaped plow added to aid in clearing snow along the right-of-way. While a sound idea, in reality, it did not perform as expected. (Nelson Tower.)

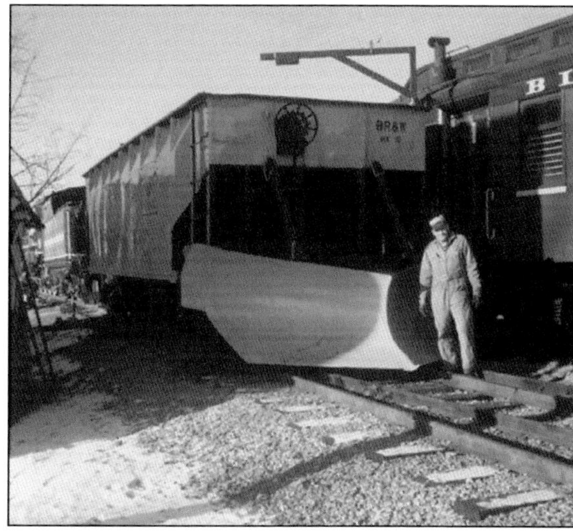

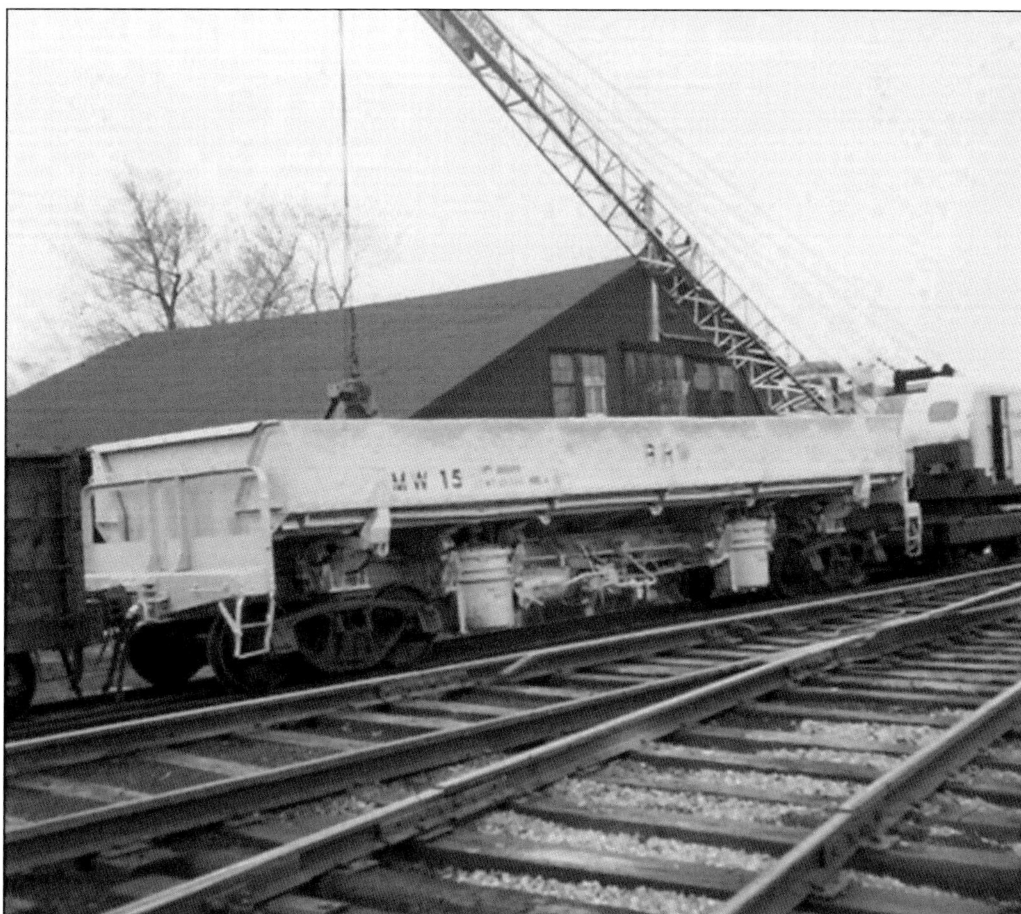

Black River used an ex-Pennsylvania dump car for maintenance-of-way service hauling fill along the right-of-way. The car, owned by Samuel Freeman and leased to the railroad, was painted yellow, and to the right of the car is the American clamshell crane MW-11. (Nelson Tower.)

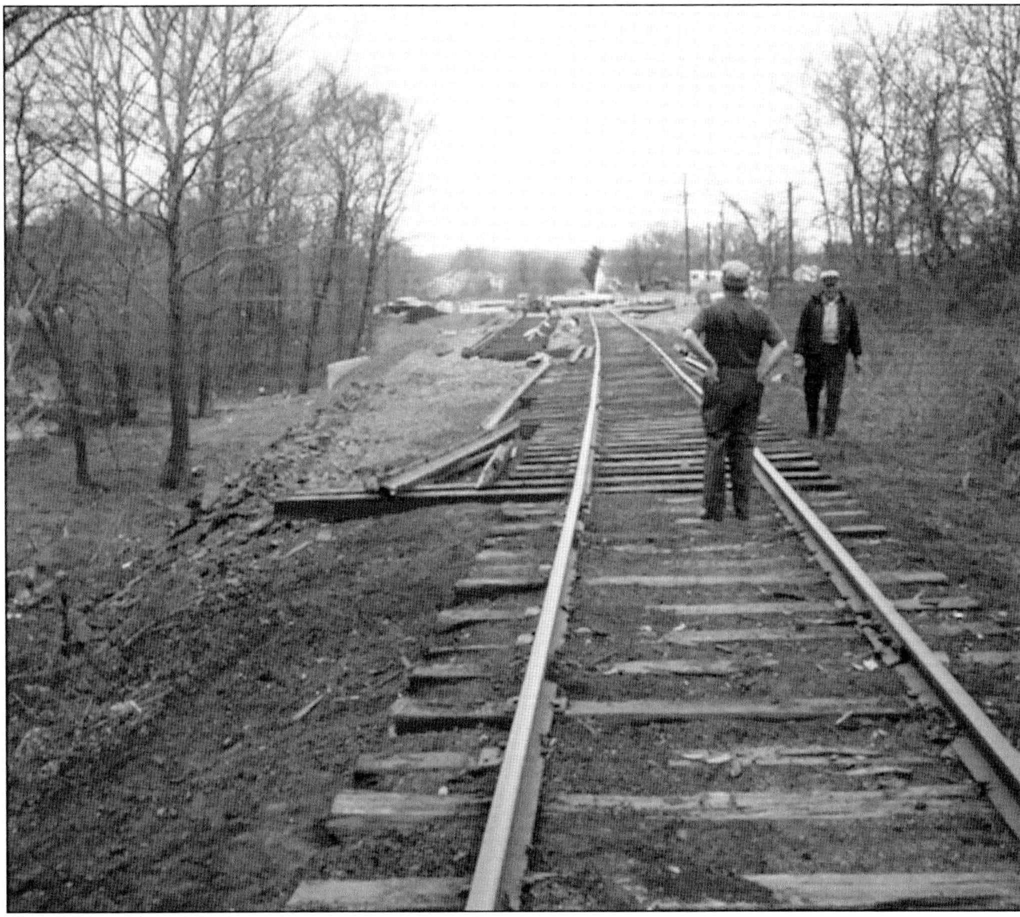

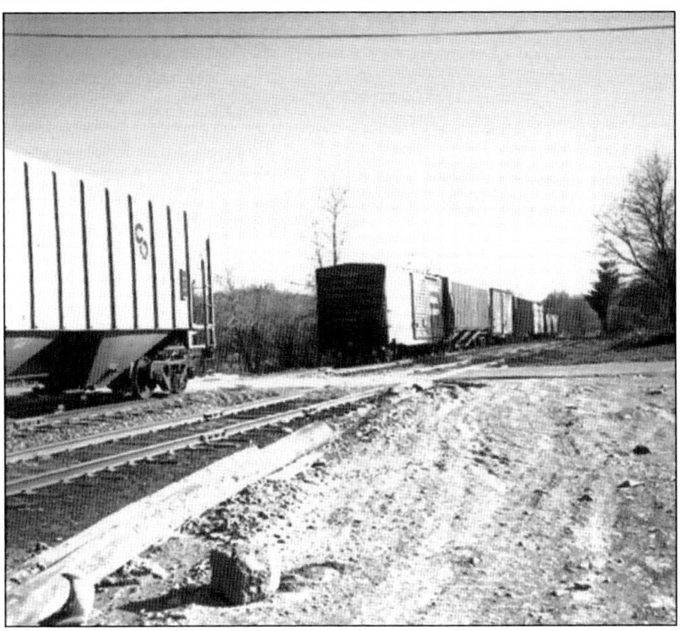

By 1971, there was a need to extend the interchange track in Lambertville over the original 10-car storage track built in 1970, thus crossing Route 29. Volunteers extended the track to accommodate the increase in freight traffic due that time period. (Nelson Tower.)

The extended interchange in Lambertville allowed for the increase in freight cars being left for the Black River crews to deliver to customers along the line. Here, the cut of cars is separated to allow traffic to pass over the road. (Nelson Tower.)

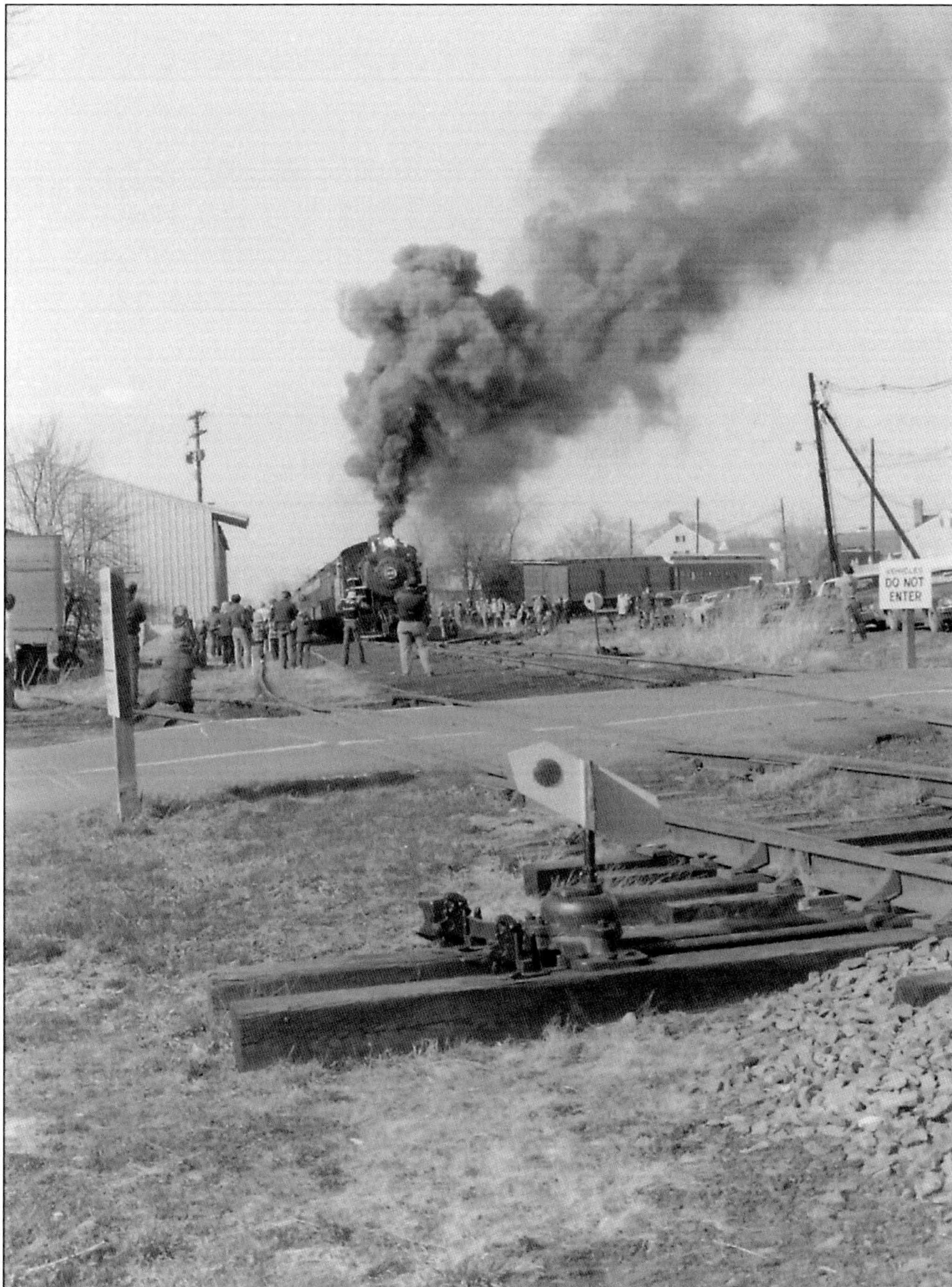

Railfans enjoy the sight of steam engine No. 60 as it heads south from the Flemington station. To the right is the Central Railroad of New Jersey track through Flemington, and on the siding are a boxcar lettered for Turntable Junction, a baggage car of the High Iron Company, and a passenger car. To the extreme left is the ex–Long Island Rail Road rotary snowplow that was brought to the Black River & Western.

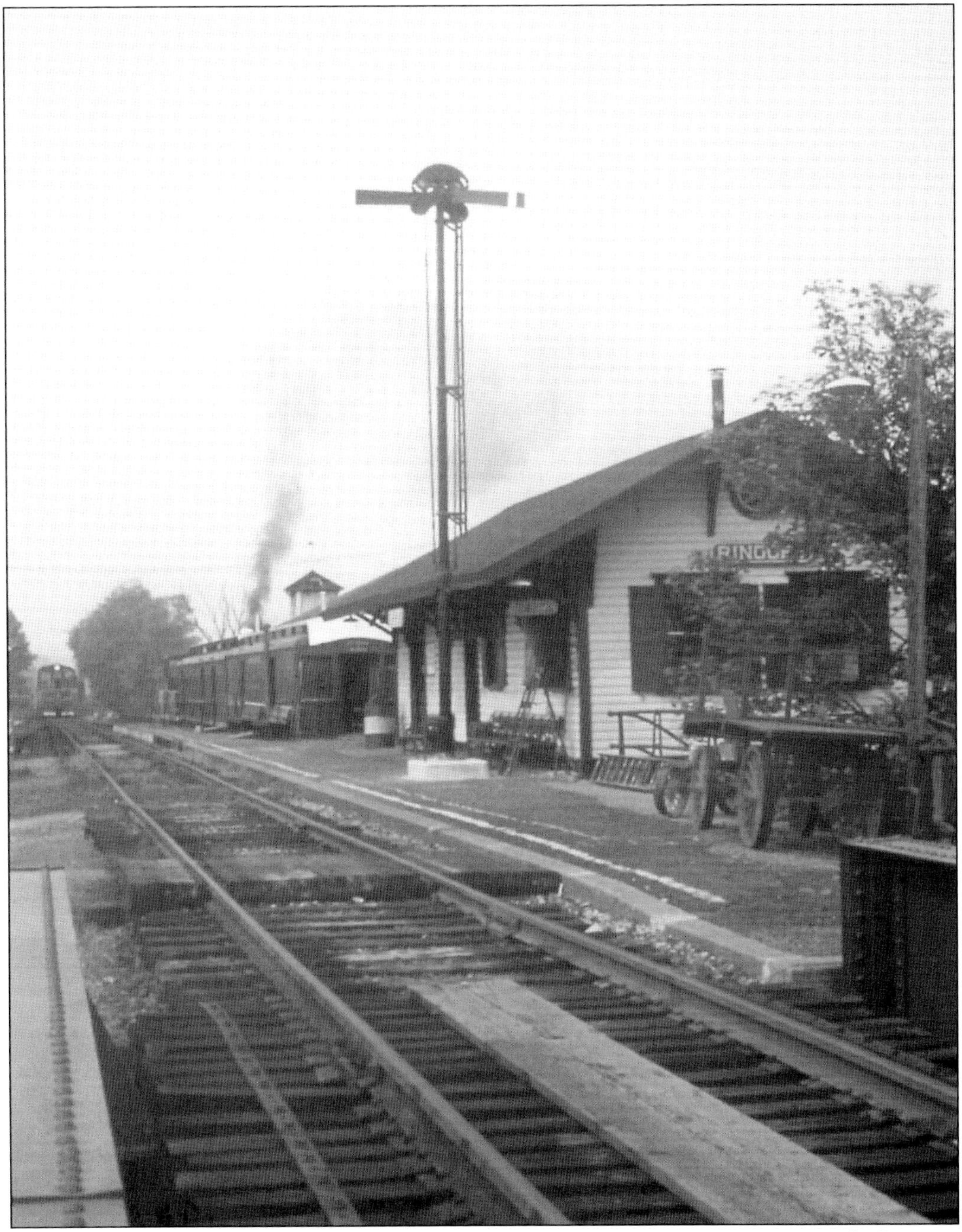

A semaphore was installed in Ringoes in 1972. Used as a signal to stop trains entering the Ringoes station platform, it allowed passengers sufficient time to enjoy snacks and purchase souvenirs prior to boarding the train for their return trip to Flemington. Obtained in 1965, the semaphore had been previously located at Swartswood Junction (JU) and used by the Lehigh & New England and the New York, Susquehanna & Western Railroads. Black River volunteers brought it to Ringoes in 1965 for storage and eventual restoration and installation. (Nelson Tower.)

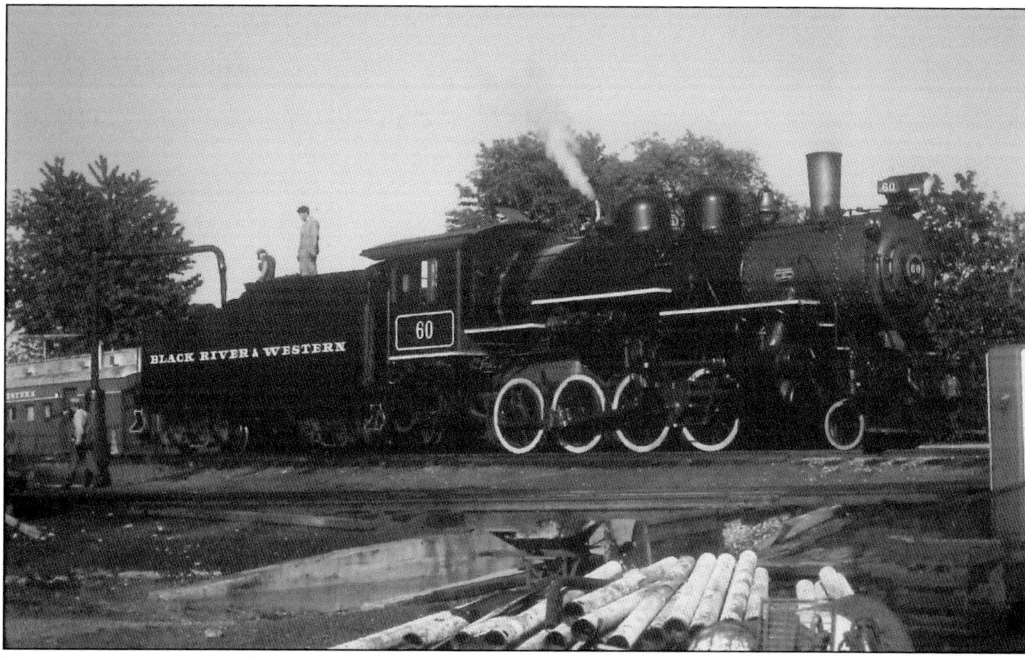

Volunteers load water from the water plug into the tender of steam engine No. 60 in Ringoes on a nice summer day in July 1973. The water plug was located next to the main track and replaced the old wooden water tank that had previously been used.

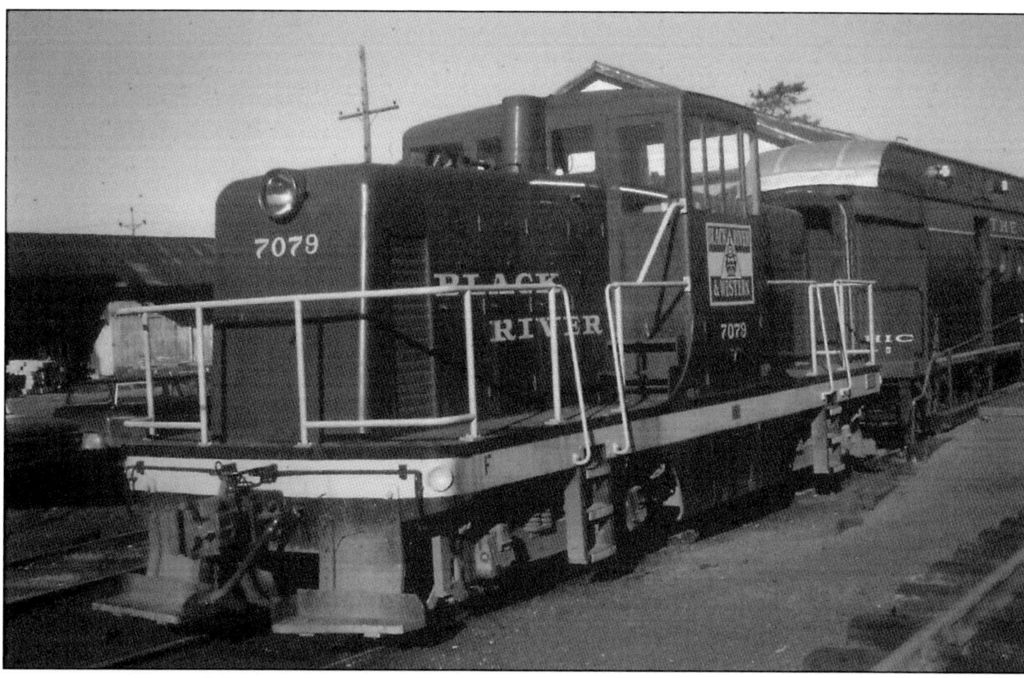

Locomotive No. 7079 was a 65-ton General Electric center cab locomotive and used in railroad service. Called "the Schoolhouse," it was owned by North Hunterdon High School and used as a rolling diesel shop.

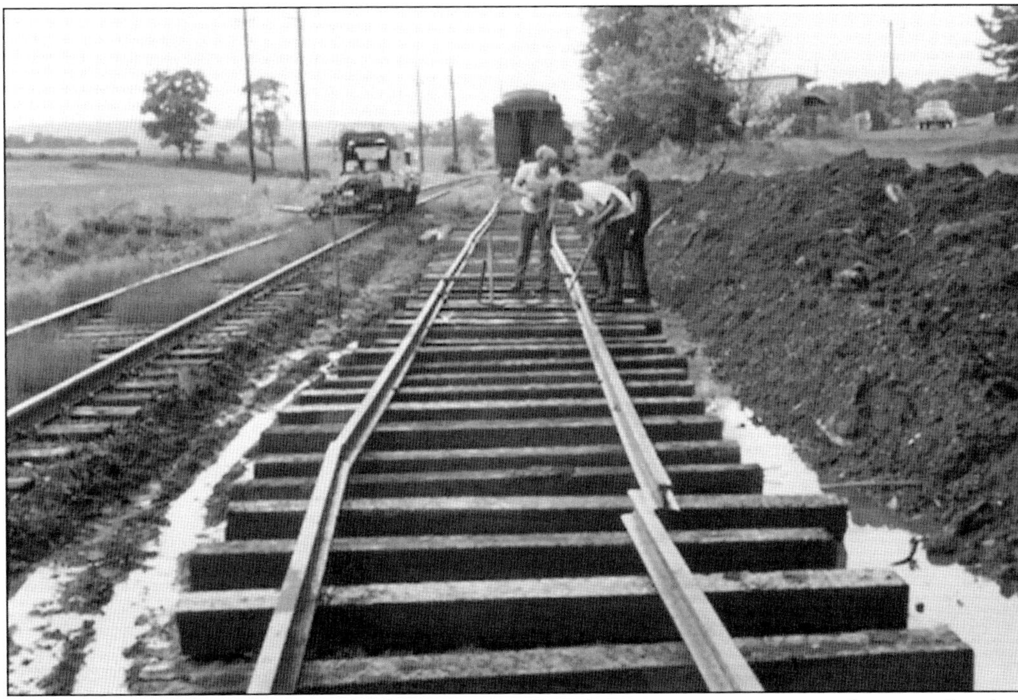

The siding at Copper Hill was rebuilt in 1972 to allow for two trains to meet and pass each other. Volunteers would clean out and repair the siding to allow for two train operations that would start in 1972. (Nelson Tower.)

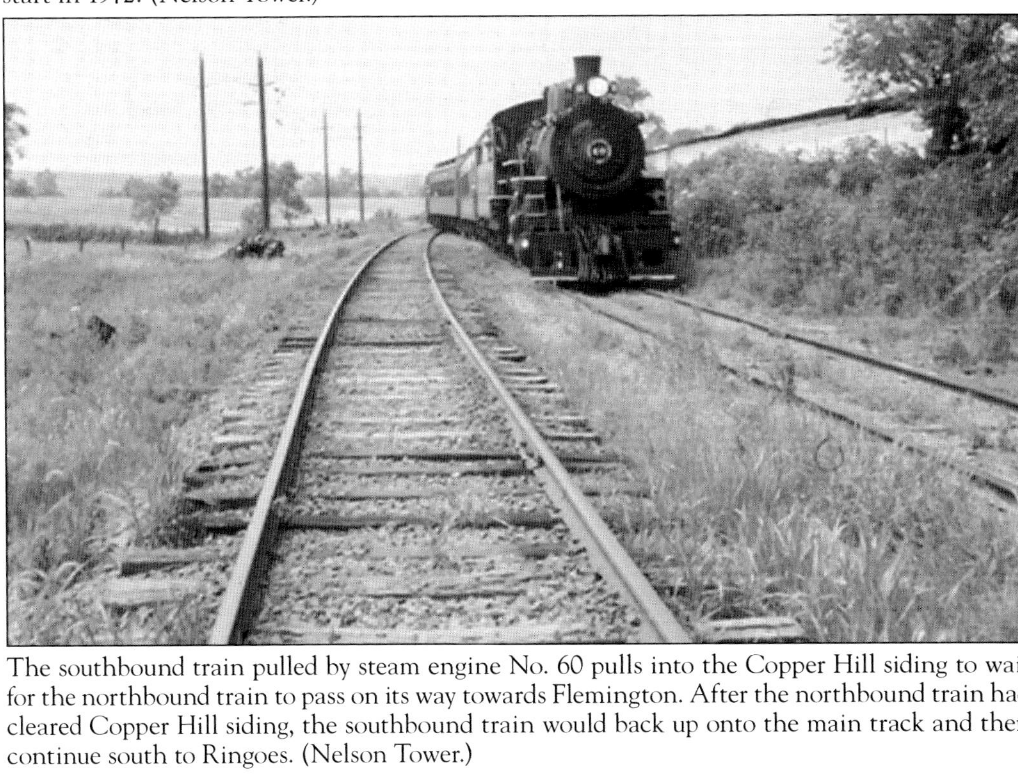

The southbound train pulled by steam engine No. 60 pulls into the Copper Hill siding to wait for the northbound train to pass on its way towards Flemington. After the northbound train had cleared Copper Hill siding, the southbound train would back up onto the main track and then continue south to Ringoes. (Nelson Tower.)

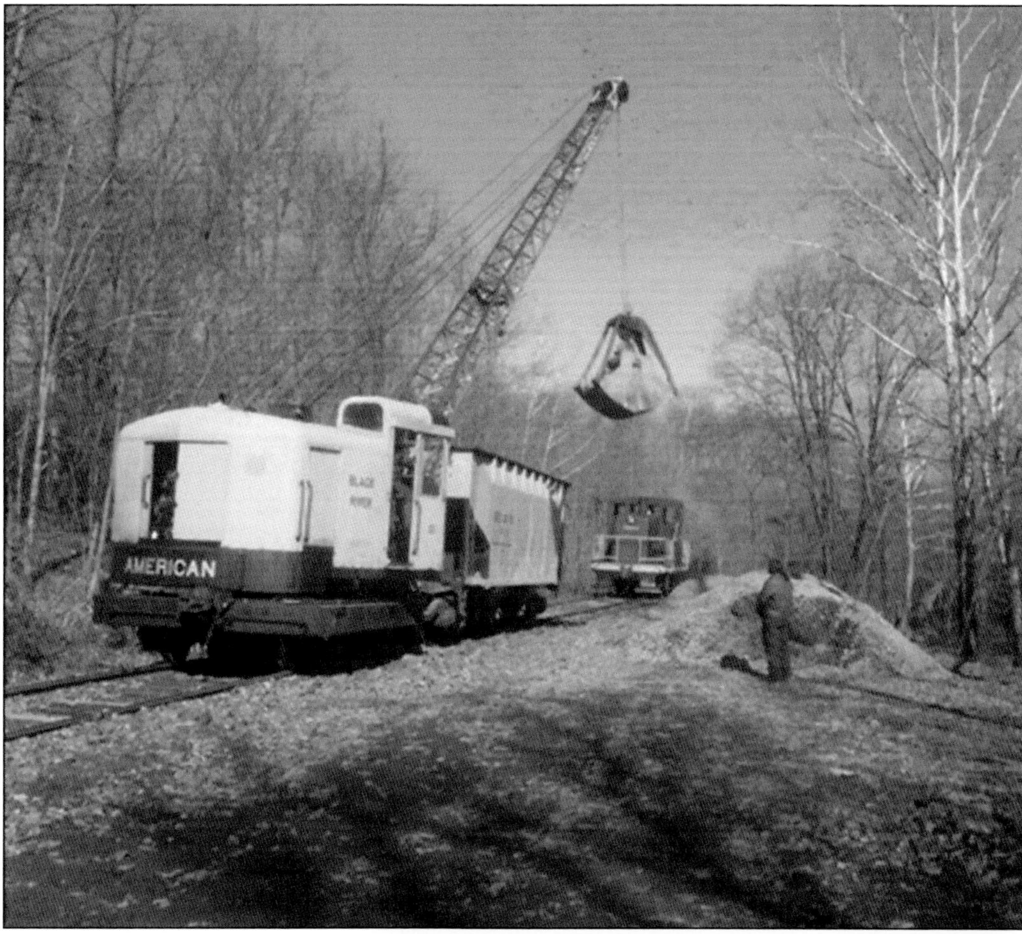

Work on the right-of-way continued in the fall of 1972. Above is the American clamshell crane MW-11 loading the ballast hopper MW-12 with gravel while locomotive No. 7079 waits. The spacing between the hopper car and the engine prevented potential damage to the locomotive and crew. (Nelson Tower.)

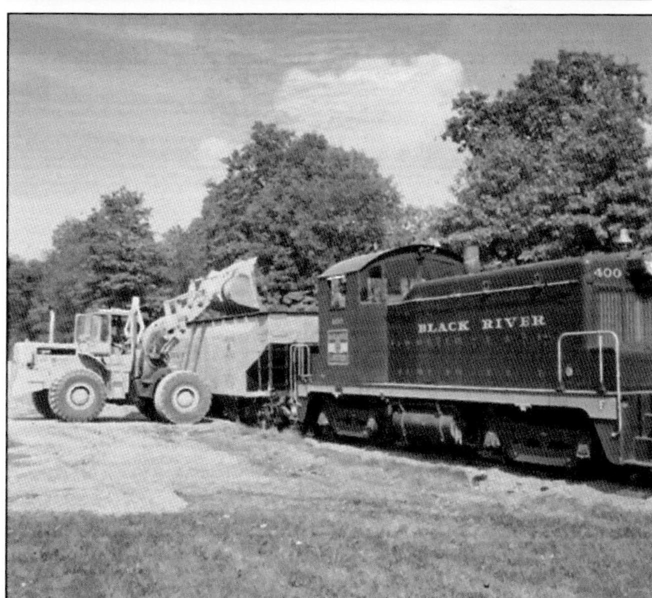

Locomotive No. 400 waits while hopper MW-12 is loaded with ballast at a local facility along the railroad. The ballast will be spread from the hopper car along the right-of-way. (Nelson Tower.)

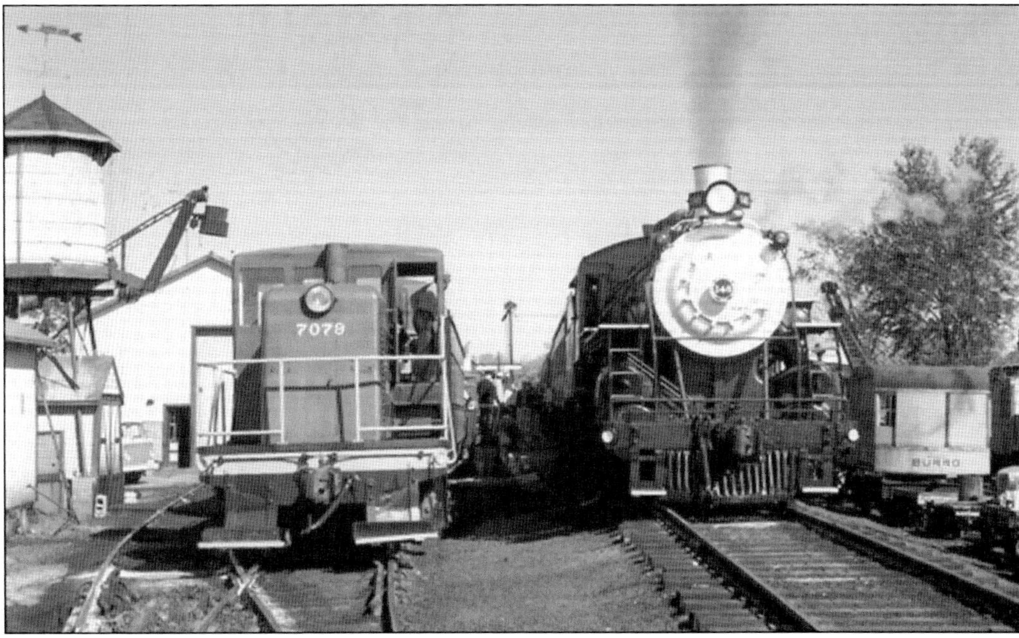

In the fall of 1973, three train operations allowed for passengers to arrive in Ringoes from Flemington by way of one of the steam engines pulling a string of coaches. Steam engine No. 148 arrives in Ringoes, and passengers can transfer to the Lambertville train shown here being pulled by locomotive No. 7079. (Nelson Tower.)

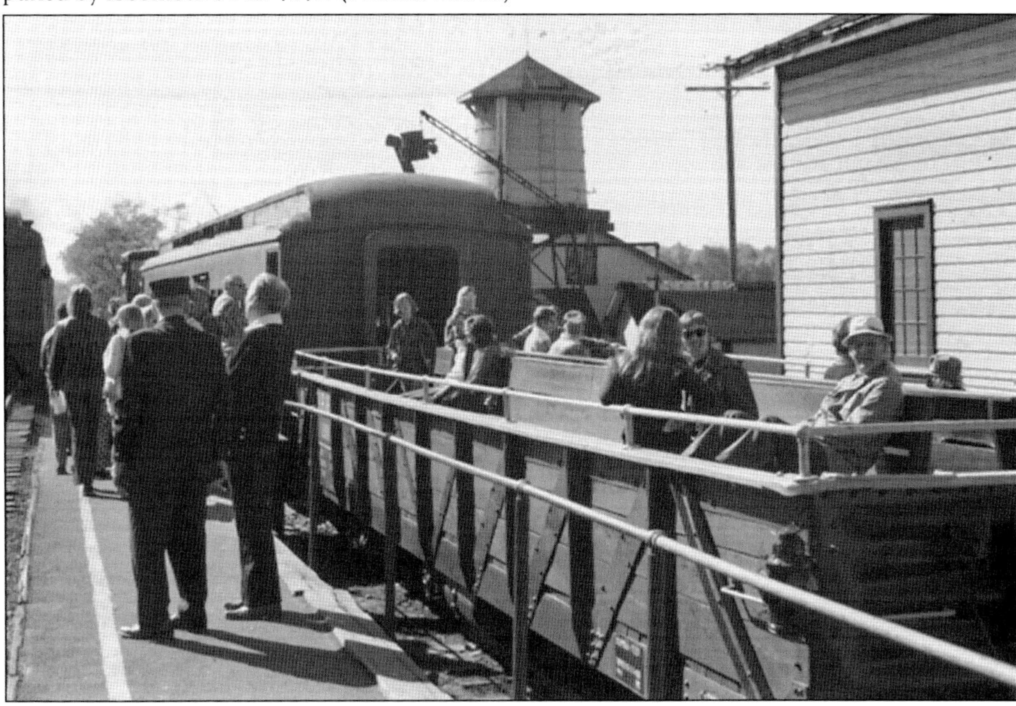

Riders to Lambertville had the choice of riding in a coach or in the open gondola car. The southbound train to Lambertville waits for the Flemington train to turn around before proceeding towards Lambertville. (Nelson Tower.)

Shown being prepared for service in Ringoes in 1973, both steam engines No. 60 and No. 148 would be used in passenger excursion service between Flemington and Ringoes. (Nelson Tower.)

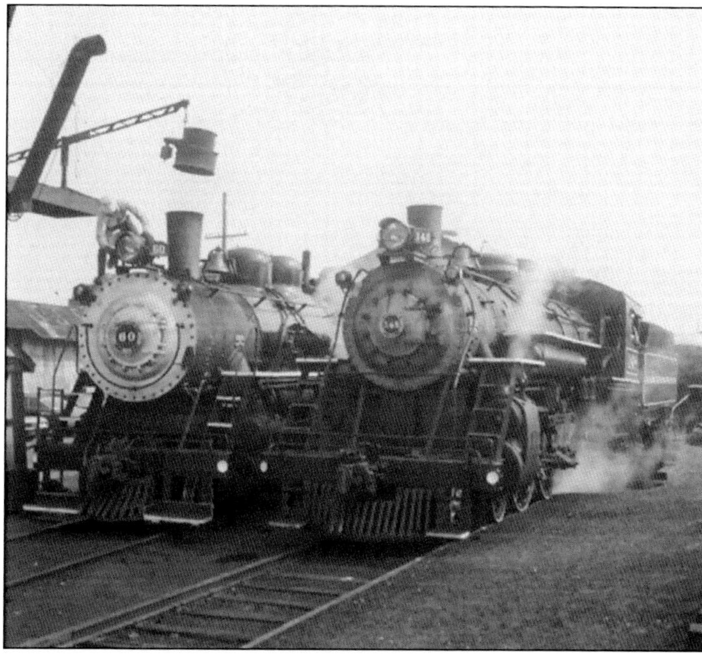

Steam engine No. 60 is ready to head for the main track while steam engine No. 148 is readied for two-train passenger excursion service between Flemington and Ringoes. The two engines would be used for steam excursions during the 1973 and 1974 seasons. (Nelson Tower.)

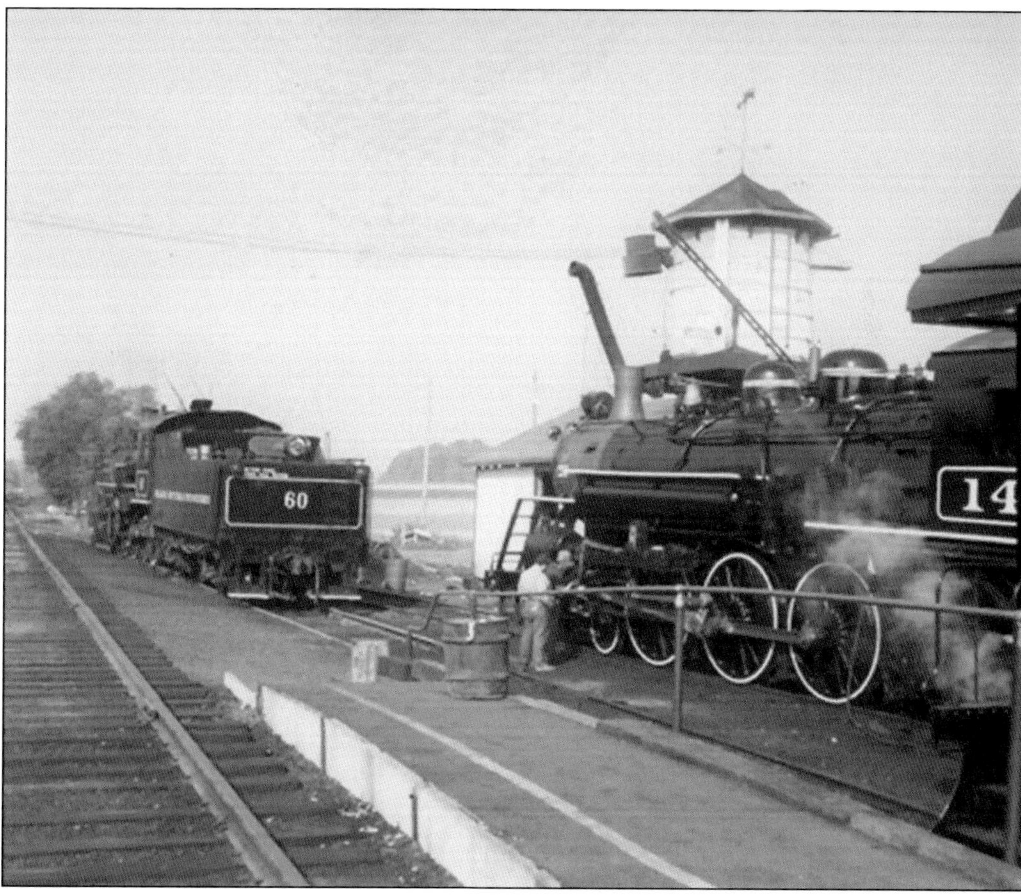

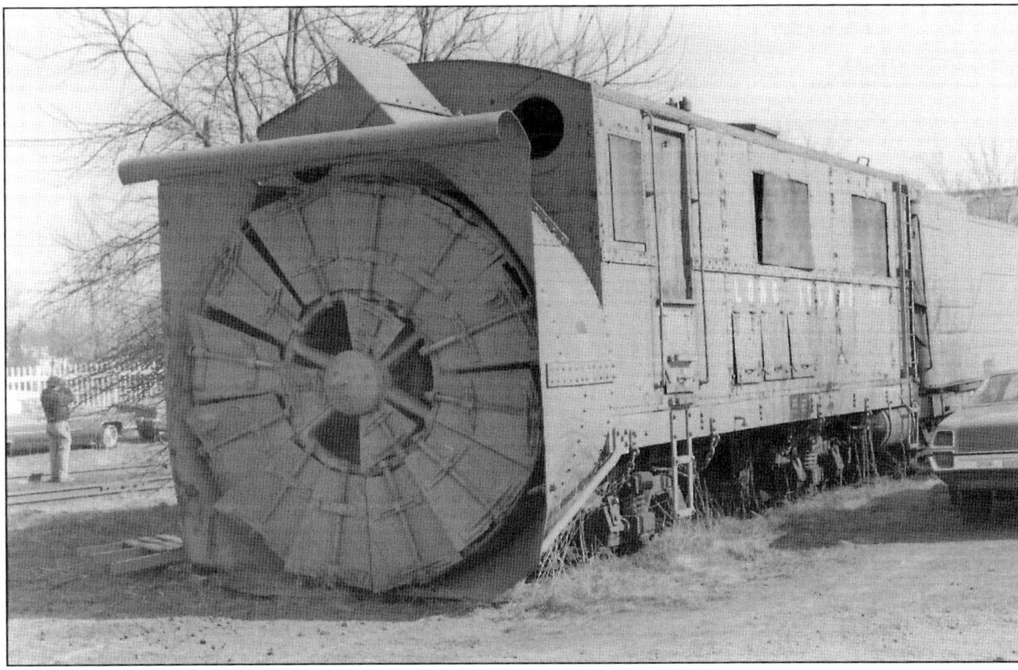

An ex–Long Island Rail Road steam-powered rotary snowplow and tender owned by Ron Ziel was brought to and leased by the Black River & Western Railroad for clearing the tracks in 1974. Never used on Black River & Western line, the rotary snowplow is now in Steamtown.

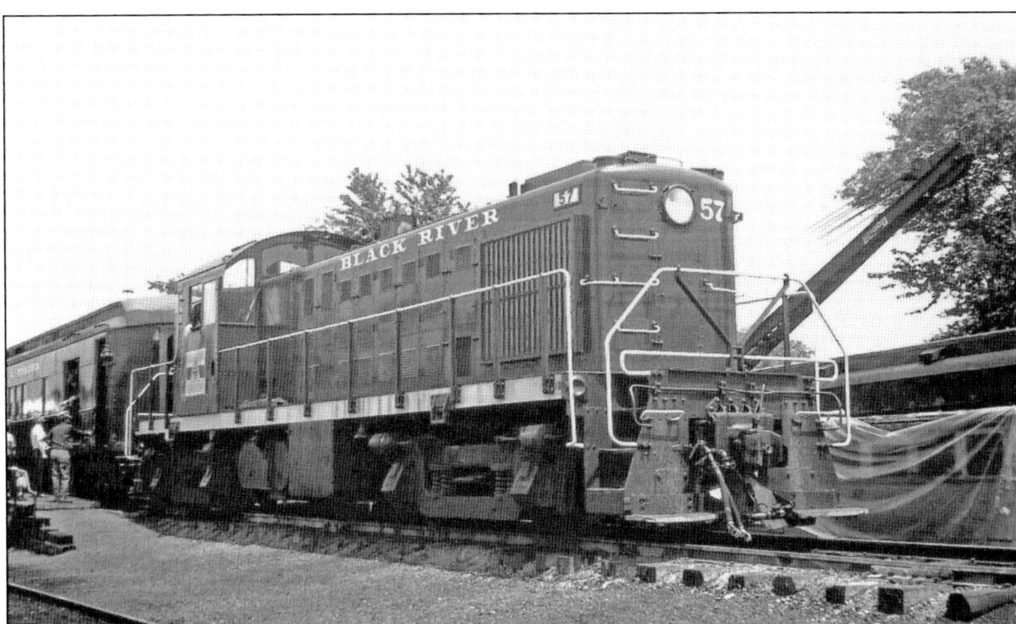

RS-1 locomotive No. 57 arrives at the Ringoes station in June 1974. Baggage car No. 297 is the first car behind the engine on the left. The boom of the burro crane can be seen on the right. The diesel engine was used when the steam engine was taken out of service.

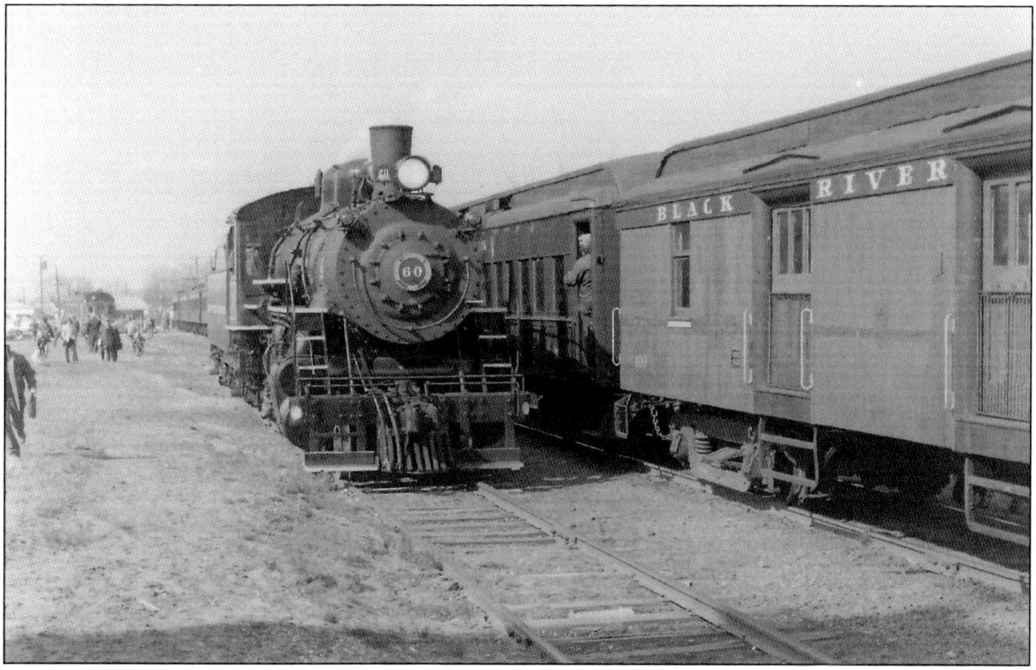

Steam engine No. 60 passes by a long string of passenger cars during a runaround maneuver in Flemington. The Railroad Post Office car No. 101 is seen on the right. The railroad's doodlebug, Pennsylvania Motorcar No. 4666, is seen in the background on the left.

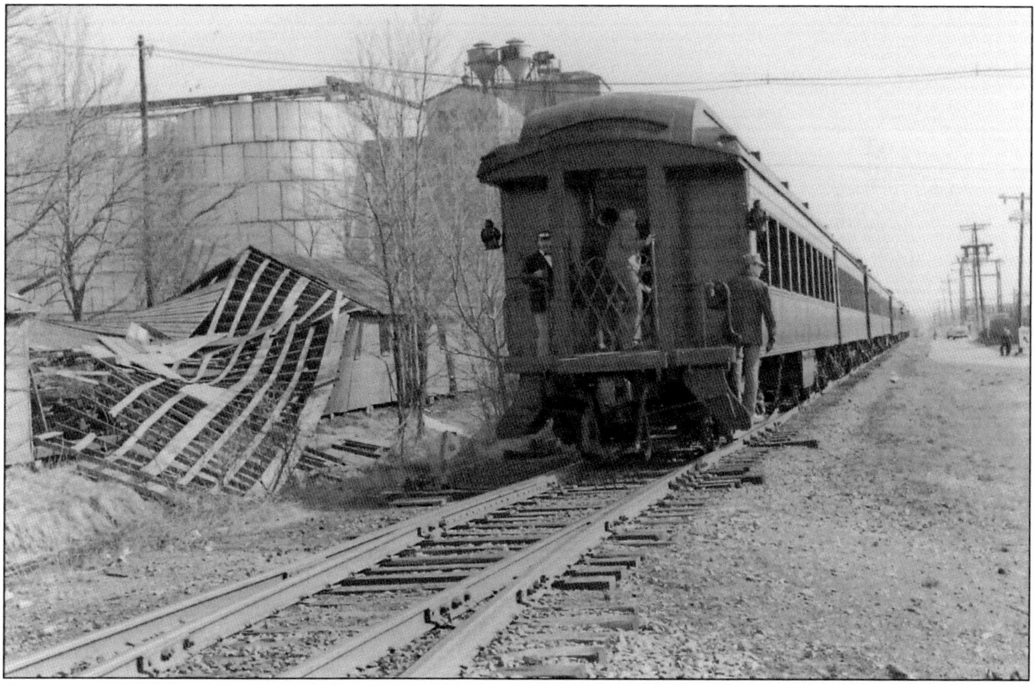

A long string of passenger cars leaves Flemington en route to Ringoes and return. Crewmen have placed marker lanterns on the rear-most passenger car to indicate the end of the train.

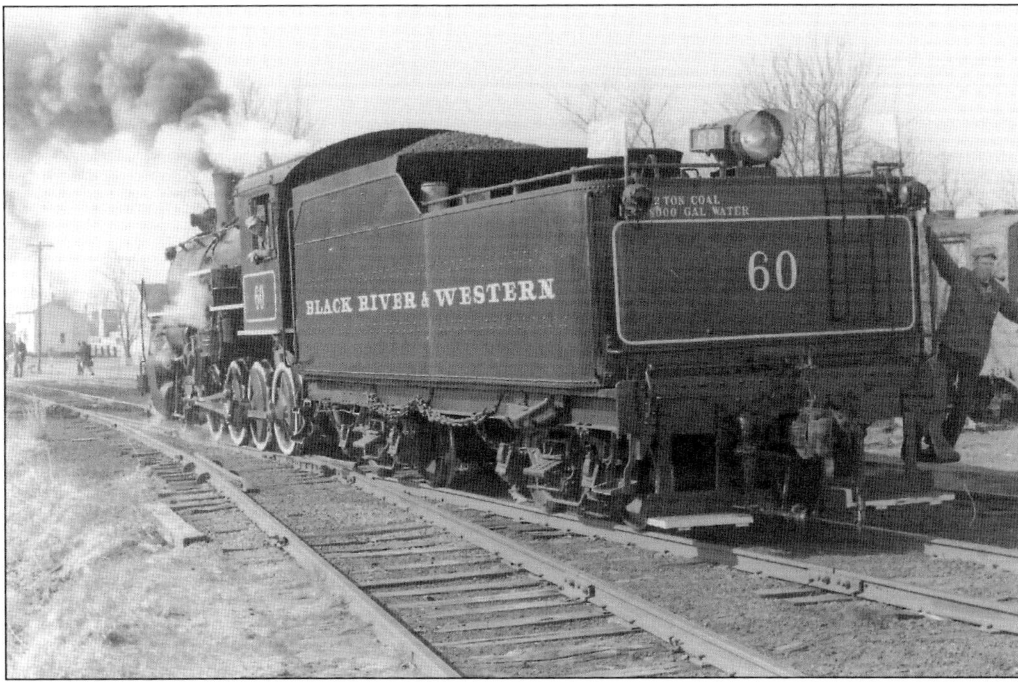

Under the direction of brakeman Gene Stains, who is seen giving hand signals to the engineer from the side of the tender, steam engine No. 60 in Flemington moves in reverse to couple up to the passenger cars.

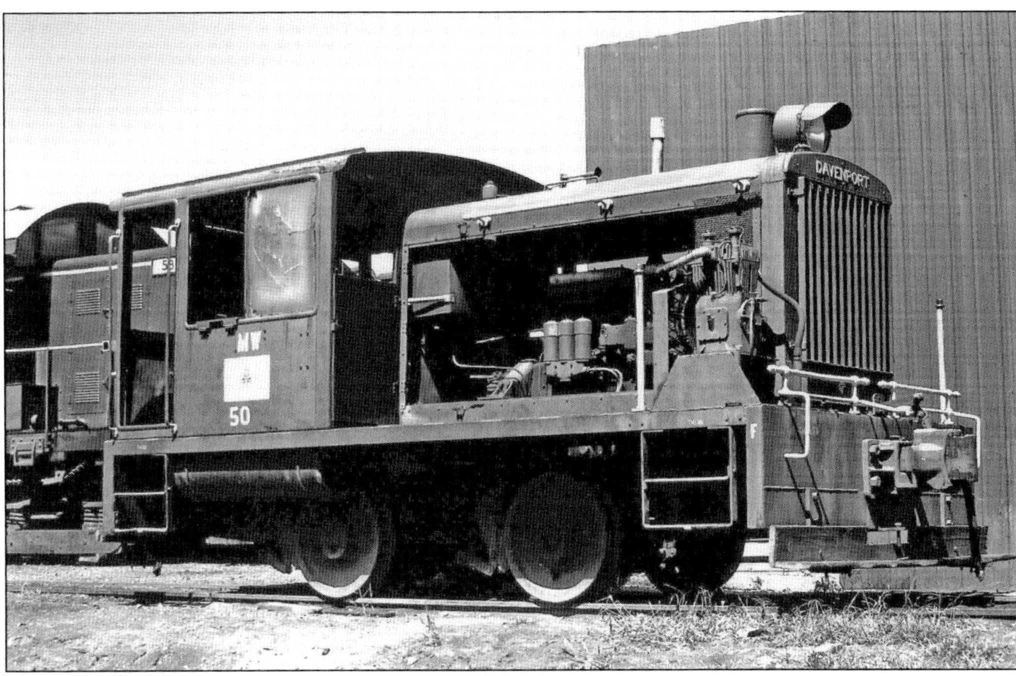

A 1925 Davenport locomotive was leased from Trap Rock Industries for use on Black River for maintenance-of-way duties. Used by the railroad for a number of years, it was returned and believed to have later been scrapped.

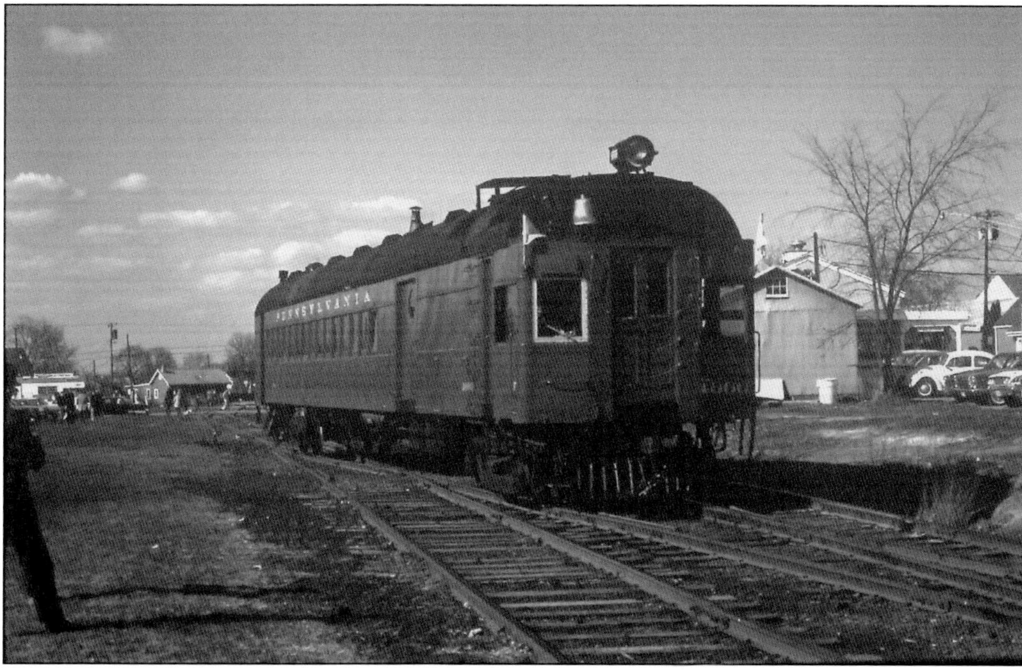

Ex–Pennsylvania Railroad No. 4666 in Flemington was used for passenger service between Flemington and Ringoes in 1975. The 1930 motorcar, known as a doodlebug, was first leased by the railroad in 1975. It was later bought in 1978, and by 1992, it was sold into private ownership.

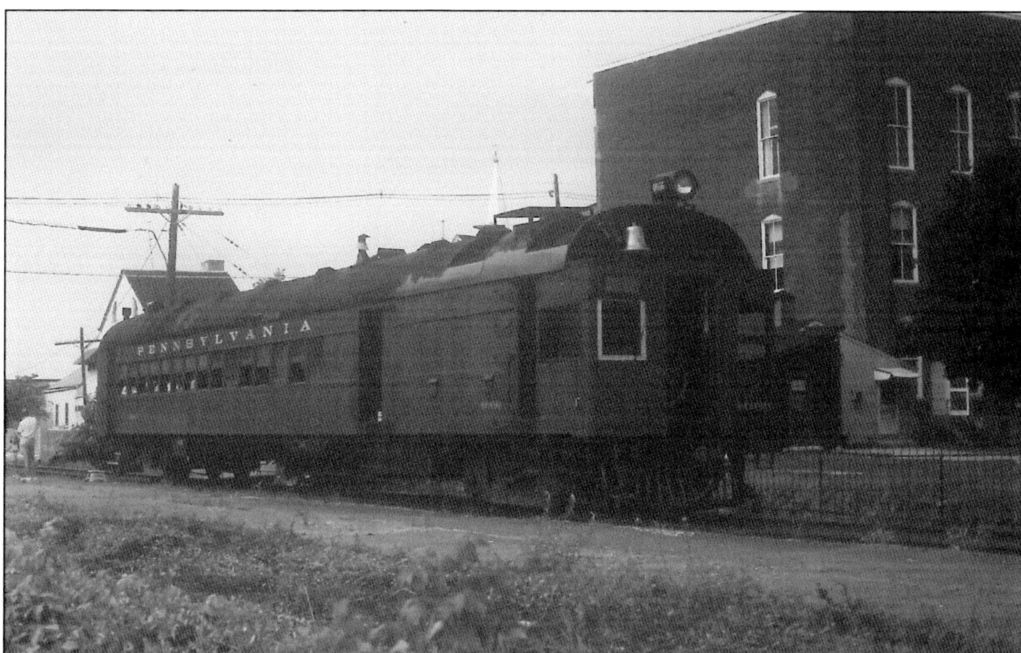

Motorcar No. 4666, shown here in Lambertville during 1977, still shows her Pennsylvania Railroad colors. The motorcar was used for excursions between Ringoes and Lambertville in place of the earlier Lambertville trains of 1973.

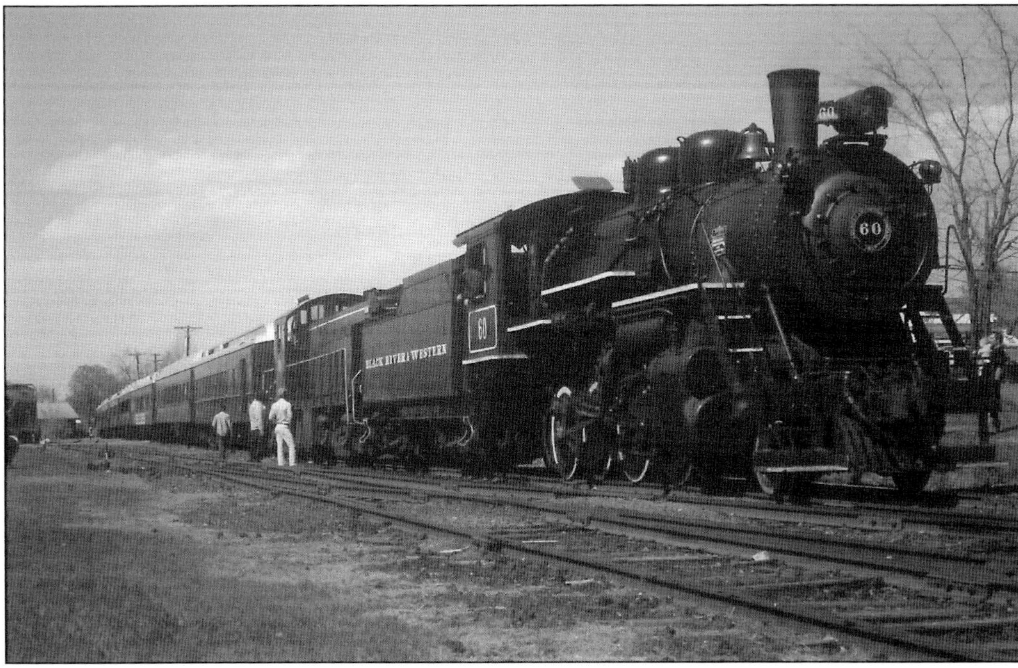

A special double-headed trip using steam locomotive No. 60 and RS-1 diesel locomotive No. 57, along with seven passenger cars, prepares for a trip south from Flemington in April 1978.

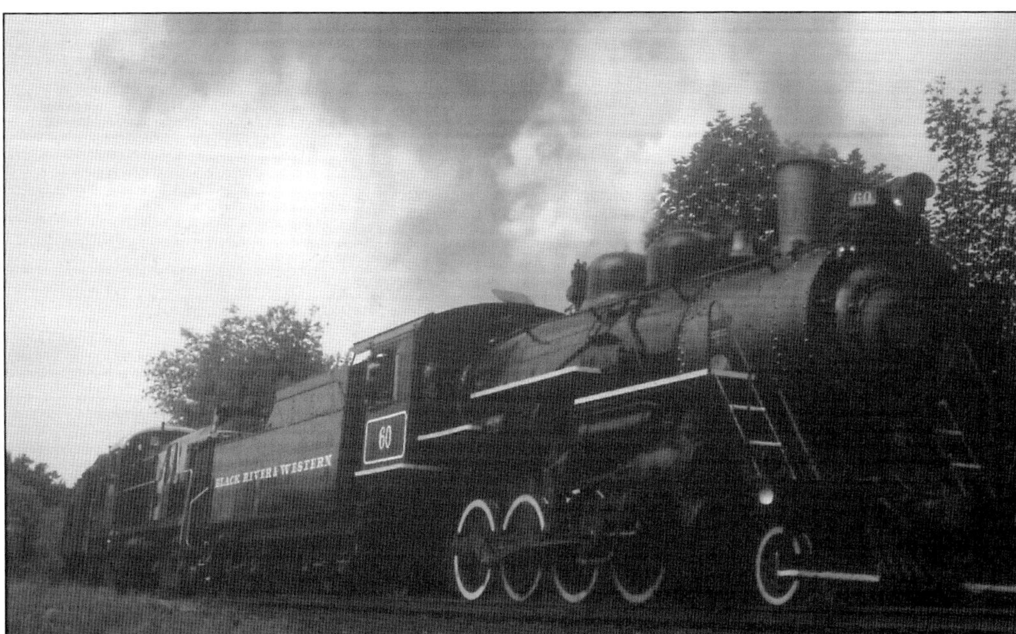

Steam engine No. 60 under steam and RS-1 diesel locomotive No. 1554 head south through the Copper Hill area toward Ringoes in February 1980. This was one of many double-headed trips that ran over the rail line during the 1980s.

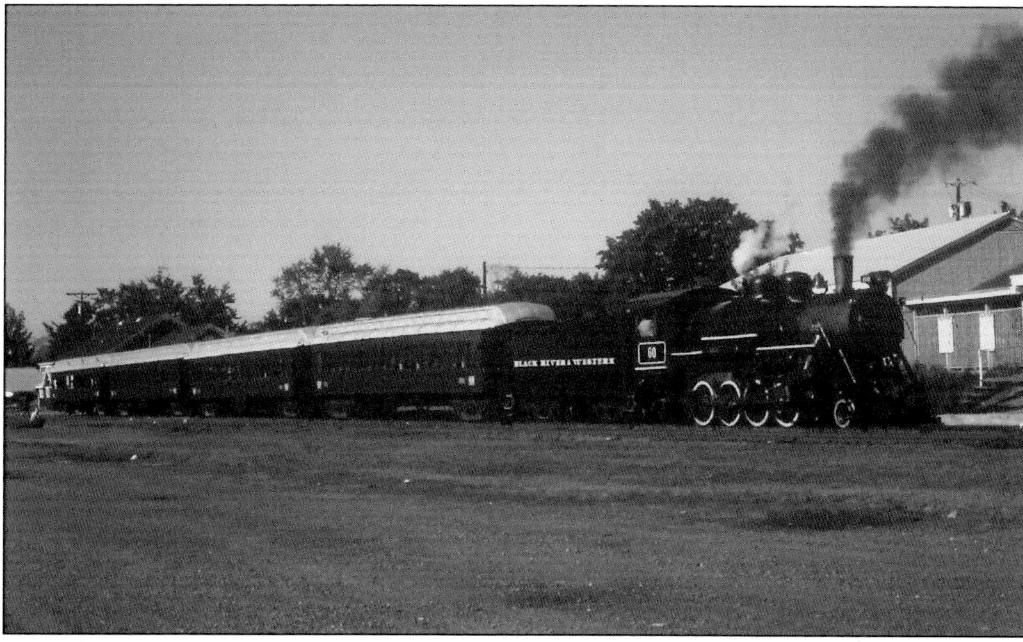

Steam locomotive No. 60 pulls passenger cars No. 301, No. 303, No. 304, and No. 302 wait while passengers board for a southbound trip to Ringoes in June 1978. The roofs of the passenger cars were painted silver in an attempt to keep the cars cooler in the summer.

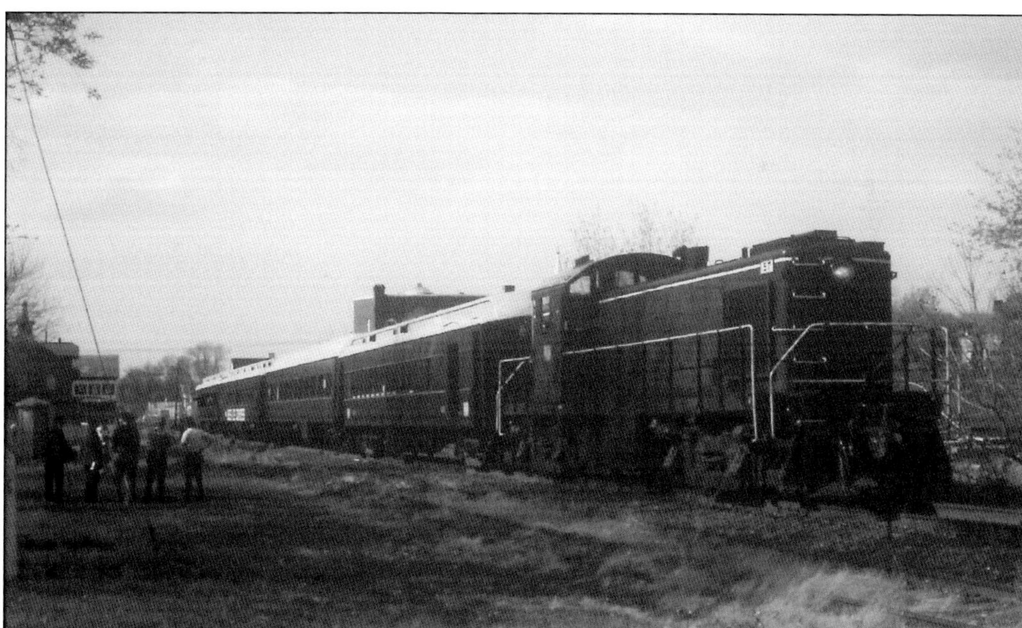

RS-1 locomotive No. 57 is pictured with four passenger cars at Lambertville in 1978. The first car behind the locomotive is combine No. 297, and the silver roofs of the cars gave the train the appearance of being a "circus train." The roofs of the cars would eventually be repainted the original black color.

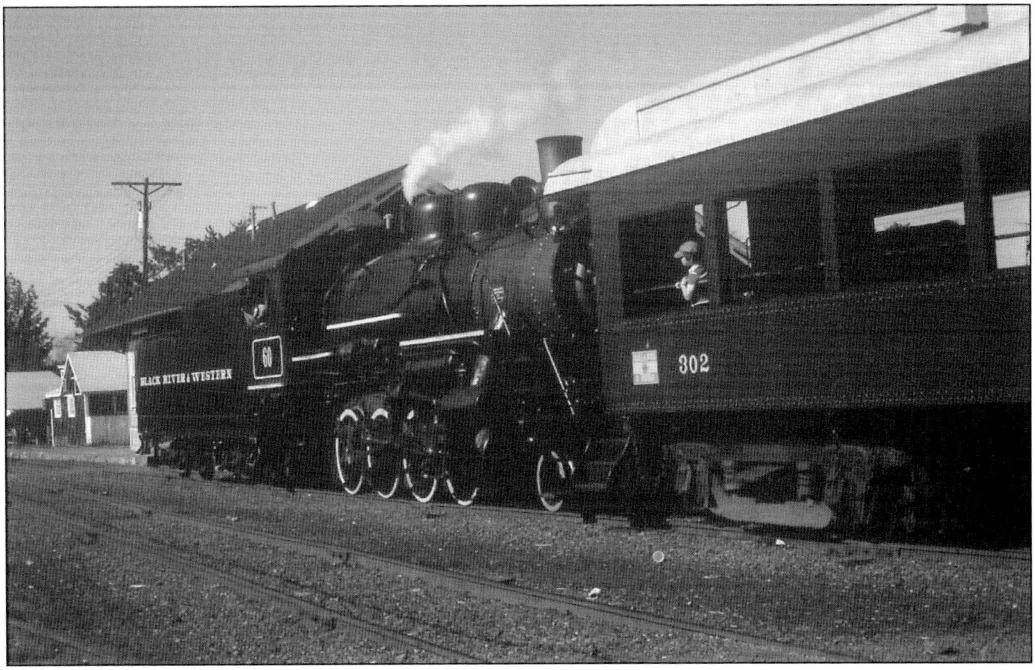

A young passenger looks on while steam engine No. 60 arrives in Flemington with passenger coach No. 302 trailing. Passenger car No. 302 had open windows and bench seats down the center of the car and was popular with passengers for the fresh air it afforded during the summer months.

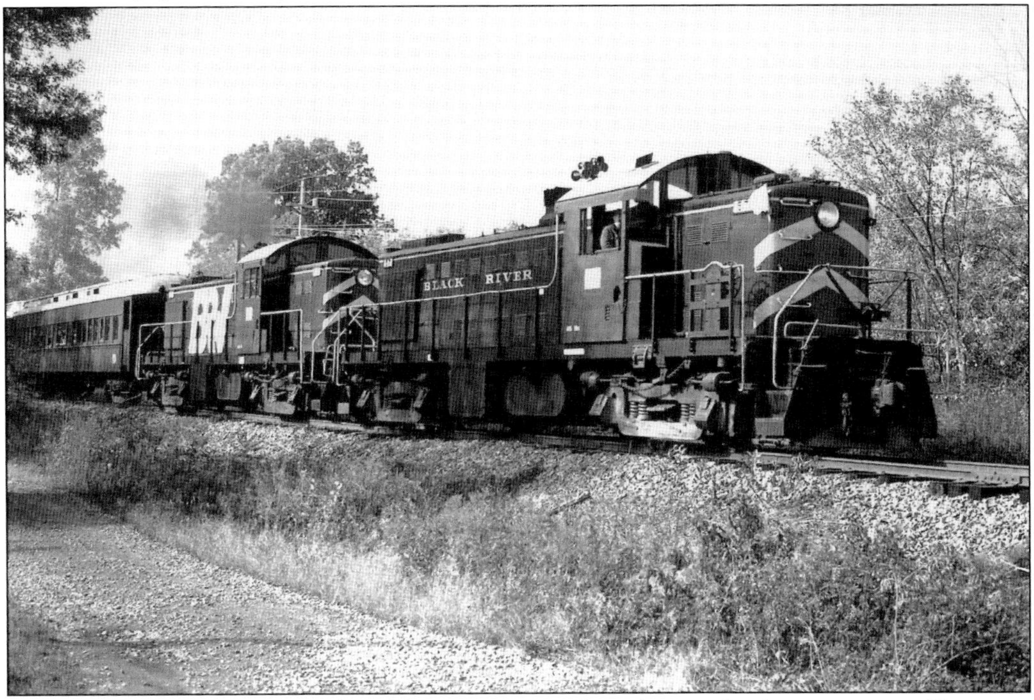

Locomotive No. 211 was renumbered locomotive No. 58 and given the distinctive speed lettering of the BR&W. It is shown here during railroad service in Lambertville led by locomotive No. 57 in 1983 during a double-header trip. The No. 58 engine was later scrapped.

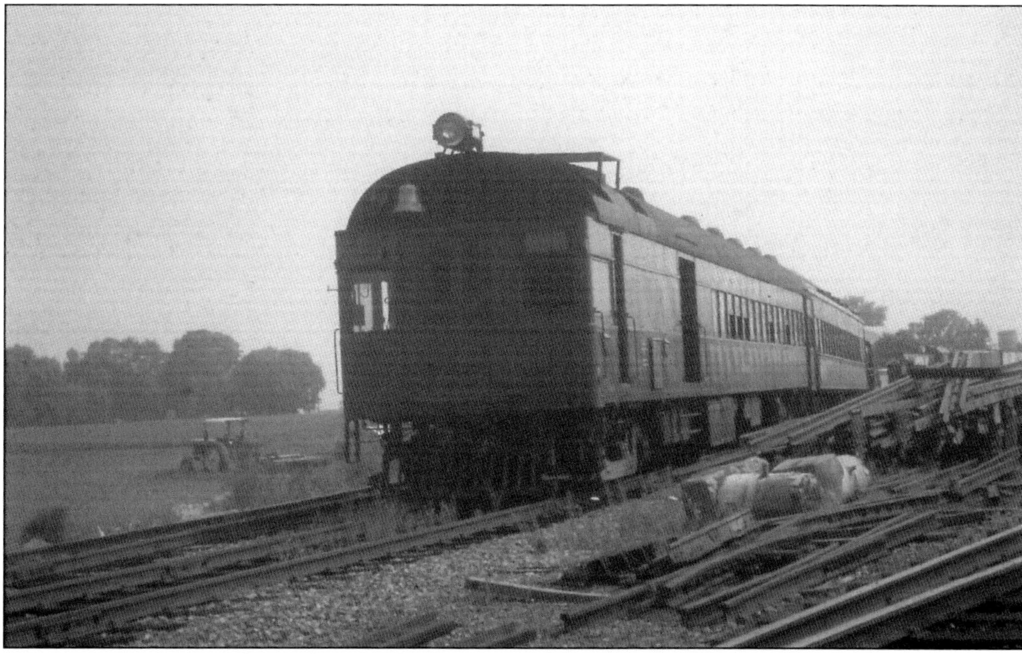

Motorcar No. 4666 is shown here with car No. 321 in Ringoes during July 1982. Passenger car No. 321 was converted from a coach to a cab car to run along with the motorcar. The cab car was a controlling unit that would allow operation of the two units in either direction.

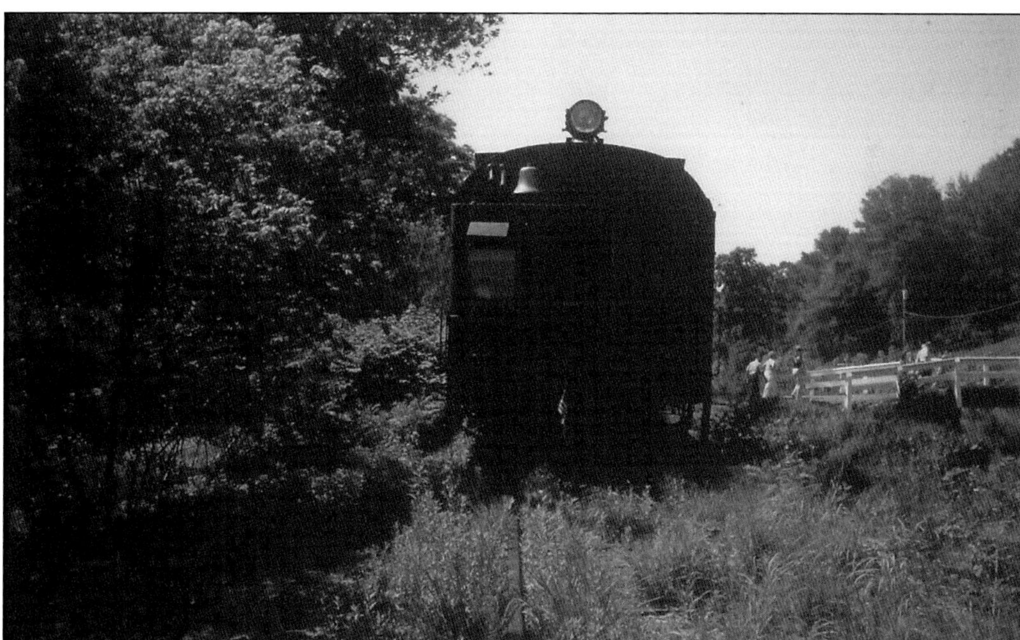

Motorcar No. 4666 occasionally ran south of Lambertville to the area near the flea market, about a mile south of Lambertville. These excursions were short-lived but showed the willingness of the railroad to try new endeavors.

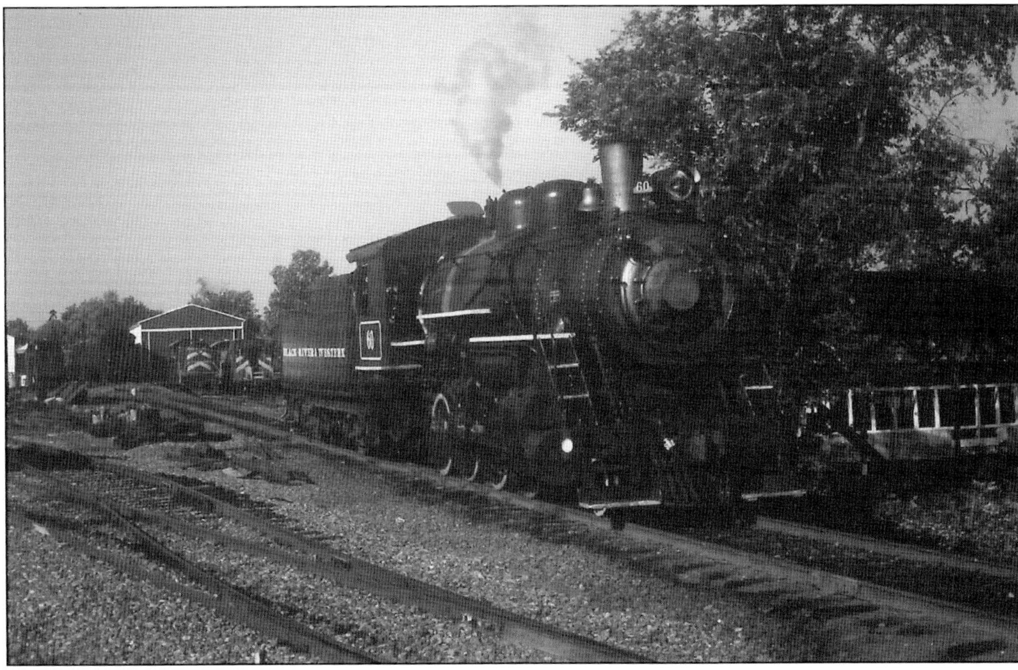

Steam engine No. 60 sported a red and gold number plate on the front of its boiler in 1983. To the right is one of the streetcars that was stored in Ringoes. In the background are motorcar No. 4666, the passenger string of cars on the main track, locomotive No. 57, locomotive No. 58, and caboose No. 35.

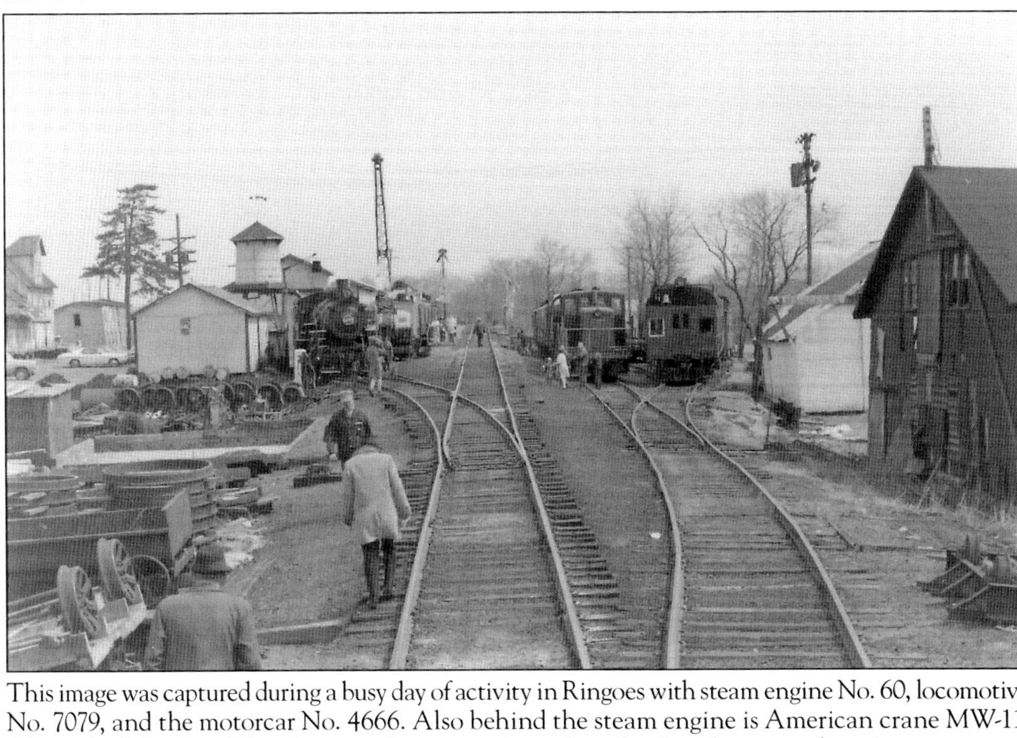

This image was captured during a busy day of activity in Ringoes with steam engine No. 60, locomotive No. 7079, and the motorcar No. 4666. Also behind the steam engine is American crane MW-11. Along the left side of the photograph are a variety of used railroad parts and equipment.

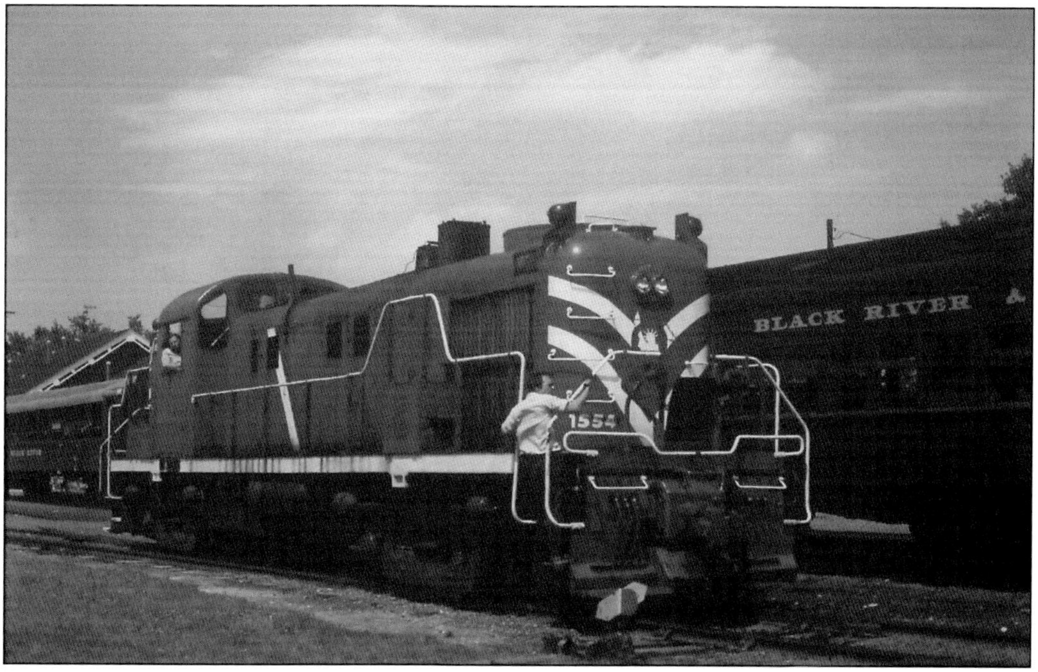

Engineer Gene Cruver runs locomotive No. 1554, which was painted in the red Central Railroad of New Jersey colors, during a runaround move in Flemington. The locomotive was obtained as part of the acquisition of the South Branch line from Flemington to Three Bridges.

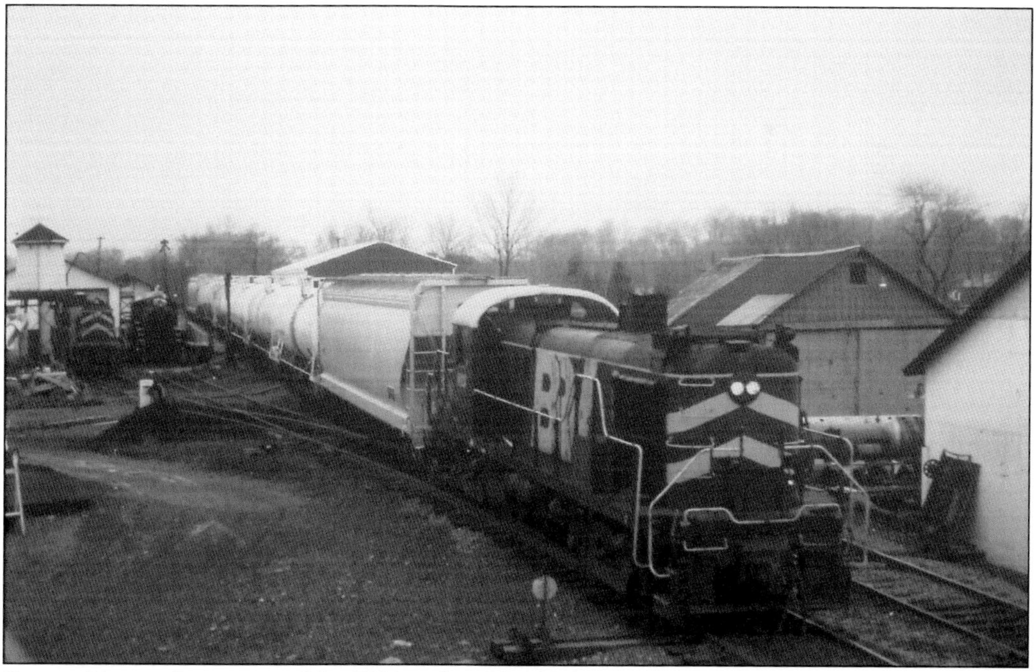

Pictured here is locomotive No. 1554, in her BR&W lettering, entering Ringoes with a string of freight cars in March 1984. Locomotive No. 51 and steam engine No. 60 can be seen in the left background.

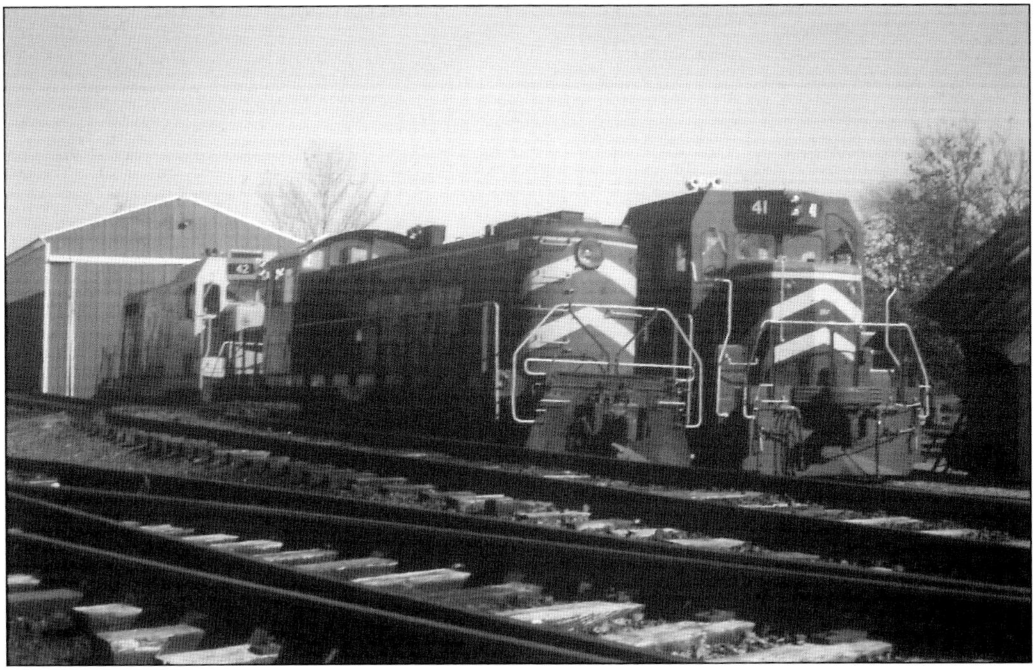
Three of the railroad diesel locomotives sit idle at Ringoes in 1985; the locomotives pictured are, from right to left, No. 42, No. 57 and No. 41.

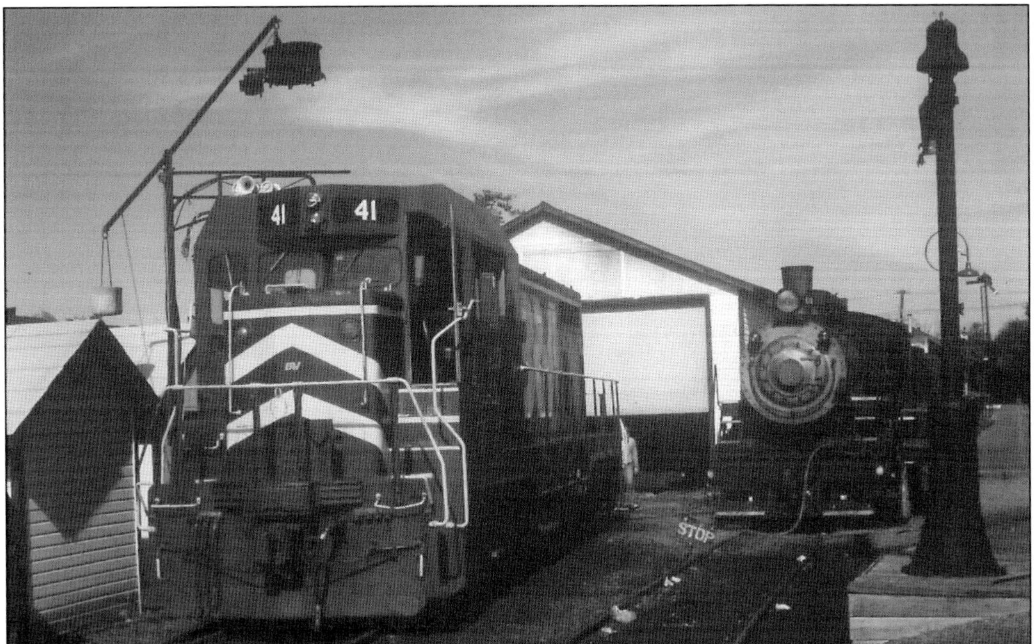

EMD model CF-7 locomotive No. 41 sits on the engine house lead track, and steam engine No. 60, sporting a red number plate, sits on the souvenir track in Ringoes in 1986. On the right is the water plug, and on the left over the engine is a stack fan used by the steam crew during the start-up of the steam engine.

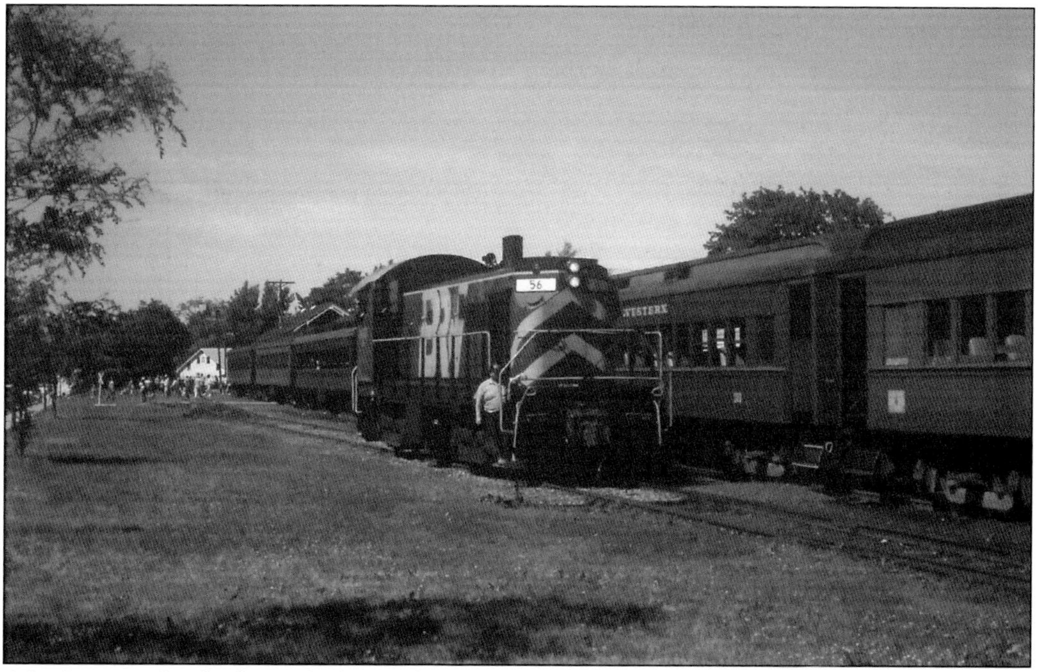

A brakeman rides the front of Alco T-6 locomotive No. 56 during a runaround move in Flemington in June 1989. Painted in the speed lettering of the day, the engine was used in both passenger and freight service.

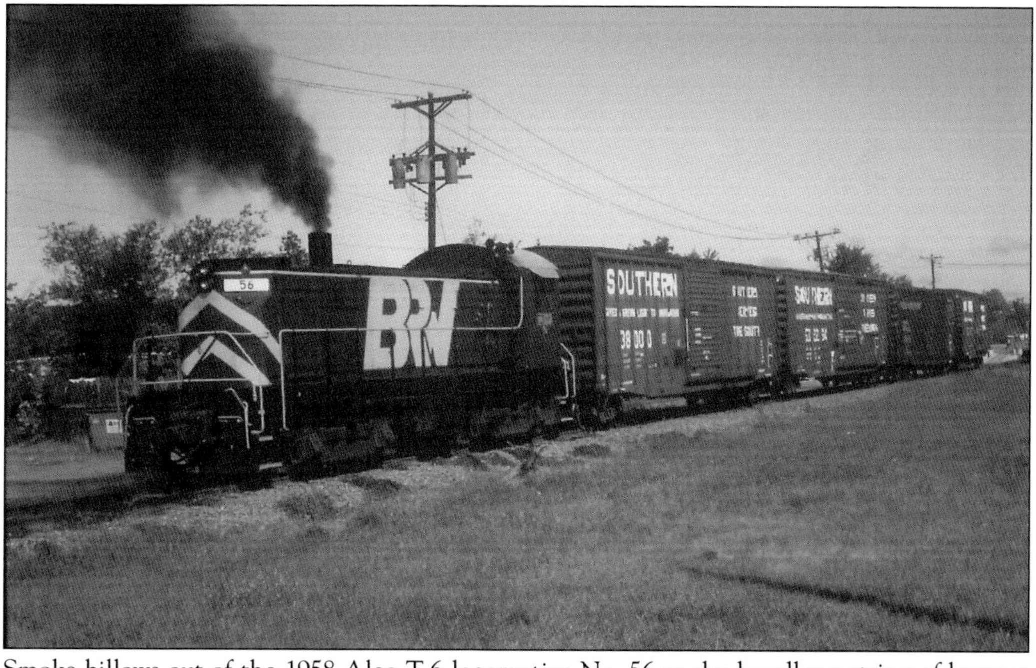

Smoke billows out of the 1958 Alco T-6 locomotive No. 56 as she handles a string of boxcars during a freight move. Acquired in 1981, the engine would serve for a number of years in service with the railroad before being sold.

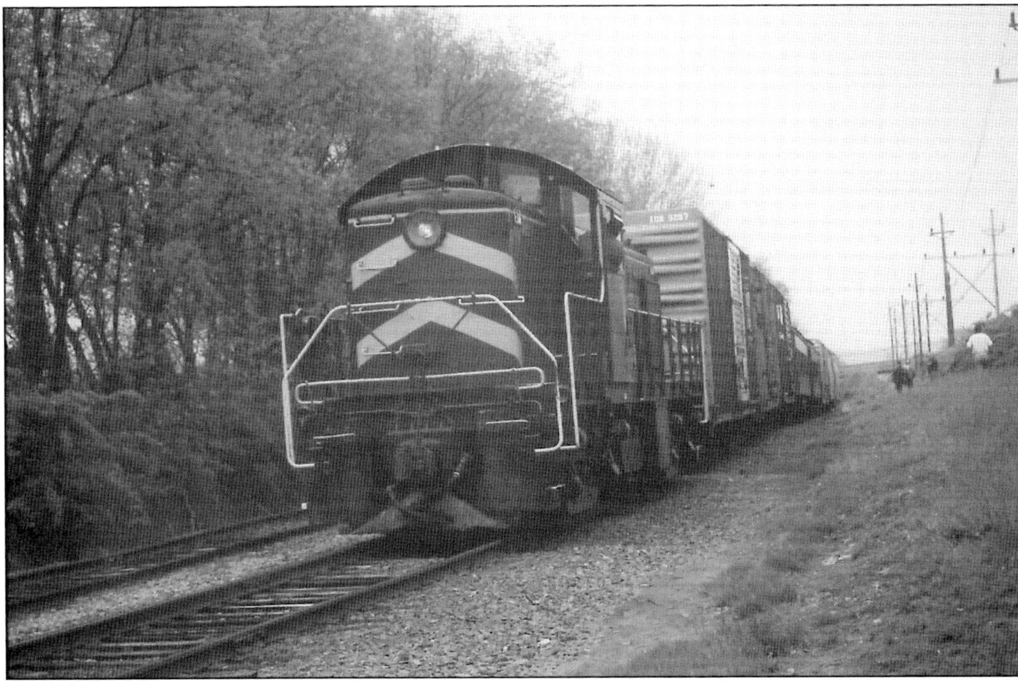

Locomotive No. 57 switches cars at the Three Bridges yard in June 1987, with a mixed consist of both freight and passenger cars. During the special excursion trip, passengers were allowed off the train and given the opportunity to photograph the event.

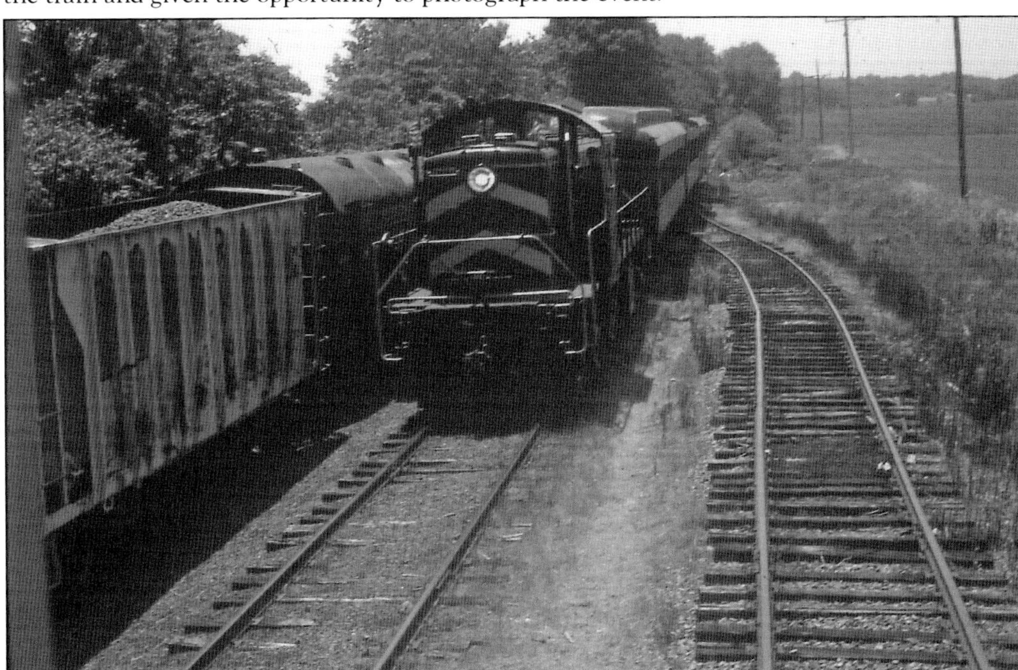

In a view looking from the cab of locomotive No. 42, locomotive No. 57 heads north through the south Ringoes yard, with a string of passenger cars, toward the Ringoes station on a return trip from Lambertville.

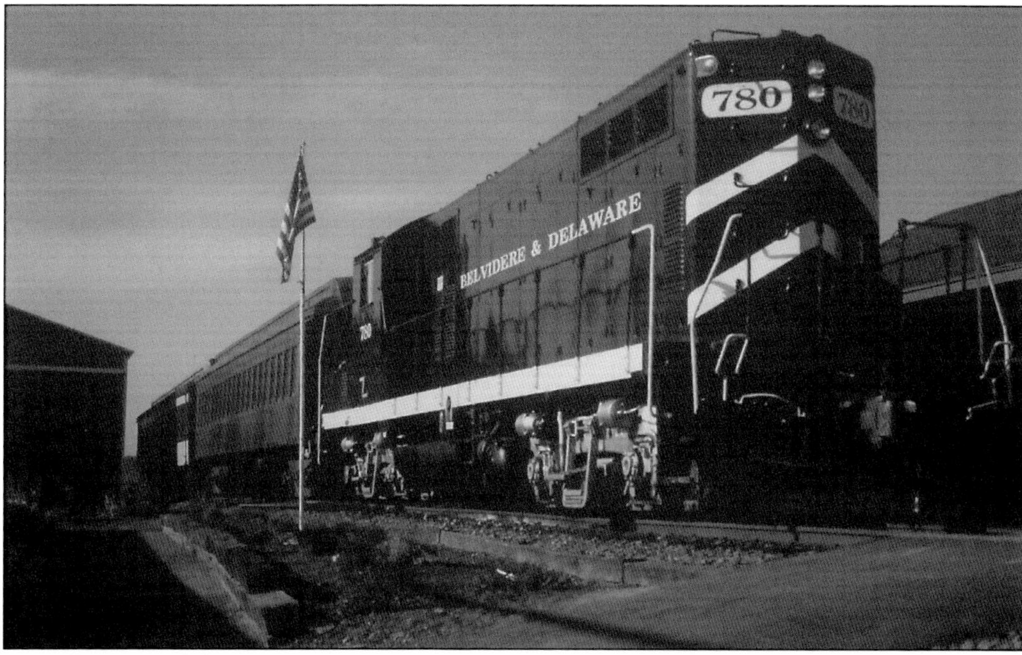

1950 EMD model GP7U Locomotive No. 780 sits at the Ringoes station in November 1998, ready to start passenger excursion service between Flemington and Ringoes with two passenger coaches.

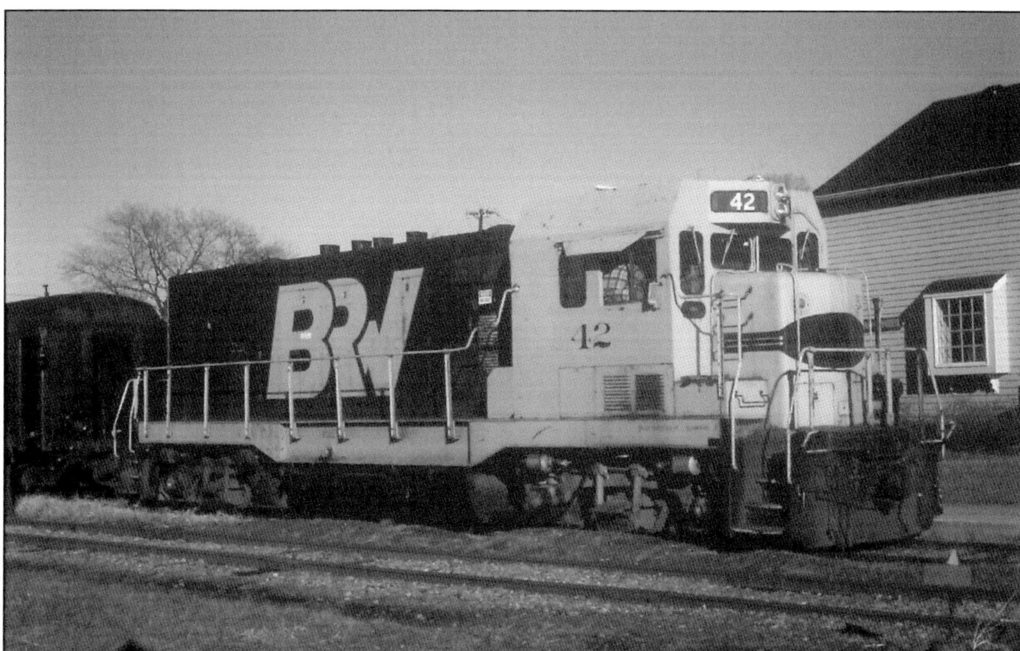

A model CF7 Locomotive No. 42, still in partial Sante Fe paint, waits for the order to proceed south from Flemington with a consist of passenger cars in 1990. The unit arrived on the railroad as Sante Fe Unit No. 2421 and would be renumbered 42 and partially painted with the BR&W speed lettering.

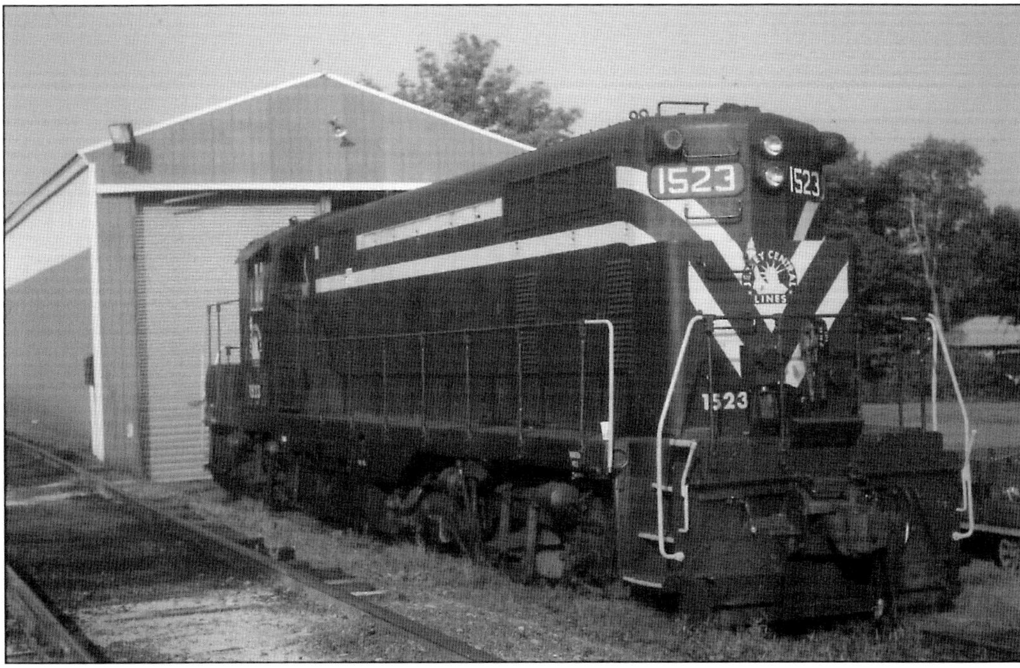

The 1952 GP-7 locomotive No. 1523 was owned by the United Railroad Historical Society of New Jersey (URHS) and leased to and used by the Black River & Western. The engine would later be returned to the URHS.

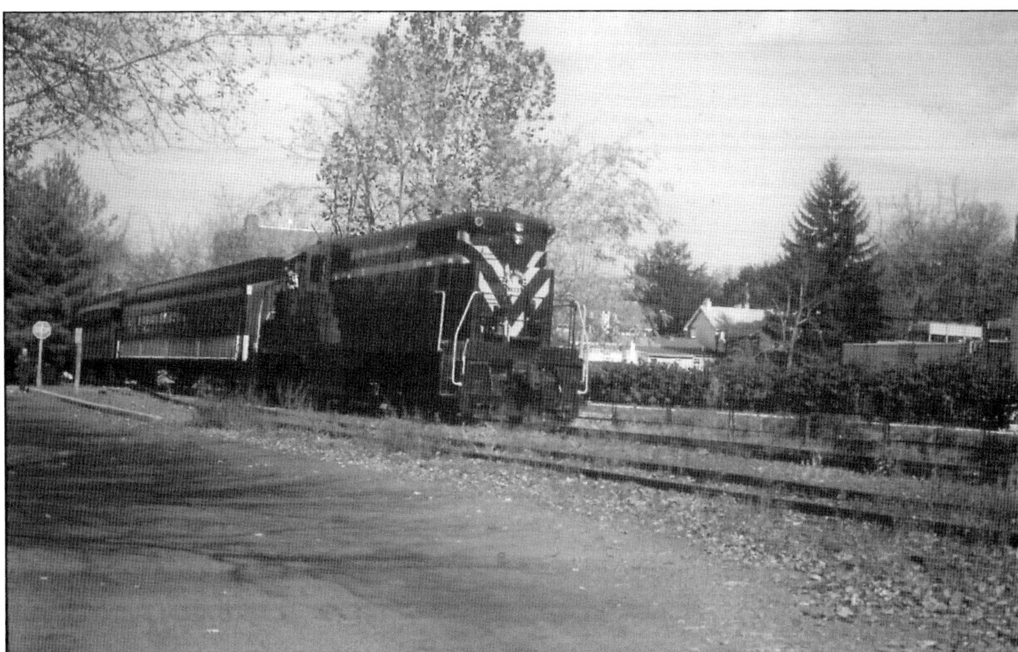

Locomotive No. 1523, with a string of ex–Canadian National passenger cars, was used in passenger excursion service and is seen heading into Lambertville along the canal in 1998. The locomotive retained its Jersey Central paint scheme while on the railroad.

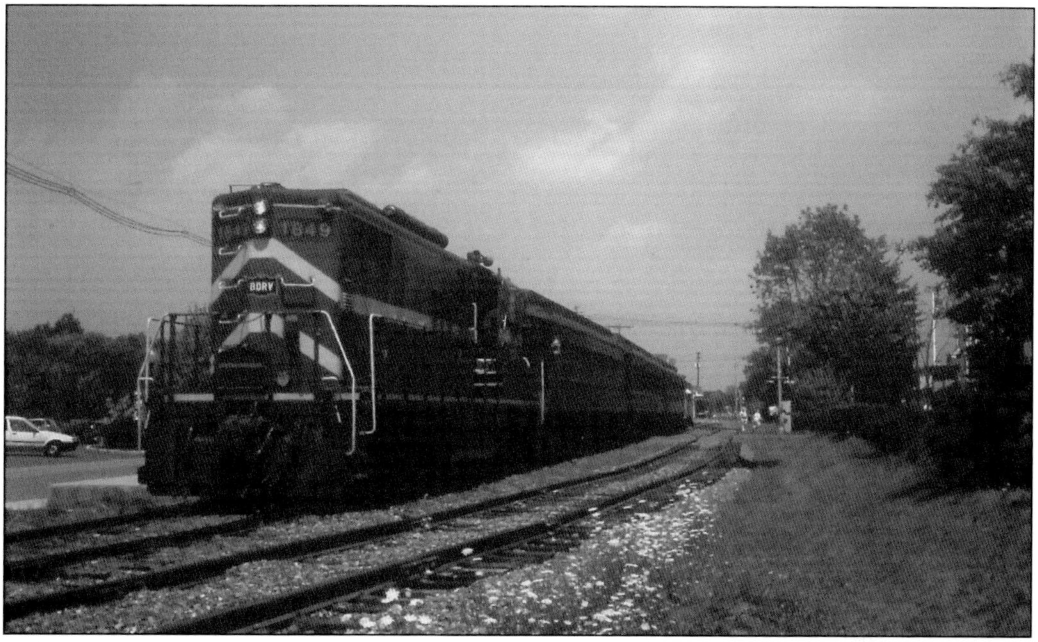

EMD model GP9 Locomotive No. 1849 waits at the new Flemington station platform on a nice August day in 1997. This locomotive was one of a few GP9s owned by the railroad and used for both passenger and freight service.

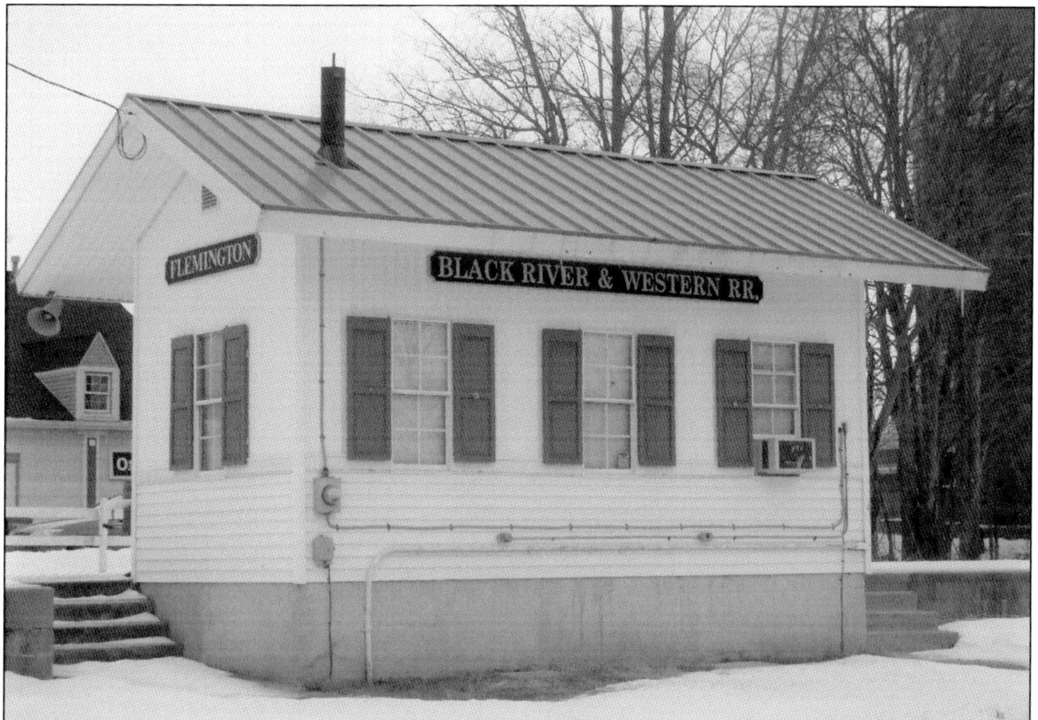

The original Flemington station started as a ticket booth, was later replaced by a larger passenger car, and was then moved farther south where the current small station and platform were built.

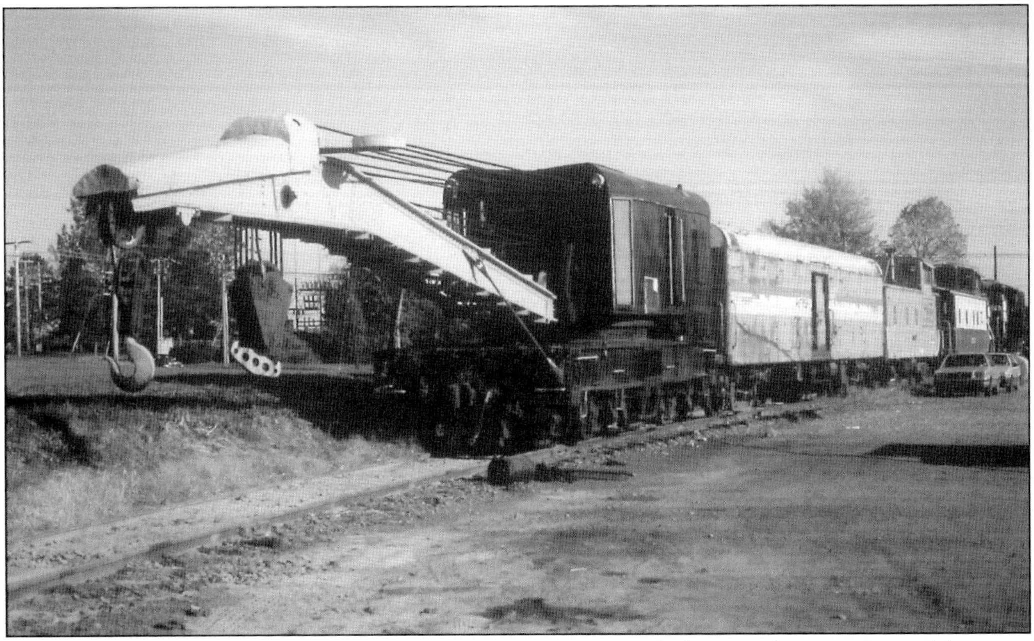

One of two 150-ton wreck cranes stored in Ringoes is pictured along with an ex-Amtrak baggage car and two cabooses. The crane was formerly used by the Long Island Rail Road. It was used for various duties on the railroad.

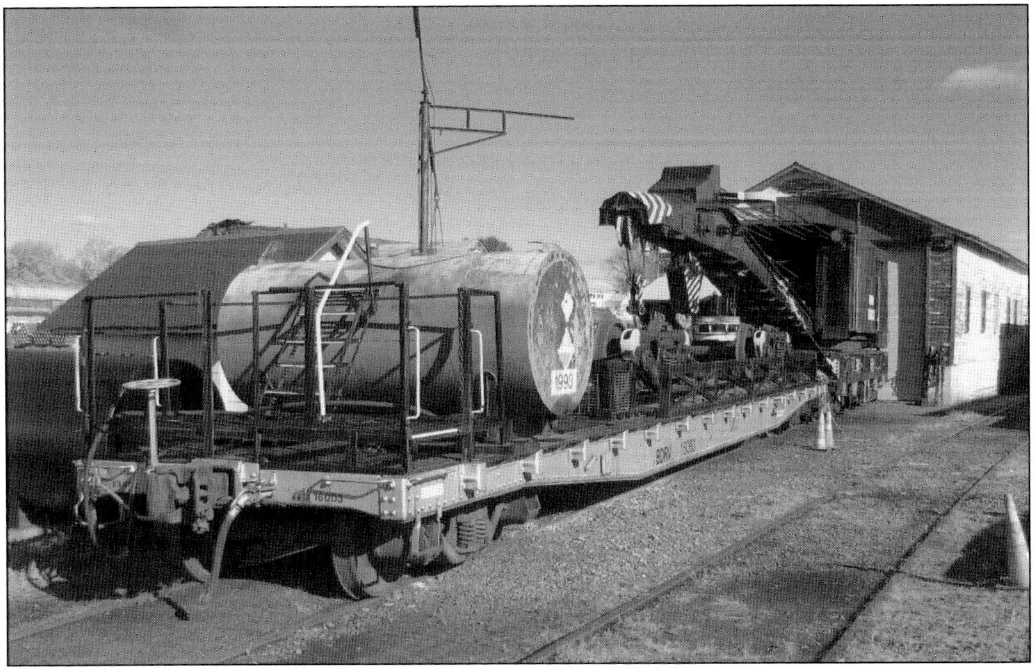

The 150-ton Belvidere & Delaware River wreck crane No. 16002 and idler car No. 16003 sit in front of the engine house in Ringoes. Both railcars were formerly used by Amtrak before being bought by the Black River & Western.

Three

Railroading in the New Millennium

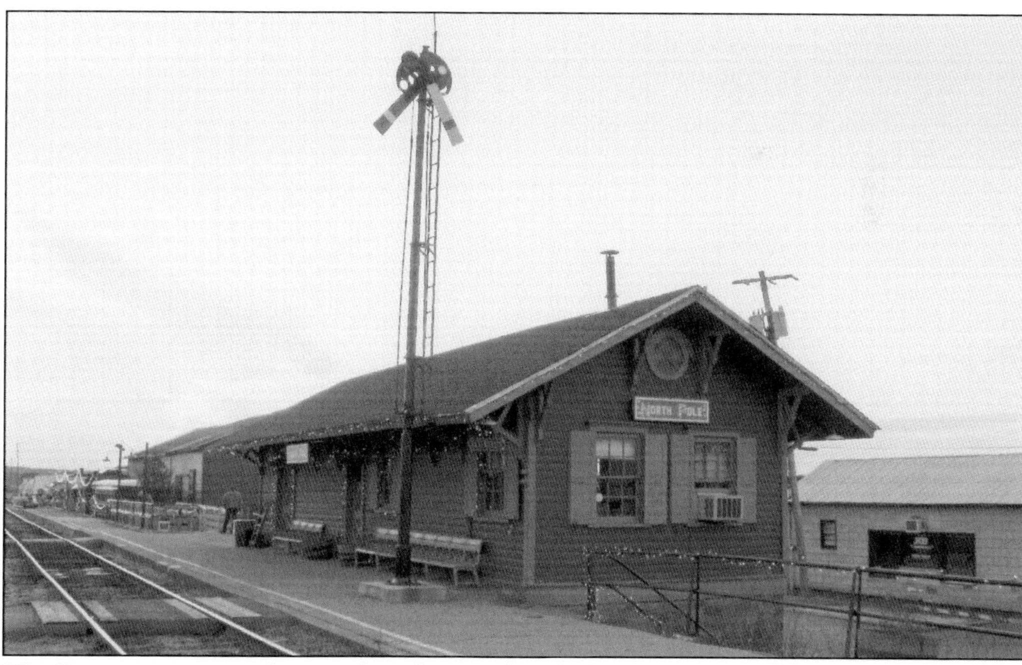

The Ringoes station is decorated as the North Pole for the seasonal Christmas trains in this 2008 photograph. The ever-popular sold-out events provide the public with holiday enjoyment, and many visitors return each year. The events featured Santa and Mrs. Claus, cookies and hot chocolate, and an enjoyable train ride.

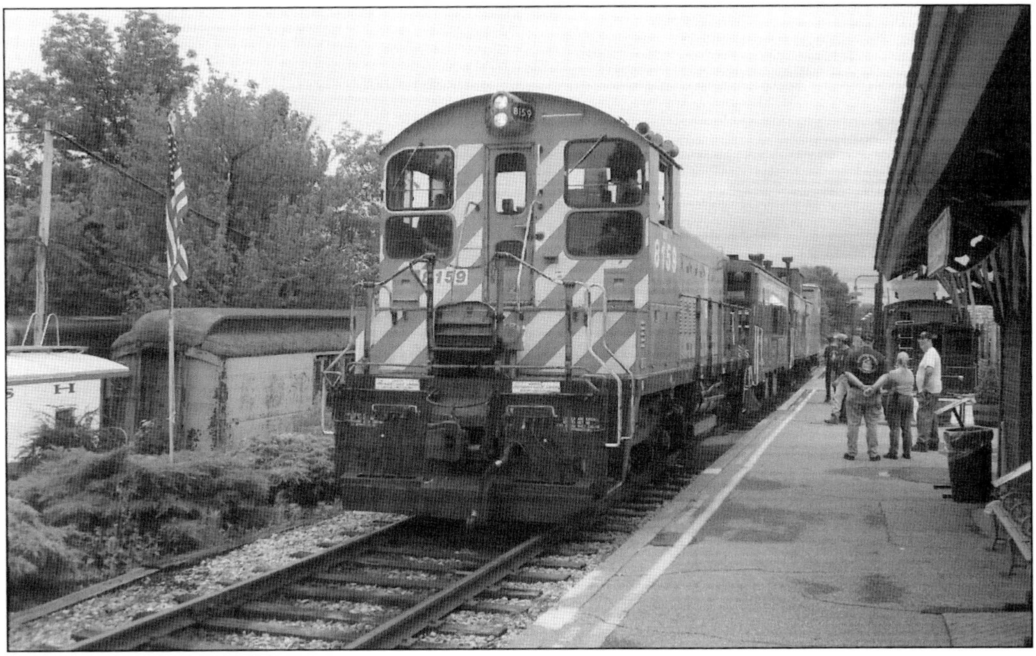

Black River Locomotive No. 8159 is ready with a string of cabooses in Ringoes for a special Saturday night "Caboose Hop" trip that ran between Ringoes and Three Bridges and back. These special trips allowed passengers to experience the ride in a caboose.

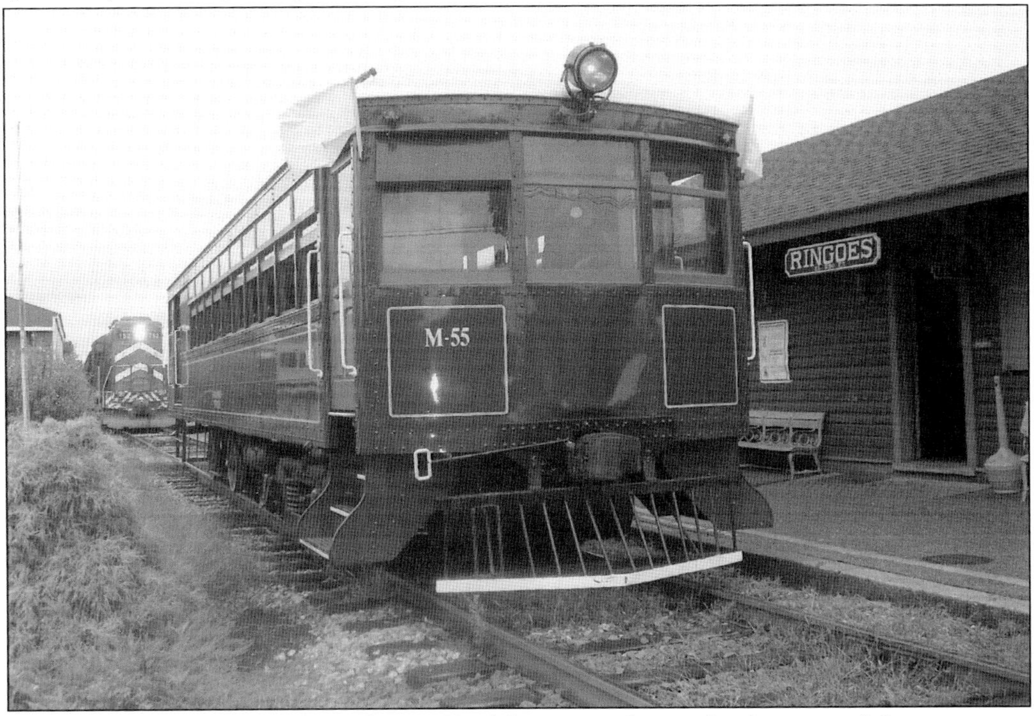

The Brill M-55 motorcar "the Delaware Turtle" was run during the first year of the corn maze trains. The car shuttled passengers to and from the corn maze, while locomotive No. 752, seen in the background, pulled the train that brought passengers to Ringoes from Flemington.

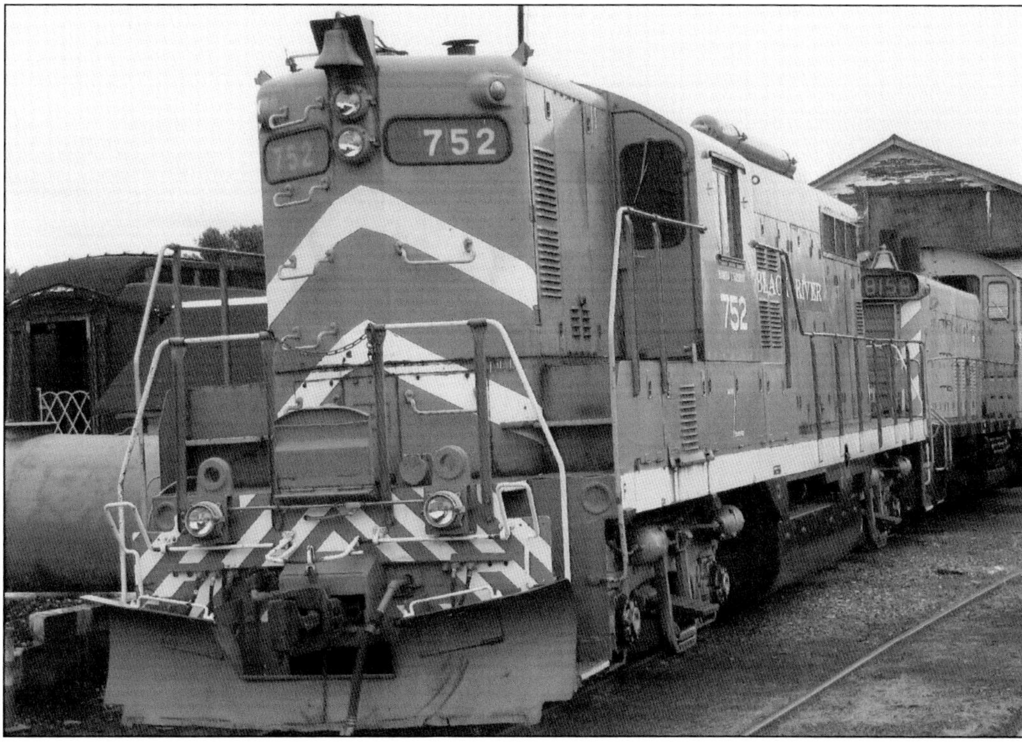

Shown in Ringoes, locomotive No.752 was named *Harold T. Filskov* in honor of one of the owners of the Vermont Railway who was also a former director of New Jersey's Raritan River Railroad. The second engine in line is a locomotive No. 8159, nicknamed "Pinky" for her faded color. The locomotive was renumbered in 2015 to No. 1259 and repainted black.

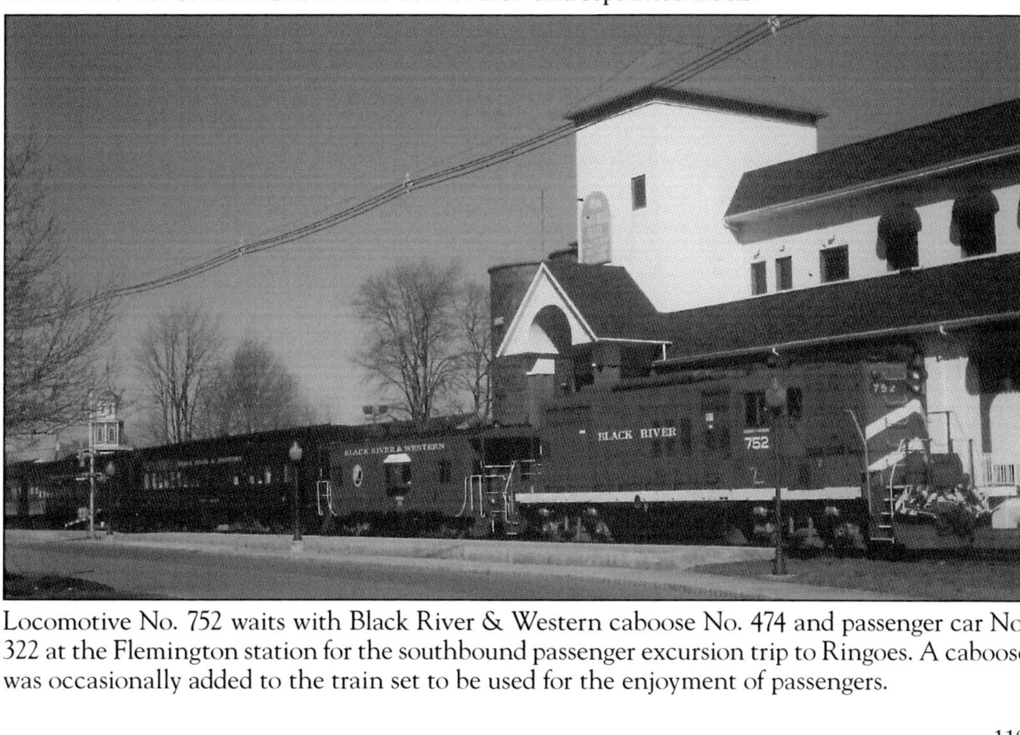

Locomotive No. 752 waits with Black River & Western caboose No. 474 and passenger car No. 322 at the Flemington station for the southbound passenger excursion trip to Ringoes. A caboose was occasionally added to the train set to be used for the enjoyment of passengers.

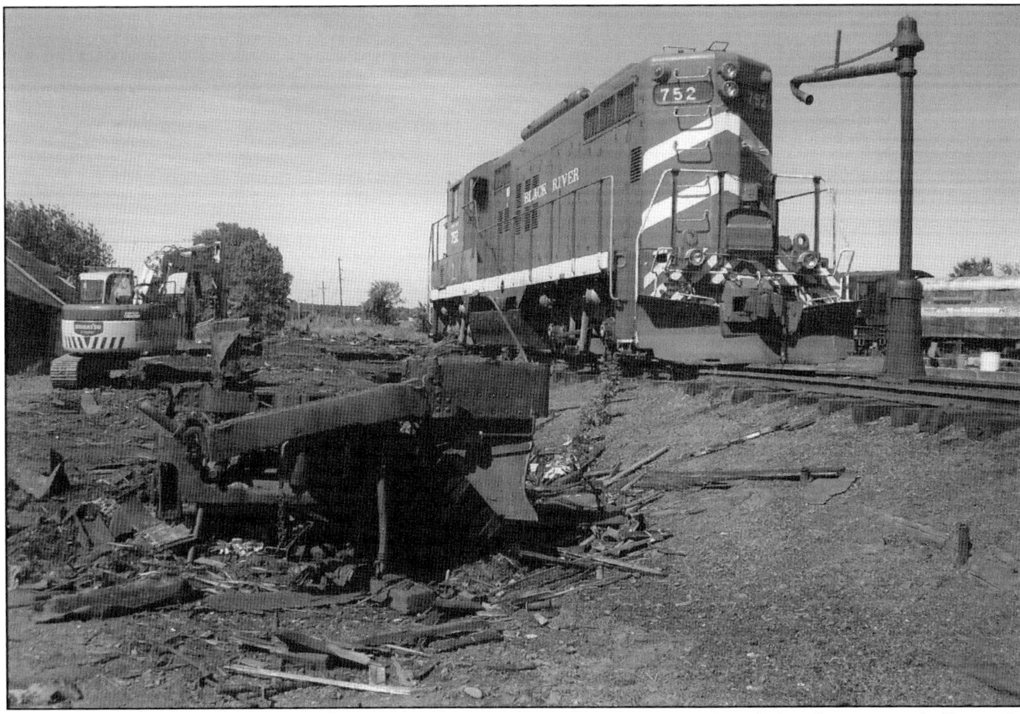

A clear day shows locomotive No. 752 sitting on the main track while there is a lull in the scrapping activity of an old railroad car. In the background are one of the 150-ton wreck cranes and an ex-Amtrak baggage car.

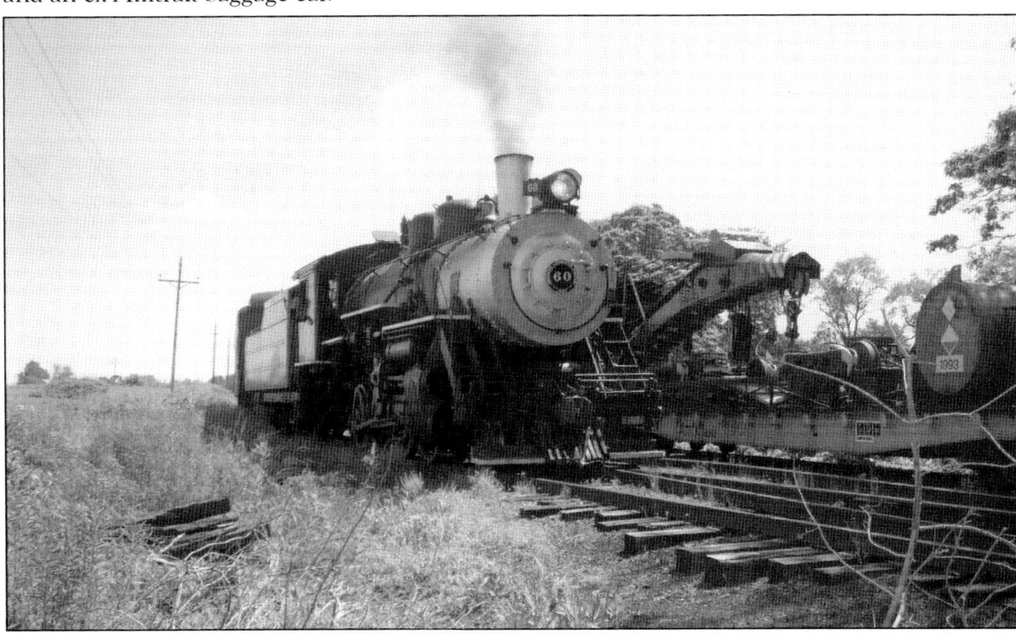

Steam engine No. 60 returned to regular passenger excursion service in 2013 after a lengthy overhaul period. Shown here in the south Ringoes yard after a day of excursion trips, she will return to the engine house for rest and routine maintenance before the next round of passenger excursions.

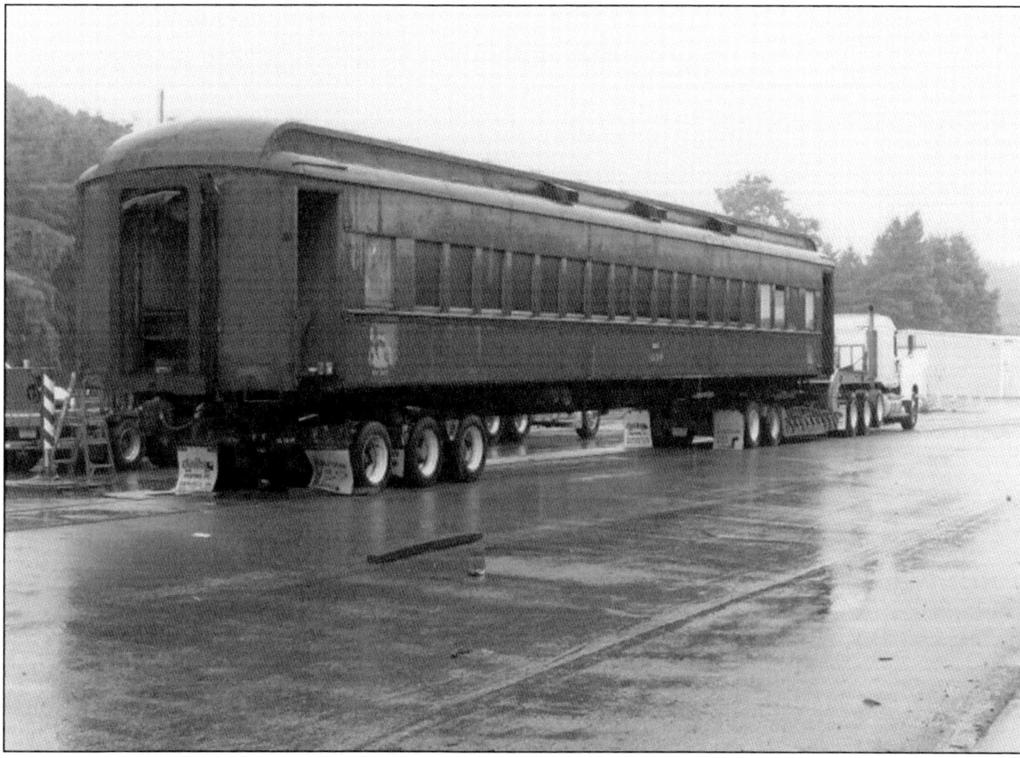

On a rainy day in July 2010, passenger car No.1009 was prepared to be trucked from Phillipsburg to Flemington. The car had been stranded in Phillipsburg and required movement by truck to the Black River Railroad Historical Trust for restoration.

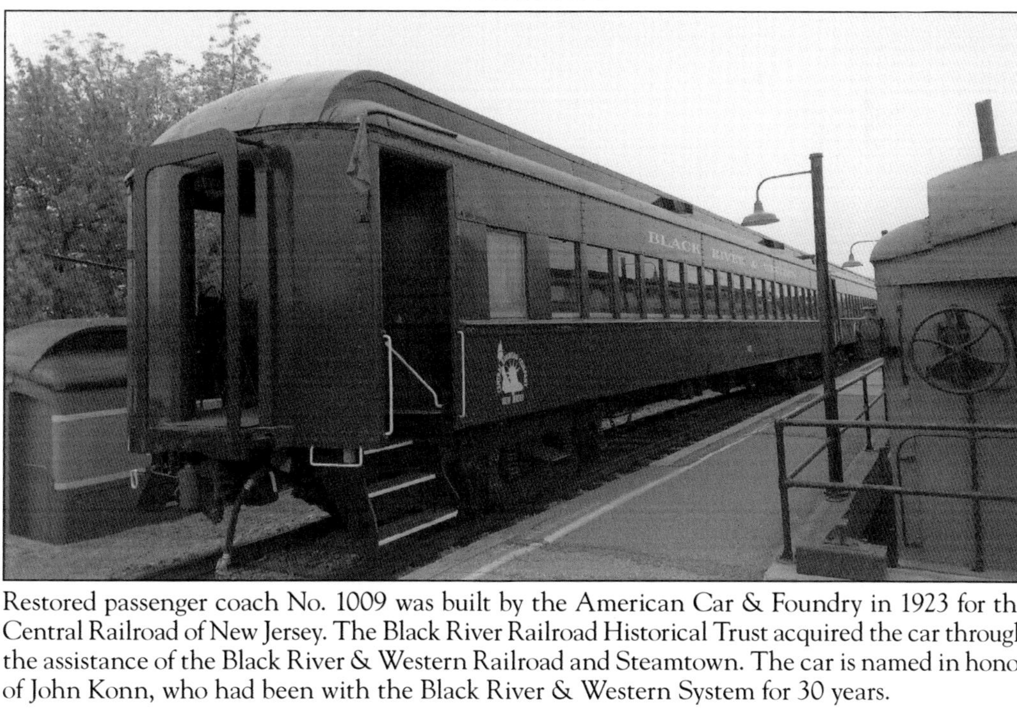

Restored passenger coach No. 1009 was built by the American Car & Foundry in 1923 for the Central Railroad of New Jersey. The Black River Railroad Historical Trust acquired the car through the assistance of the Black River & Western Railroad and Steamtown. The car is named in honor of John Konn, who had been with the Black River & Western System for 30 years.

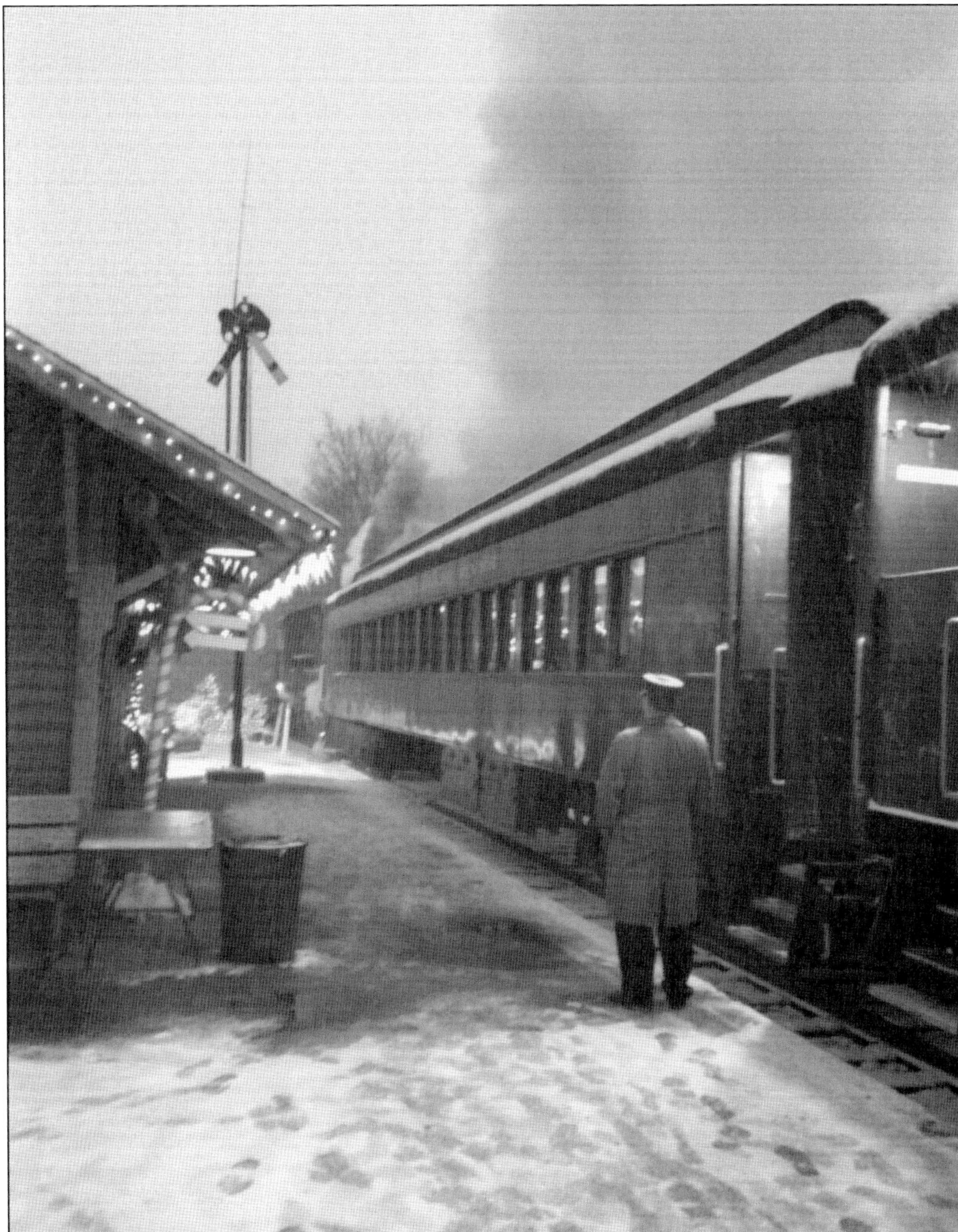

A lone trainman waits on a cold, snowy day for the departure of the North Pole Express. Each holiday season, the Ringoes station is transformed into the North Pole. Passengers are treated to a visit with Santa and Mrs. Claus, served hot chocolate and cookies, and treated to other activities while visiting.

Steam engine No. 60 arrives at the North Pole, where Santa and Mrs. Claus wait on the platform for the arrival of a North Pole Express train. The Clauses wave to all the passengers on the train as it passes during the Christmas season.

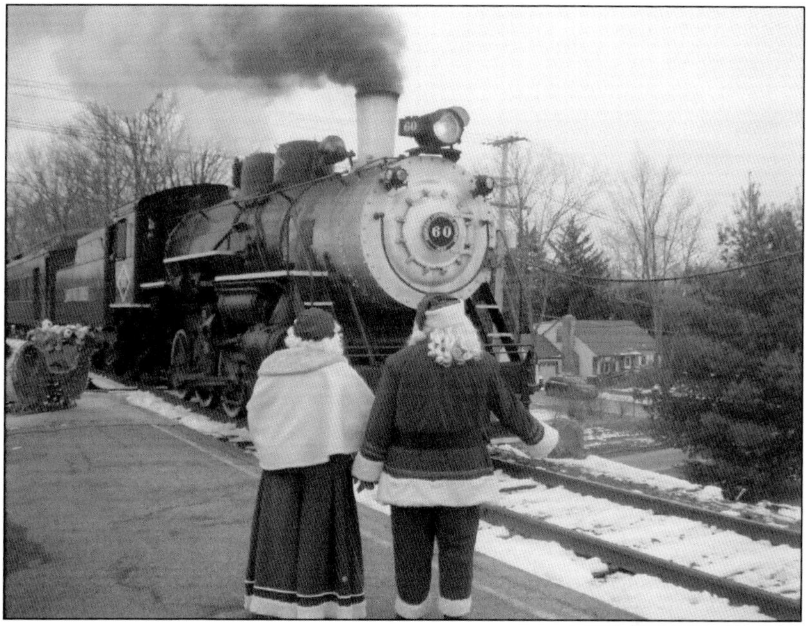

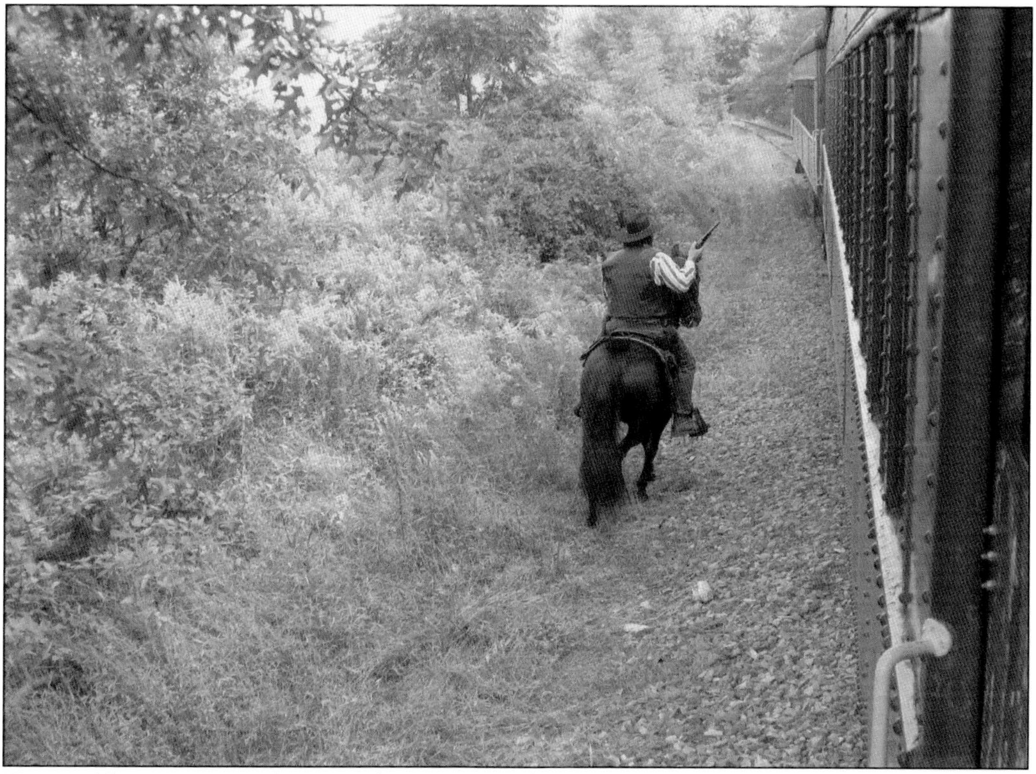

Train robberies are another popular event on the Black River & Western Railroad. Bandits aboard the train rob the passengers of "Black River Bucks" while armed gunmen on horses ride alongside the train. Once arriving at the Ringoes station, the children are encouraged to help the Sheriff with the bandits.

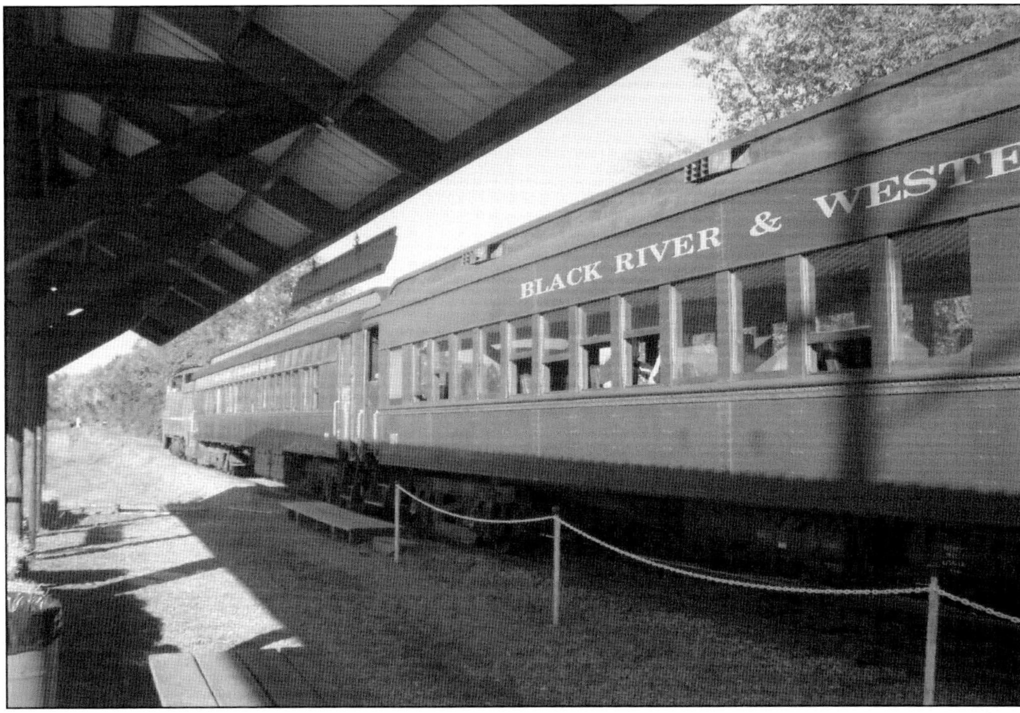

The Pumpkin Junction Express train waits at Pumpkin Junction for passengers to return from pumpkin picking and the corn maze before heading north to Flemington. Pumpkin trains are just one of several family events held throughout the year.

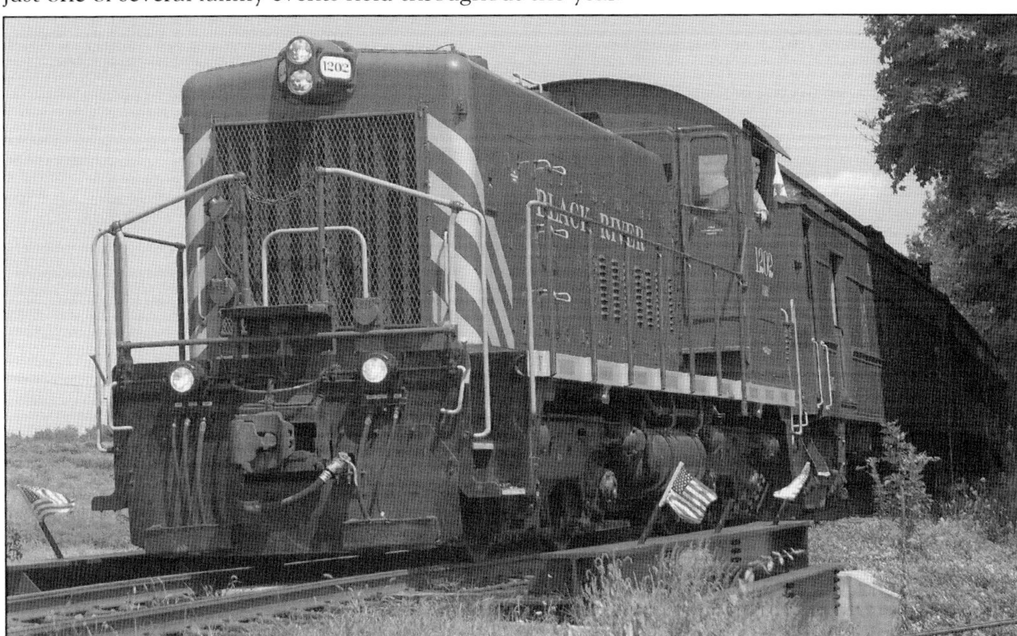

Black River Locomotive No. 1202 arrives in Ringoes with a string of passenger cars over the railroad bridge that has been decorated with American flags. The first car behind the engine is combine No. 297. Locomotive 1202 was used on numerous occasions to pull the passenger trains.

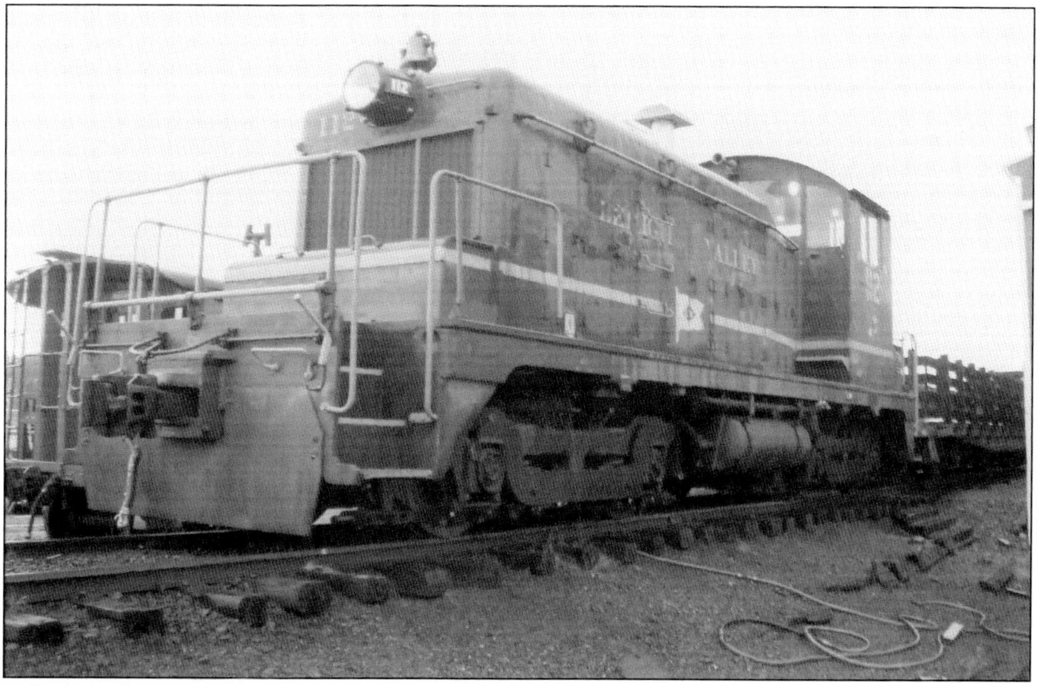

Lehigh Valley Locomotive No. 112 was called into service and used for passenger excursions. The 1939 EMC model SW-1 is privately owned by Pennsy Railcar Restorations, LLC and leased by the Black River Railroad Historical Trust as needed.

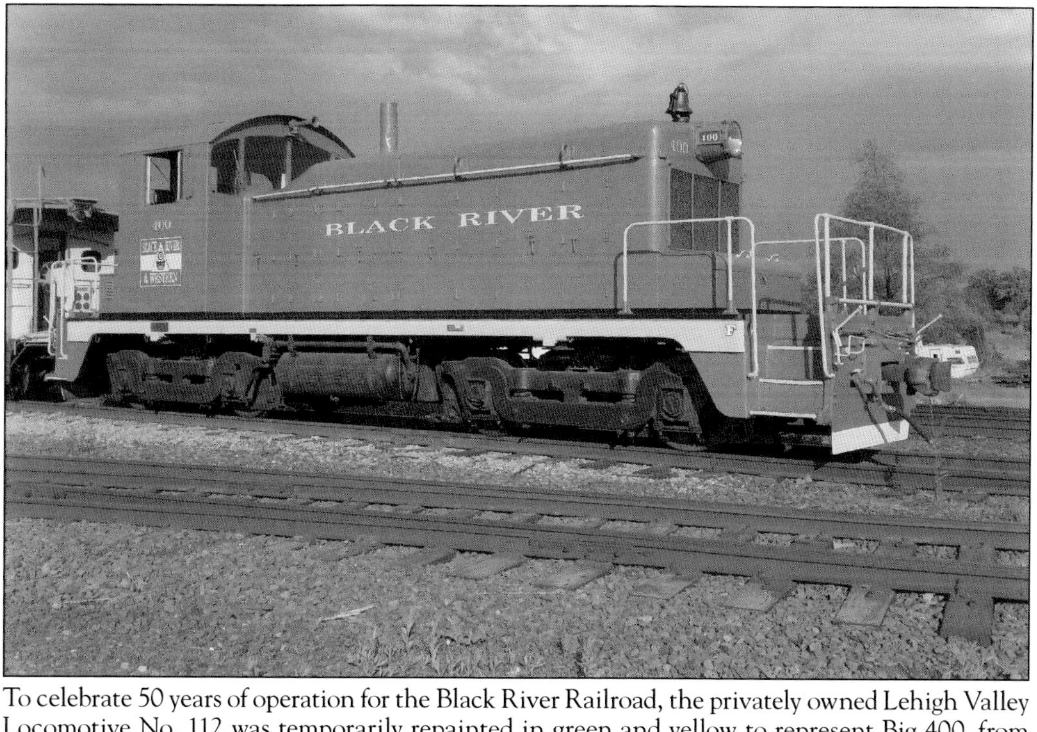

To celebrate 50 years of operation for the Black River Railroad, the privately owned Lehigh Valley Locomotive No. 112 was temporarily repainted in green and yellow to represent Big 400, from the early days of operation on the railroad.

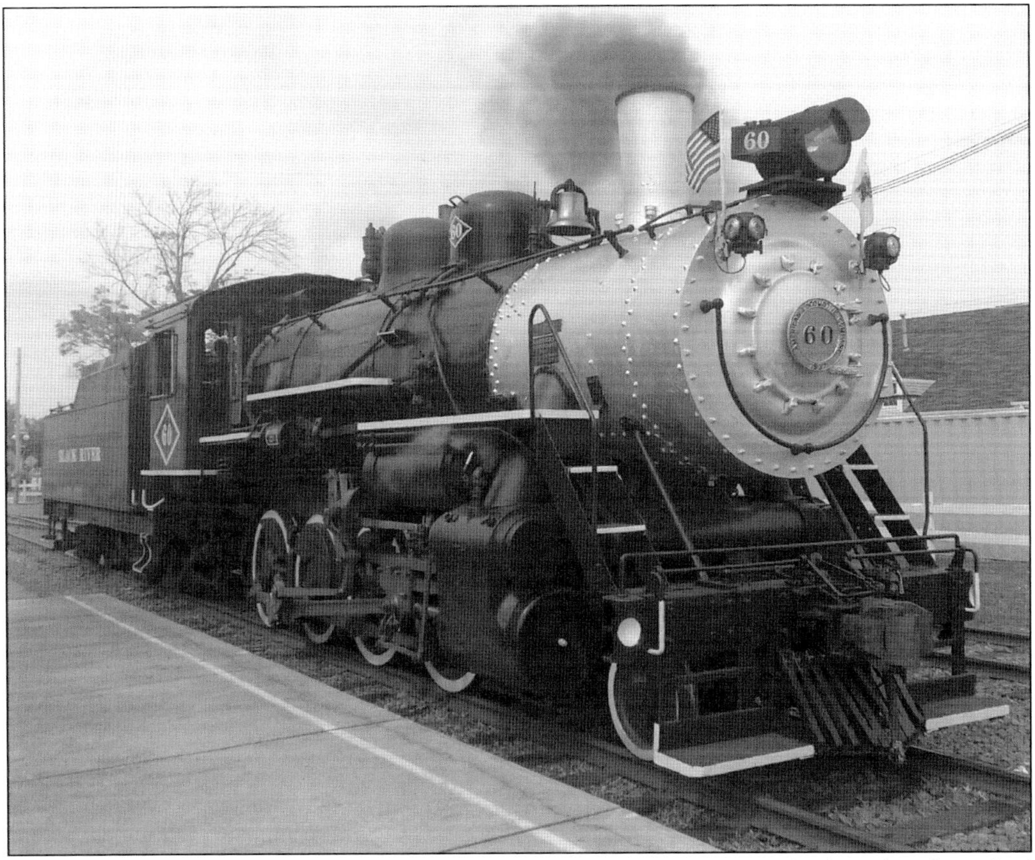

Steam engine No. 60 was used for the 50th anniversary on May 16, 2015. Shined and touched up, she sported a gold number plate on the front of the boiler in commemoration of 50 years of service to the Black River & Western Railroad. She also sported the American and New Jersey flags, like she had in 1965. The steam engine that pulled the first excursion train in 1965, No. 60 was the same engine that pulled the excursion train 50 years later and on the same date.

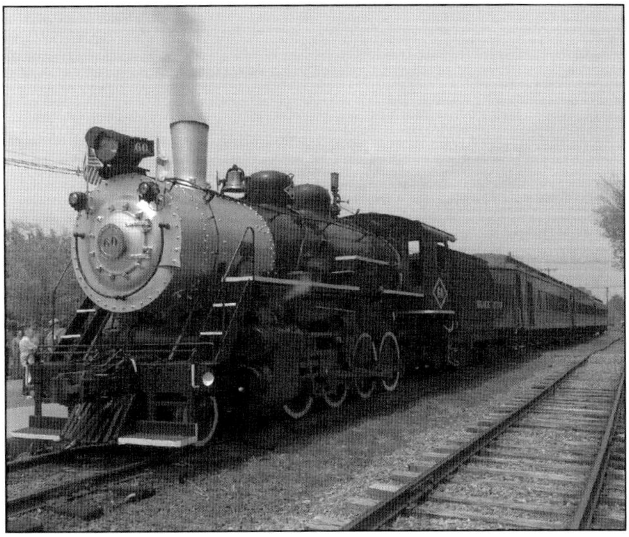

BLACK RIVER

1965 2015

50 YEARS

Started as a steam-powered tourist attraction, the Black River & Western Railroad has grown though the past 50 years to become a successful short line. It has continuously provided weekend passenger excursions over the past 50 years and is expected to continue this service well into the future. The railroad has adapted to changes over the years and will continue to do so. Preserving railroad history and educating the public on railroading has been the mission of the volunteer-based Black River Railroad Historical Trust, which works closely with the railroad. The enthusiasm and growth shown by the volunteers over the past 15-plus years is a reflection of the bright future for the railroad. For more information about the Black River & Western Railroad and their events please visit the website at www.blackriverrailroad.com

Consistent with our mission to preserve history on a local level, this book was printed in South Carolina on American-made paper and manufactured entirely in the United States. Products carrying the accredited Forest Stewardship Council (FSC) label are printed on 100 percent FSC-certified paper.

MADE IN THE USA